THE BIBLE ON

A Checklist,
1897-1980

FILM

Richard H. Campbell
and Michael R. Pitts

THE SCARECROW PRESS
Metuchen, N.J., & London
1981

Library of Congress Cataloging in Publication Data

Campbell, Richard H., 1959-
    The Bible on film.

    Includes indexes.
    1. Bible films--Catalogs. I. Pitts, Michael R.
II. Title.
PN1995.9.B53C3   011'.37   81-13560
ISBN 0-8108-1473-0   AACR2

Manufactured in the United States of America

For

ANGELA MICHELLE PITTS
                    - Michael R. Pitts -

and

To the memory of my friend, Toby,
who will be with me always.
                    - Richard H. Campbell -

TABLE OF CONTENTS

ARRANGEMENT OF ENTRIES

The films are arranged by year of issue, and then alphabetically when there is more than one entry in a given year.

INTRODUCTION

The idea of trying to index every film, either motion picture or television program, based on The Bible seemed rather easy at first, but research has uncovered hundreds of such films, dating back to 1897. As a result, many problems began to arise: many of the silent titles are lost to the ages, or are seldom screened today, and only sketchy information could be found on many others. Another problem arose in describing each film. The stories of The Bible are too well known to be retold here and in many cases the films based upon them are literal translations to the screen. In the case of the story of Jesus Christ, there have been well over fifty screen adaptations; telling the story of The Saviour in each annotation would clearly be redundant.

What we have tried to do in this book is to present a listing of the movies based on The Bible, both the Old and New Testaments, with as much technical information as possible, but giving only a synopsis of the individual films' plotlines. To have gone into great detail in plot synopsis would only have diminished the inspirational quality of the stories themselves. This book is intended only to provide a checklist to the films derived from The Bible. Anyone who wishes a more thorough knowledge of the individual stories should consult the ultimate authority, The Bible itself.

The main problem in the compilation of this volume was trying to list every film connected with The Bible. Information on foreign films is sometimes scarce, and the same is true of early American and foreign silent films. Information is just as scarce about television programs. We have gathered information on all the Biblical titles we could find from a number of sources and have detailed them herein. To list all of the programs produced for television from The Bible would probably take a volume in itself; therefore we have closed with a section on selected television programs derived from the Good Book. We have, however, listed only television programs on film, in keeping with the title of our book, and not those done live or on tape.

No doubt there are still a number of film titles that are missing from the text and the authors would appreciate any additions or corrections from readers, sent in care of the publisher.

The main reason we wrote this book is because there is no volume in existence which has attempted to chronicle all the films based on The Bible. A few deal with religion or with aspects of The Bible, but here we have tried to compile all the films derived from that source. At one time it was thought that to put Biblical stories on film was irreverent or a sacrilege, but today people read less and look at pictures more; by watching movies, some people have come to understand the meaning of The Bible, more than through the actual texts themselves. Perhaps how one learns is not as important as what is learned. As for the films themselves, many people would rather see a film that has the true meaning of The Bible (e. g., JESUS CHRIST SUPERSTAR or THE KING OF KINGS [1927]), than watch an historically accurate movie made only for money and devoid of all inspiration.

The Bible on Film is divided into three sections: The Films of the Old Testament, The Films of the New Testament, and Selected Television Programs based on both the Testaments. Only films actually based on The Bible or containing Biblical characters are included. Omitted are movies that may contain some Biblical aspects but are certainly not religious in content; e. g., OH GOD! In listing the individual films, the following information is included where possible: title, release year, country of origin (all films are presumed to be of United States origin unless otherwise listed), release company, running time, and whether in color or black and white (the latter listed as B/W). All known production credits are included for each film and as complete a cast listing as possible is provided. Where known, the character names are included with the cast. Films issued prior to 1929 are silent, unless otherwise noted.

It should be noted that the films included in the text are those which received either theatrical release or have been shown on television as feature films. In some cases motion pictures have been made only for church or educational purposes but have been exhibited in theatres or on television. Movies made expressly for television (called telefeatures or telefilms) are included in the text, and in many cases these have been released abroad as theatrical films. Those who wish to research further into films made for church or educational purposes should consult catalogues from such filmmakers as Family Films (14622 Lanark Street, Panorama City, California 91402) or Cathedral Films (2282 Townsgate Road, Westlake Village, California 91359). Many cities also have rental libraries for both theatrical and non-theatrical films, both features and short subjects; The Sacred Film Library (Box 55164, Indianapolis, Indiana 46205) is an example.

For the most part, the authors are in agreement on the opinions expressed about the films in this book. Where there is a difference of opinion, or one writer has a very strong feeling about a certain film, the comments are individually signed.

In closing, we believe in The Bible and are glad to see its stories glorified in any form of the media. The appearance of Biblical stories on film, and their use as a source for the cinema since its inception, make it all the better.

The authors would like to thank the following individuals and organizations for their help in writing this book: Academy of Motion Picture Arts and Sciences' National Film Information Service (Val Almendarez), The American Film Institute (Laura Masoner), Jim Ashton, Ball State University Library Reference Department (Neal A. Coil), Richard Bojarski, Tara Maria Campbell, Cathedral Films (Leonard Skibitzke), CBS-TV Entertainment Press Information (Patricia Diehl), Mark Day (Indiana University Libraries' Reference Department), Family Films (Robert W. Garmatz), Family Theatre Productions, Tim Ferrante, Historical Films (Bebe Bergsten), Dr. Conrad Lane, The Library of Congress, Dave McConnell, Don Miller, Carolyn Pitts, Sacred Film Library of Indianapolis, Indiana, Anthony Slide, Wayne Smith, John Wooley and Barry Yingling.

Richard H. Campbell
Michael R. Pitts

February, 1981

PART I

THE FILMS OF THE OLD TESTAMENT

SAMSON AND DELILAH
1903
France
Pathé
15 minutes B/W
Director: Ferdinand Zecca
        Perhaps the first film version of the story of mighty
Samson, from the Book of Judges, whose physical strength
could not keep him from falling under the spell of the beautiful, but evil, Delilah.

BELSHAZZAR'S FEAST
1905
France
Pathé
1 reel B/W
        Taken from the Book of Daniel, this short theatrical
film told of the court of Belshazzar in ancient Babylon and
included the Biblical account of the handwriting on the wall.
The film was remade, with the same title, by the French
Gaumont studio in 1913.

DANIEL IN THE LION'S DEN
1905
France
Pathé
135 feet B/W
        The earliest known screen adaptation of the Book of

Daniel story, relating how God saved young Hebrew Daniel from being eaten by lions. This version showed an angel, sent by God, saving Daniel.

GIUDETTA E OLOFERNE (Judith and Holofernes)
1906
Italy
Cines
1 reel   B/W
    Taken from the Apocrypha, GIUDETTA E OLOFERNE was the screen's first production of the story of Jewish girl Giudetta (Judith) saving the town of Bethulia from Babylonian conqueror Oloferne (Holofernes) by enticing him with drink and then cutting off his head.
    The film, with the same title, was remade in Italy in 1928 and again in 1960 (q. v.), although the best version of the story was done by D. W. Griffith in 1914 with his JUDITH OF BETHULIA (q. v.).

MOSES AND THE EXODUS FROM EGYPT
1907
France
Pathé
478 feet   B/W
    Another short film in Pathé's series of Biblical movies, this outing was perhaps the first flicker to tell the story of Moses. Included in this lost silent were the scenes of Moses receiving the Ten Commandments and the falling of the manna from Heaven.

DAVID AND GOLIATH
1908
Kalem
800 feet   B/W
Director-Screenplay: Sidney Olcott
    An early film of the Old Testament story of shepherd boy David slaying the giant Goliath. The film's main emphasis was on the gaining of strength through faith. Its adapter and director, Sidney Olcott, would go on to direct the first definitive religious film ever made, FROM THE MANGER TO THE CROSS (q. v.) in 1912, also for Kalem.

SAMSON AND DELILAH
1908
France
Pathé
1082 feet   B/W
Director: Ferdinand Zecca
     Director Ferdinand Zecca remade his 1903 version
(q. v.) of the Samson story, with the screen time being more
than doubled.   Besides the usual plot, Samson is shown going
to Heaven at the film's finale.

NOAH'S ARK
1909
Great Britain
Alpha
350 feet   B/W
Producer: Arthur Melbourne Cooper
     NOAH'S ARK, a British presentation, has a couple of
motion picture firsts to its credit.   Besides being the first
film to tell the story of Noah and his Ark, it was also one
of the very first movies to interpolate live-action with puppet
animation.   The story tells of a little girl who has a dream
in which her toys act out the story of Noah's Ark.   The live-
action portion of the film revolved around the present-day
scenes with the child, while the puppet animation had the
toys acting out the Deluge story.

SAUL AND DAVID
1909
Vitagraph
1000 feet   B/W
Director: J. Stuart Blackton
Screenplay: Rev. Madison C. Peters
     CAST: Maurice Costello, Florence Lawrence, William
Ranous.
     After making the successful five-part THE LIFE OF
MOSES (q. v.) for Vitagraph, director J. Stuart Blackton and
writer Rev. Madison C. Peters turned their attention to a
screen adaptation of the story of young David and King Saul
in ancient Israel.   The film retold the events surrounding the
fall of Saul and David's being the new king of the Hebrews.
     Two more films on the subject of David appeared

three years later. DAVID, KING OF ISRAEL was a 1912 release made in the United States and it emphasized the slaying of Goliath by David. The Italian-made DAVID, also issued in 1912, appears to be lost to the ages.

THE LIFE OF MOSES
1909-1910
Vitagraph
5 reels B/W
Director: J. Stuart Blackton
Screenplay: Rev. Madison C. Peters
  CAST: William Humphrey, Charles Kent, Julia Arthur, Earle Williams, Edith Storey.
  Vitagraph released THE LIFE OF MOSES in five parts, beginning December 11, 1909 and culminating February 19, 1910. The whole film told the story of Moses and how he led the Israelites out of Egypt and into the Promised Land. The portions of the film and their release dates are:
  Part One: "The Life of Moses" (December 11, 1909).
  Part Two: "Forty Years in the Land of Midian" (December 31, 1909).
  Part Three: "The Plagues of Egypt and the Deliverance of the Hebrews" (February 5, 1910).
  Part Four: "The Victory of Israel" (February 12, 1910).
  Part Five: "The Promised Land" (February 19, 1910).
  The first of a supposed series of Biblical pictures from Vitagraph, THE LIFE OF MOSES showed such happenings as the pillar of fire, the parting of the Red Sea and the giving of The Ten Commandments. The Moving Picture World called it "a picture that is deserving of the greatest praise and commendations as a whole."

ADAM AND EVE
1910
Great Britain
Bruns Films
8 minutes B/W
Producer-Director: Phil Bruns
  CAST: Phil Bruns (Adam).
  Producer-director Phil Bruns basically had almost a one-man show in this early flicker from Great Britain. Not only did he make the film for his own company but he also enacted the role of Adam in this adaptation of the Creation saga.

CAIN AND ABEL
1910
France
Gaumont
10 minutes   B/W
  In the early days of the French cinema producer Louis Gaumont turned out a whole series of short films based on the Old Testament, beginning with CAIN AND ABEL.   The film retold the Biblical story of the murder of Abel by his brother Cain and the tribulations Cain faced for his evil deed.
  Other Old Testament films made by Gaumont, and now lost to the ages, include ESTHER AND MORDECAI (1910), JEPHTHAH'S DAUGHTER (1910), THE MARRIAGE OF ESTHER (1910), PHARAOH, or ISRAEL IN EGYPT (1910), SAUL AND DAVID (1911), and THE SON OF SHUNAMITE (1911), which had Elisha raising a Shunamite woman's son from the grave.
  Other French studios turned out a number of Old Testament-based films prior to World War I.   The studio C. G. P. I. issued CAIN AND ABEL (1911), INFANCY OF MOSES (1911), in color; ABRAHAM'S SACRIFICE (1912) and SAUL AND DAVID (1912).   Also Pathé released in 1914 a tinted film called JOSEPH'S TRIALS IN EGYPT.
  In 1911 another film called CAIN AND ABEL was issued in the United States, a production of the Vitagraph Company.

DAVID AND GOLIATH
1910
France
Pathé
1000 feet   B/W
  CAST: Berthe Bovy, René Alexander, L. Ravet.
  Another in the series of French Pathé films adapted from Old Testament stories.   This version of David's slaying of the giant Goliath, at 1,000 feet, was a bit longer than most of the series entries.

I MACABEI (The Maccabees)
1910
Italy
1 reel   B/W
Director: Enrico Guazzoni
  As detailed in the Apocrypha, I MACABEI took place

in 166 B. C. and told the story of a Jewish family, the
Maccabees, and their struggle for religious freedom against
the ruler of the Selecuid Empire. The resulting film, however, was a conglomerate of Biblical plots and ancient world
costuming which resulted in a muddled effort. A far better
version of the story was made in Italy a half-century later
as IL VECCHIO TESTAMENTO (q. v.).

THE DELUGE
1911
Vitagraph
978 feet   B/W
  THE DELUGE was the American cinema's first pictorial presentation of the Great Flood and it was a faithful
adaptation of the Old Testament story.
  The film told how God looked upon the wickedness of
the human race and decided, in 3317 B. C., to destroy the
world except for Noah and his family. He instructs Noah to
build an ark and take two of each living creature aboard it
along with his family. After forty days of inundation the
water subsides and eventually the ark rests on Mt. Ararat,
where Noah builds an altar to the Lord for their deliverance.
God then sets a rainbow in the sky as a promise that He will
never again destroy the world by flood.
  Released in February, 1911, THE DELUGE was part
of a brief series of Biblical films made by Vitagraph at the
time, starting with the five-part THE LIFE OF MOSES
(q. v.) in 1909.

ADAM AND EVE
1912
Serbia
B/W
Director: Ivo Urbanic
  ADAM AND EVE is another example of an early silent
film from Europe based on the Book of Genesis and telling
pictorially the story of the Creation and of Adam and Eve,
the first man and woman. The film was produced in Serbia,
which became part of the state of Montenegro, now known as
Yugoslavia.
  The same year, an American company, Vitagraph,
also released a film called ADAM AND EVE, but this was a
modern-day retelling of the Genesis story. Here Adam was

a poor gardener whose wife, Eve, persuades him to steal from a peddler in order to possess luxuries. Although they try to flee from their crime, the two are eventually caught and their punishment is banishment from their neighbors.

DANIEL
1913
Vitagraph
2 Reels   B/W
Director: Fred Thomson
Screenplay: Madison C. Peters
    CAST: Charles Kent, Courtney Foote, L. Rogers Lytton.
    Taken from the Old Testament Book of Daniel, this film related how God saved young Daniel from being devoured by lions while he was a political prisoner of the King of Babylon.

THE WIFE OF CAIN
1913
Helgar Corporation
3 reels   B/W
Director-Screenplay: Charles L. Gaskill
    CAST: Helen Gardner.
    Early silent screen vamp Helen Gardner, who also starred in THE ILLUMINATION (q. v.), starred in this Old Testament-based film for her own company, Helen Gardner Picture Players.
    The Old Testament relates that after Cain killed his brother, Abel, God cast him out and he went to dwell in the land of Nod, on the east of Eden, and there he knew his wife. This film, replete with Cain's brand on the forehead, told the story of Cain and his wife.

JUDITH OF BETHULIA
1914
Biograph
4 reels   B/W
Producer-Director: D. W. Griffith
Screenplay: D. W. Griffith, from the play by Thomas
               Bailey Aldrich and the narrative poem "Judith
               and Holofernes"

Henry B. Walthall and Blanche Sweet in JUDITH OF
BETHULIA (Biograph, 1914).

Titles: Frank Woods
Photography: G. W. Bitzer
Editor: James Smith
     CAST: Blanche Sweet (Judith), Henry B. Walthall
(Holofernes), Mae Marsh (Naomi): Robert Harron (Nathan),
Lillian Gish (Young Mother), Dorothy Gish (Crippled Beg-
gar), Kate Bruce (Judith's Maid), G. Jiguel Lance (Eunuch
Attendant of Holofernes), Harry Carey (Traitor); W. Chrys-
tie Miller, Gertrude Robinson, Charles Hill Mailes, Eddie
Dillon.
     Bethulia, in the hill country of Judea, is besieged by
the troops of the Assyrian Holofernes (Henry B. Walthall).
The strength of the city holds and the invaders decide to
surround its walls and starve the population into surrender.
Judith (Blanche Sweet), a rich young widow who is beloved
by her people, decides to end the famine by disguising herself as a courtesan and entering Holofernes' camp, where
the general becomes enamored of her. He chooses her as
his handmaiden and she gets him drunk and decapitates him.
She takes the head back to her people to give them the

courage to continue the battle. The death of Holofernes, however, causes anarchy among his troops and the army flees.

Obviously influenced by the length and scope of QUO VADIS (q.v.), the Italian import, D. W. Griffith set out to make his first feature length film, and JUDITH OF BETHU-LIA was shot in California in the summer of 1913. It is credited with being the first film to employ an orchestra on set during production. The Moving Picture World called the film "A fascinating work of high artistry." The success of the film gave Griffith the impetus to leave Biograph and produce the first of his classic epic features, THE BIRTH OF A NATION (Wark Releasing, 1915).

In 1917 Biograph reissued JUDITH OF BETHULIA with an additional two reels and with new subtitles and called it HER CONDONED SIN.

For the record, "Judith" is a book of The Apocrypha, which was deleted from The Bible.

SAMSON
1914
Universal
6 reels B/W
Producer: J. Farrell MacDonald
CAST: J. Warren Kerrigan (Samson), Mayme Kelso (Delilah); Harold Lloyd, Hal Roach (Extras).

Universal produced this version of the Old Testament story of strong-man Samson (J. Warren Kerrigan), who was a great crusader who did the will of God until he let himself be seduced by the Philistine Delilah (Mayme Kelso), who cut off his hair and thus removed his strength. Blinded, he is cast into prison, but his hair grows back and when he is brought to court to be taunted by his captors he prays to God to return his strength. He destroys the pillars of the court, thus killing himself and his Philistine captors, including Delilah.

The picture contained some well executed sets, especially the temple of Dagon. It was also well acted, especially by J. Warren Kerrigan in the title role, and its mob scenes were thrilling to audiences of its day. The scenario for the film, however, was weak and The Moving Picture World said, "We cannot say that it adequately fulfills its mission ... when compared with others in the same class with which it must compete."

JOSEPH IN THE LAND OF EGYPT
1915
Thanhouser
4 reels   B/W
Director: Eugene Moore
            CAST: James Cruze (Joseph), Marguerite Snow.
    Popular screen players James Cruze and Marguerite
Snow starred in this four-reel version of the trials and tribulation of Joseph, sold by his brothers into slavery in Egypt
and rising up to become a powerful political figure who eventually forgives his siblings for their transgressions against
him.
    James Cruze, who played Joseph, would soon develop
into a very prolific film director, his most noted vehicle
being THE COVERED WAGON (Paramount, 1923).

SAMSON
1915
Box Office Attractions
5 reels   B/W
Director: Ben Lewis
Screenplay: Garfield Thompson, from the play by Henri
              Bernstein
            CAST: William Farnum (Samson); Maud Gilbert, Ed-
gar L. Davenport, Agnes Everitt, Harry Springler, Charles
Guthrie, Carey Leigh, George De Carlton, Elmer Peterson,
Edward Kyle.
    Producer William Fox, who at the time was trying to
break the film trust, produced this Biblical melodrama,
which was in direct competition with Universal's SAMSON
(q. v.), produced the year before. In this outing, popular
screen idol William Farnum played the man of great
strength, but sadly this epic has apparently been lost to the
ages.

MAMA'S AFFAIR
1921
Associated First National Pictures
6 reels   B/W
Producer: Joseph Schenck
Director: Victor Fleming
Screenplay: John Emerson & Anita Loos, from the play by
              Rachel Barton Butler

Photography: Oliver Marsh
     CAST: Constance Talmadge (Eve Orrin), Kenneth
Harlan (Dr. Harmon), Effie Shannon (Mrs. Orrin), Katherine
Kaelred (Mrs. Marchant), George Le Guere (Henry Marchant), Gertrude Le Brandt (Bundy).
     The Constance Talmadge Film Company produced this
drama about a selfish mother (Effie Shannon) who tries to
force her daughter (Constance Talmadge) to marry her best
friend's son (George Le Guere) when the girl really loves a
doctor (Kenneth Harlan). A brief prologue burlesques Eve
eating of the forbidden fruit in the Garden of Eden.

THE QUEEN OF SHEBA
1921
Fox
9 reels B/W
Director: J. Gordon Edwards
Screenplay: Virginia Tracy
Photography: John W. Boyle
Assistant Director: Mike Miggins
Chariot Race Supervisor: Tom Mix
     CAST: Betty Blythe (The Queen of Sheba), Fritz
Leiber (King Solomon), Claire De Lorey (Queen Amrath),
George Siegmann (King Armud), Herbert Heyes (Tamaran),
Herschel Mayall (Mentor), G. Raymond Nye (Adonijah),
George Nichols (King David), Genevieve Blinn (Bathsheba),
Pat Moore (Sheba's Son), Joan Gordon (Nomis), William
Hardy (Olos), Paul Cazeneuve (Pharaoh's Envoy), John Cosgrove (King of Tyre), Nell Craig (Princess Vashti), Al Fremont (Captain), Earl Crain (Joab).
     THE QUEEN OF SHEBA was a spectacular recounting
of the love affair between Solomon (Fritz Leiber) and the
beautiful Sheba (Betty Blythe). The story tells of how a
maiden, who is a prisoner when King Armud (George Siegmann) captures the land of Sheba, seduces the king and kills
him on their wedding night, thus attaining the throne. She
then visits Solomon, who has been crowned king of Israel in
deference to his brother Adonijah (G. Raymond Nye), now
his bitter enemy. Solomon and Sheba fall in love and incur
the wrath of Queen Amrath (Claire De Lorey), Solomon's
wife. Amrath's father, the Pharaoh of Egypt, promises war
on Israel if Solomon and Sheba marry, so the Queen of Sheba
returns to her homeland with their infant son. When the boy
is four years old Sheba sends him to Solomon but he is ab-
ducted by Adonijah, who does battle with Solomon. Sheba's

troops, however, repulse the forces of Adonijah, and the Queen again parts with Solomon and returns to her homeland with her son.

Director J. Gordon Edwards, the grandfather of producer-director Blake Edwards, wanted to create a new approach to screen sex symbols after having directed many of Theda Bara's vehicles at Fox. Although Fox was near bankruptcy, producer William Fox managed to raise the money to film this epic feature, which was a big box-office success. Among its many assets were the sensational chariot races (staged by Western star Tom Mix), beautifully conceived night battle scenes, and a fine performance by beautiful Betty Blythe in the title role.

SKIRTS
1921
Fox
5 reels B/W
Director-Screenplay: Hampton Del Ruth
     CAST: Clyde Cook, Chester Conklin, Polly Moran, Jack Cooper, Billy Armstrong, Ethel Teare, Glen Cavender, Slim Summerville, Harry McCoy, Bobby Dunn, Tom Kennedy, Ed Kennedy, William Tracy, Harry Booker, Alta Allen, Laura La Verne, Alice Davenport, The Singer Midgets.
     Slapstick comedy about a supposed circus handyman (Clyde Cook) who tries to undermine his millionaire father's fortunes. A brief animated prologue had clay figures representing Adam and Eve in the Garden of Eden.

THE BIBLE
1921-1922
Sacred Films, Inc.
1 reel series B/W
     Most of the stories from The Old Testament are included in this series, such as the story of Creation, Cain and Abel, and Noah's Ark. The one-reelers, which came to a halt just before the start of the story of Moses, were produced by the Weiss Brothers, producers noted for cheap dramas and westerns whose careers spanned from the 1920s to the 1960s.
     In addition to the above films, in 1928 Major Herbert M. Dawley directed a group of one- and two-reelers based on the life of Jesus Christ, but it is not known if they were

released theatrically. Among the titles were "The Unwelcome Guest," "Forgive Us Our Debts," "The Rich Young Ruler" and "Christ Confronts His Critics."

SAMSON AND DELILAH
("Tense Moments from Opera #5")
1922
Great Britain
Master Films
1100 feet B/W
Producer: H. B. Parkinson
Director: Edwin J. Collins
Screenplay: Frank Miller
       CAST: Valia (Delilah), W. D. Waxman (Samson).
       This silent short was shown with live musical accompaniment and was one of the entries in the "Tense Moments from Opera" series produced in Great Britain. The film was derived from the opera about Samson and Delilah written by Camille Saint-Saëns. Despite the public apathy toward silent film opera with musical accompaniment, the film was remade in 1927.

SAMSON UND DELILA (Samson and Delilah)
1922
Austria
Corda-Film/Vita-Film
6004 feet B/W
Director: Alexander Korda
Screenplay: Sidney Garrick, Alexander Korda & Ernest Vajda
Photography: Anton Ziedler & Nikolaus Forkas
Editor: H. Leslie Brittain
Art Director: Alexander Ferenczy
Cutter: Zoltan Korda
Assistant Director: Karl Hartl
       CAST: Maria Corda (Delilah/Opera Singer); Franz Herterich, Paul Lukas, Ernst Arndt, Oskar Hugelmann, Alfredo Galaor.
       Filmed in Vienna by Alexander Korda, this version of SAMSON UND DELILA used over seven hundred extras and the largest set ever built for a film in Europe up to that time. Like many Biblical films of its period, the picture interpolated a modern and a Biblical storyline. Here a Jewish scholar attempts to interest an opera singer (Maria

Corda) in the role of Delilah, with the singer refusing the part. The film then re-enacts the Samson and Delilah story.

SAMSON UND DELILA cost a fortune for its period and it lost a great deal of money for its backer, Dr. Szucs, a one-time Hungarian film distributor. The film was also plagued with production problems, especially the giant temple set, which would not tumble under the might of Samson (aided by a dozen pulling oxen out of camera range). Ironically, the huge set collapsed of its own volition while the cast and crew were on a lunch break.

For all its pomp and splendor, this costly film did not get many showings outside its native Europe.

Cecil B. DeMille and Hedy Lamarr
on the set of SAMSON AND DELILAH
(Paramount, 1949).

Some sources credit Mikhaly Kertesz (known as Michael Curtiz when he came to Hollywood) as the supervising director for SAMSON UND DELILA. He had previously helmed the two-part SODOM UND GOMORRAH (q. v.) and would soon direct DIE SKLAVENKÖNIGIN (q. v.), which also starred Maria Corda, before coming to Hollywood to turn out NOAH'S ARK (q. v.) in 1928.

SODOM UND GOMORRAH (Sodom and Gomorrah)
1922 (Part One) & 1923 (Part Two)
Austria
Sascha-Film
80 minutes each Part B/W
Director: Michael Curtiz [Mikhaly Kertesz]
Screenplay: Ladislaus Vajda
Assistant Photography: Gustav Ucicky
     CAST: Lucy Doraine, Victor Varconi, Willy Forst, Walter Slezak, Erica Wagner, Gelog Reimers.
     Filmed in two parts and shot outside the Sascha-Film's studio in Sievering, Austria, this Biblical opus attempted to imitate the successful formula used by Cecil B. DeMille in the United States by telling parallel stories in ancient and modern times. Part One of SODOM UND GOMORRAH had a modern-day woman marrying a wealthy elderly man for his money and then corrupting her step-son by seducing him. Eventually her guilt is so great that she has a nightmare about the destruction of Sodom and Gomorrah. Part Two then took up with the evil life in the twin cities of sin and how God destroyed Sodom and Gomorrah, as envisioned in the woman's dream. As a result she is soon justly rewarded for her evil schemes of power. As seen today, the seduction scenes are merely humorous.
     SODOM UND GOMORRAH proved to be quite popular in Europe and director Michael Curtiz and screenwriter Ladislaus Vajda teamed again for the Biblical spectacle DIE SKLAVENKÖNIGIN (Moon of Israel) (q. v.), which resulted in Curtiz coming to Hollywood.

THE SHEPHERD KING
1923
Fox
9 reels B/W
Director: J. Gordon Edwards

Screenplay: Virginia Tracy, from the play by Wright Lori-
           mer & Arnold Reeves
Photography: Bennie Miggins
        CAST: Violet Marsereau (Princess Michal), Edy
Darclea (Princess Herab), Virginia Lucchetti (Adora), Nero
Bernardi (David), Guido Trento (Saul), Ferrucio Biancini
(Jonathan), Alessandro Salvini (Doeg), Mariano Bottino
(Adriel), Samuel Balestre (Goliath), Adriano Bocanera (Sam-
uel), Enzo Di Felice (Ozem), Eduardo Balsarno (Abimelech),
Ameriga Di Giorgio (Omah), Gordon McEdward (Prisoner),
Ernesto Tranquili (Jesse), Isabelle De Leaso (Jesse's Wife).

     THE SHEPHERD KING recounted the rise to power of
shepherd boy David (Nero Bernardi), fulfilling the prophecy
of Samuel (Adriano Bocanera), who warned King Saul (Guido
Trento) not to battle the Philistines. Samuel predicts Saul
will lose the battle and his throne, and says David will be
the new king of Israel. Saul's son Jonathan (Ferrucio
Biancini) befriends David, who later slays the giant Philistine Goliath (Samuel Balestre). Fearing the loss of his
throne, Saul sets a trap for David in the battle with the
Philistines but David is victorious. Gathering his forces,
David routs the Philistines when they attack and during the
battle Saul and Jonathan are killed. The victorious David
becomes king and marries Saul's daughter, Michal (Violet
Marsereau).

     This film was one of five features to be made in
Italy by producer William Fox and director J. Gordon Edwards, following their success with THE QUEEN OF SHEBA
(q. v.) two years before. Photoplay called this spectacular
production "An interesting story about David the Psalmist,
done by a capable Italian cast. " The mainly Italian cast,
however, was a box office drawback in the United States,
where the film did not fare nearly as well as THE QUEEN
OF SHEBA.

THE TEN COMMANDMENTS
1923
Paramount
13 reels B/W with Color prologue
Producer-Director: Cecil B. DeMille
Screenplay: Jeanie MacPherson
Photography: Bert Glennon, Pervell Marley, Archie Stout &
              J. F. Westerberg
Editor: Anne Bauchens
Art Director: Paul Iribe

Theodore Roberts in THE TEN COMMANDMENTS (Paramount, 1923).

Technical Director: Roy Pomeroy
Cutter: Anne Bauchens
Assistant Director: Cullen Tate
    CAST: Prologue: Theodore Roberts (Moses), Estelle
Taylor (Miriam), Julia Faye (Pharaoh's Wife), Charles de
Roche (Rameses), Terrence Moore (Pharaoh's Son), James
Neill (Aaron), Lawson Butt (Dathan), Clarence Burton (Task-
master), Noble Johnson (Bronze Man). Part Two: Richard
Dix (John McTavish), Edythe Chapman (Mrs. McTavish),
Rod La Rocque (Dan McTavish), Leatrice Joy (Mary Leigh),
Nita Naldi (Sally Long), Robert Edeson (Redding), Charles
Ogle (Doctor), Agnes Ayres (Outcast), Viscount Glerowly.
    The first American epic film of the 1920s to be based
on The Bible, THE TEN COMMANDMENTS told its story in
two parts, a concept popular with producer-director Cecil B.
DeMille. The Technicolor prologue depicted the Biblical
stories from Exodus, followed by a modern-day story set in
San Francisco about two brothers (Richard Dix, Rod La
Rocque) who love the same girl (Leatrice Joy). The girl
marries one brother (Rod La Rocque) who proves to be a

crook; he makes a fortune using inferior building materials and bribes the building inspector. Later he kills his mistress (Nita Naldi) and then finds out that she may have given him leprosy. The man meets his death in a motorboat accident and his widow then marries the good brother (Richard Dix).

When viewed today, this silent version remains quite good, especially since it was filmed in a restrained manner. When the film was issued Photoplay called it "one of the greatest pictures ever made. A wonderful entertainment and a marvelous sermon." Today this silent feature takes a back seat to Cecil B. DeMille's remake in 1956 (q. v.), which deleted the modern story and expanded the filming of the events surrounding the Exodus.

DIE SKLAVENKÖNIGIN (Moon of Israel)
1924
Austria
6680 feet B/W
Producer-Director: Michael Curtiz [Mikhaly Kertesz]
Screenplay: Ladislaus Vajda, from the book Moon of Israel
           by H. Rider Haggard
Creative Supervisor & Titles: H. Rider Haggard
Editor: Herbert Hoagland
         CAST: Maria Corda, Arlette Marchal, Adelqui Miller, Oscar Beregi, Ferdinand Onno, Lya de Putti, Mans Marr, Hans Thimig, Adolf Weisse, Reinhold Haeusseumann.
         Basically a retelling of THE TEN COMMANDMENTS (q. v.), DIE SKLAVENKÖNIGIN was the film that brought Hungarian producer-director Michael Curtiz to the attention of Hollywood studios, thus leading to his long and illustrious American film career as a top director. Released in the United States in 1927 by Films Booking Office (FBO) as MOON OF ISRAEL, the film had the additional prestige of having popular fiction writer H. Rider Haggard, from whose book the film was adapted, as the creative supervisor for the project as well as the writer of the feature's titles. Despite all of these assets, Photoplay said of the film, "It should not have been let by Ellis Island."
         DIE SKLAVENKÖNIGIN retold the story of how Moses led the Israelites out of Egypt and into the "promised land," with the tale being framed around the story of a young Jewish girl (Maria Corda) who is victimized by the Egyptian Pharaoh. A highlight of the production was Curtiz' scenes showing the parting of the Red Sea.

FIG LEAVES
1926
Fox
7 reels   B/W
Director-Story: Howard Hawks
Screenplay: Hope Loring & Louis D. Lighton
Photography: Joseph August
Costumes: Adrian
Assistant Director: James Tinling
          CAST: George O'Brien (Adam Smith), Olive Borden
(Eve Smith), Phyllis Haver (Alice Atkins), Andre de Beranger
(Josef Andre), William Austin (Andre's Assistant), Heinie
Conklin (Eddie McSwiggen), Eulalie Jensen (Madame Gris-
wald).
          FIG LEAVES was a comedy contrasting the modern
trials and tribulations of a married couple with those of
Adam (George O'Brien) and Eve (Olive Borden).   A prologue
has the duo living in a primitive apartment, Adam riding a
cart pulled by a dinosaur to work, and Eve going to a big
fig-leaf sale where she is tempted by the serpent.

SAMSON AND DELILAH
("Cameo Operas # 2")
1927
Great Britian
Song Films
2000 feet   B/W
Producer: John E. Blakeley
Director: H. B. Parkinson
          CAST: William Anderson (Samson).
          Camille Saint-Saëns' operatic version of the story of
Samson and Delilah was again put on film in the silent days
with a live musical accompaniment in this entry in the
"Cameo Operas" series produced in Great Britain.   The
first such version of the Saint-Saëns' work was done in 1922
as part of the "Tense Moments from Opera" series (q. v.).
While the previous version ran only about three reels, this
outing expanded the opera to feature length.

NOAH'S ARK
1928
Warner Brothers
9 reels   B/W

The building of the Ark, from NOAH'S ARK (Warner
Brothers, 1928).

Silent & Sound versions
Director: Michael Curtiz
Screenplay & Dialogue: Anthony Coldeway
Story: Darryl F. Zanuck
Titles: De Leon Anthony
Photography: Hal Mohr & Barney McGill
Editor: Harold McCord
Music: Louis Silvers
Song: Billy Rose & Louis Silvers
Miniature Effects: Fred Jackman
   CAST: Dolores Costello (Mary/Miriam), George
O'Brien (Travis/Japheth), Noah Beery (Nickloff/King Nephil-
im), Louise Fazenda (Hilda/Tavern Maid), Guinn Williams
(Al/Ham), Paul McAllister (Minister/Noah), Nigel de Brulier
(Soldier/High Priest), Anders Randolf (The German/Leader
of Soldiers), Armand Kaliz (The Frenchman/Leader of King's
Guards), Myrna Loy (Dancer/Slave Girl), William V. Mong
(Innkeeper/Guard), Malcolm White (Balkan/Shem), Noble
Johnson (Broker), Otto Hoffman (Trader), Joe Bonomo (Aide

to Leader of Soldiers).

Hungarian director Michael Curtiz, who had previously produced such Biblical epics as SODOM UND GOMORRAH, Part One (1922) and Part Two (1923), and DIE SKLAVEN-KÖNIGIN (Moon of Israel) (1924) (qq. v.), directed this lavish spectacle which premiered November, 1928 but did not get national release until the summer of 1929. In the interim a Vitaphone talking sequence was added to make the film a part-talkie and give it further box office appeal at a time when most theaters were wiring for sound. Photoplay commented about the feature, "Big cast, big theme, big flood. Your money's worth."

Like THE TEN COMMANDMENTS (q. v.) and other Biblical films of the period, NOAH'S ARK told a modern story in tandem with an Old Testament saga, with cast members having roles in both segments. The modern-day story took place in 1914 as a train is wrecked and a number of people are involved with each other as a result. Taking place just at the outbreak of World War I, this story is contrasted to the Biblical account of the Flood and the construction of Noah's Ark.

There is a sad footnote to this film, which was issued in both silent and part-talkie versions: several extras were drowned during the filming of the Deluge sequence.

NOAH'S ARK, minus the talkie-version's dialogue sequences, was reissued theatrically in 1957 with sound effects and narration. Portions of the film were also used in the short MAGIC MOVIE MOMENTS (Warner Brothers, 1953).

FORGOTTEN COMMANDMENTS
1932
Paramount
65 minutes   B/W
Directors: Louis Gasnier & William Schorr
Screenplay-Story: James Bernard Fagan & Agnes Brandy
               Leahy
Photography: Karl Struss
       CAST: Sari Maritza (Anya), Gene Raymond (Paul Ossip), Marguerite Churchill (Marya Ossip), Irving Pichel (Professor Marinoff), Harry Beresford (Priest), Edward Van Sloan (Doctor), Kent Taylor (Gregor), Frankie Adams (Registrar), John Peter Richmond [John Carradine], William Shawhan (Orators), Joseph [Sawyer] Sauers (Ivan Ivanovitch), Boris Bullock (Burly Student), Allen Fox (Student), John

Deering (Room Clerk), Harry Cording (Officer), Florence Shreve (Divorce Clerk), Helen Caryle (Nurse).

A grade "B" programmer, FORGOTTEN COMMAND-MENTS served as the American film debut of exotic actress Sari Maritza and used some 20 minutes of footage from Cecil B. DeMille's 1923 version of THE TEN COMMANDMENTS (q. v.).

The story told of a Russian girl (Sari Maritza) who had been the mistress of a noted scientist (Irving Pichel) who set her amorous intentions at a weak-willed husband (Gene Raymond). The duo are among a group of students who hear a priest (Harry Beresford), who is risking his life to tell the story of Moses and The Ten Commandments. The girl is then torn between wanting to believe in religion and the scoffing of the Bolshevik professor who favors the Russian government's anti-religious policies.

The stock footage from THE TEN COMMANDMENTS is the chief interest in this feature, although FORGOTTEN COMMANDMENTS is one of the first films to take notice of the Russian policy of opposition to organized religion. Interestingly, Irving Pichel, who played the chief advocate of the government policy, later directed such religious films as THE GREAT COMMANDMENT and DAY OF TRIUMPH (both q. v.).

LOT IN SODOM
1933
Amateur production
27 minutes B/W
Producer-Directors: James Sibeley Watson & Melville Web-
                      ber
Music: Louis Siegel
        CAST: Frederick Haak, Hildegarde Watson, Louis Whilbeck, Jr.

An amateur production telling the Old Testament story of Lot and his family fleeing the destruction of Sodom and Gomorrah, this film included the angels coming to warn Lot to leave the sin cities and his wife being turned into a pillar of salt.

GOOD MORNING, EVE!
1934
Warner Brothers-Vitaphone

2 reels B/W
Director: Roy Mack
Screenplay: Cyrus Woods, Eddie Moran & A. Dorian Otvos
      CAST: Leon Errol (Adam), June MacCloy (Eve);
Vernon Dent, Maxine Doyle.
      An entry in the Leon Errol comedy short series,
GOOD MORNING, EVE! concerned itself with a humorous
look at Adam and Eve as they put up with changing life sty-
les through the ages. The short is sometimes called LEON
ERROL'S ADAM AND EVE.

THE GREEN PASTURES
1936
Warner Brothers
92 minutes B/W
Producer: Henry Blanke
Directors: Marc Connelly and William Keighley
Screenplay: Marc Connelly and Sheridan Gibney, from the
      play by Marc Connelly
Photography: Hal Mohr
Editor: George Amy
Art Directors: Allen Sealburg & Stanley Fleischer
Special Effects: Fred Jackman
Sound: Major Nathan Levinson
Costumes: Milo Anderson
Assistant Director: Sherry Shourds
      CAST: Rex Ingram ("De Lawd"/Adam/Hezdrel),
Oscar Polk (Gabriel), George Reed (Deshea/Issac), Eddie
"Rochester" Anderson (Noah), Frank Wilson (Moses/Sexton),
Ernest Whitman (Pharaoh), Abraham Gleaves (Archangel),
Myrtle Anderson (Eve), Al Stokes (Cain), Edna M. Harris
(Zeba), James Fuller (Cain the Sixth), George Randol (High
Priest), Ida Forsyne (Mrs. Noah), Ray Martin (Shem),
Charles Andrews (Flatfoot/Gambler), Dudley Dickerson
(Ham), James Burress (Japheth), William "Billy" Cumby
(Abraham/King of Babylon/Head Magician), Ivory Williams
(Jacob), David Bethea (Aaron), Rosena Weston (Zipproah),
Reginald Fenderson (Joshua), Slim Thomson (Master of
Ceremonies/Man on the Ground), Clinton Rosemond (Proph-
et), The Hall Johnson Choir (Angel Chorus), John Alexander
(Dancer), William Broadus (Mr. Randall), Amanda Drayton
(Mrs. Randall), Fred "Snowflake" Toone (Zubo), Minnie Gray
(Mrs. Ham), Bessie Guy (Mrs. Shem), Dorothy Bishop (Mrs.
Japheth), Ben Carter (Gambler), Jesse Graves (General),
Duke Upshaw (Abel/Dancer), Bessie Lyle (Mrs. Prohack),

Oscar Polk and Rex Ingram in THE GREEN PASTURES
(Warner Brothers, 1936).

Lillian Davis (Viney Prohack), Charlotte Sneed (Carlotta
Prohack), Willie Best (Henry/Angel), Johnny Lee (Angel),
Philip "Lucky" Hurlick (Carlisle).
Variety termed THE GREEN PASTURES "a simple,
enchanting, audience-captivating cinematic fable." Marc
Connelly co-directed this feature, based on his play which
in turn was derived from the Southern sketches, "Ol' Man
Adam and His Chillun" by Roark Bradford. With an all-
Negro cast, the film told various Biblical stories as imag-
ined by black children in a small Southern Sunday school
class. The film begins with the famous fish fry in heaven
and goes through the stories of Adam, Noah, Moses, Cain
and Abel, etc.
While hardly an accurate account of the Old Testament stories, THE GREEN PASTURES did present a delight-
ful retelling of these fables as seen through the eyes of
good, simple and devout people, projecting their own mores
and standards on the people of Biblical times. While some
criticism has been aimed at the film as being racist and
"Uncle Tom" in its attitudes toward blacks, the movie actually contained none of the really overt submissive racial
overtones often aimed at Negroes during this period. * What
the film did try to project was how uneducated folk, really
of any race or religion, felt about their faith.
THE GREEN PASTURES greatly benefitted from good
production numbers and fine performances, especially from
Rex Ingram as "De Lawd," Oscar Polk as Gabriel and Eddie "Rochester" Anderson as Noah. Filled with well-staged
production numbers, the film also contained good dialogue,
some of it quite amusing, as when God said to Noah, just
before the flood, "What's the most rain you ever had about
these parts?"
While the film met with good critical and audience
reception, its release in 1936 was protested by the Ku Klux
Klan. The feature also resulted in two spin-off satires, the

---

*One such feature, WONDER BAR (Warner Brothers, 1934),
does deserve mention here because of a production number
which showed the concept of heaven through the eyes of an
aged black man (Al Jolson, in blackface) going to the promised land on a mule. The sequence literally flowed over
with racial overtones as the Negro's concept of heaven was
shown to be a place with plenty of singing, dancing and crap-
shooting, plus an endless array of hams and watermelons.
The music for this sequence is available on the record album Al Jolson--The Vitaphone Years (A-Jay Records 3749).

Vitaphone short, CLEAN PASTURES (1937), and a Canadian feature, GRIM PASTURES (1943).

DER APFEL IST AB (The Apple Has Been Eaten)
1948
West Germany
Camera Films
105 minutes
Director: Helmut Kautner
  CAST: Bobby Todd, Joana Maria Gorvin, Bettina Maissi, Helmut Kautner, Arno Assmann (Satan).
  The story of the creation and the lives of Adam and Eve were told in this satirical musical-comedy using fantasy and dream sequences. Cheaply made in West Germany in 1947, and shown there a year later, the film was not issued in the United States until 1950, when Lopert Films released it as THE ORIGINAL SIN, with ten minutes shorn from its running time. For all practical purposes, it was not a long enough delay.

QUEEN ESTHER
1948
Cathedral Films
50 minutes B/W
Producer: Rev. James F. Fredrich
Director: John T. Coyle
Screenplay: Rev. James F. Fredrich, John T. Coyle &
     H. W. Romberg
Photography: C. Arthur Ferndell
Editor: Thomas Neff
  CAST: Attile Kruger (Queen Esther), Richard Hale (Mordecai), Addison Richards (Haman), Charles Evans (King Xerxes), Charles Jordan (Scribe), Michael Ansara (Zubal), Virginia Wave (Haman's Wife), Douglas McEachin (Court Judge), Cy Kendall (Chamberlain).
  QUEEN ESTHER opens and closes in a modern Jewish home during the Feast of Purim, or days of Thanksgiving, when the Book of Esther is read to recall the Jews' rescue from death at Shushan. The film then reverts to Biblical times and tells the story of how a Judean slave girl, Esther (Attile Kruger), is chosen to marry Persian King Xerxes (Charles Evans) and how she fights to save her people from persecution. At the climax, Esther appears, unannounced,

Attile Kruger and Charles Evans in QUEEN ESTHER
(Cathedral Films, 1948).

before the king, asks for mercy for her people and tells him
of the deceit that surrounds him.   As a result, Xerxes
spares the Jews and elevates Mordecai (Richard Hale) to the
highest office in the kingdom.   Meanwhile, the evil Haman
(Addison Richards) is executed on the gallows he had built
for Mordecai.

Made for church distribution, QUEEN ESTHER was
also released to television and it is a finely compact pictorial version of the story in the Book of Esther.   A later
Italian version, ESTHER E IL RE (Esther and the King)
(q. v.), was more colorful but not nearly as reverent as
this version.

SAMSON AND DELILAH
1949
Paramount
127 minutes   Color

Producer-Director: Cecil B. DeMille
Screenplay: Jesse Lasky & Frederick M. Frank
Adaptation: Vladimir Jabofinsky & Harold Lamb, from the
novel Judge and Fool by Vladimir Jabofinsky
Photography: George Barnes
Editor: Anne Bauchens
Music: Victor Young
Art Director: Hans Drier & Walter Taylor
Set Decorators: Sam Comer & Ray Moyer
Technicolor Directors: Natalie Kalmus & Robert Brower
Assistant Director: Edward Slaven
Makeup: Wally Westmore, Harold Lierly & William Wood
Costumes: Edith Head, Gus Peters, Dorothy Jeakins, Gwen
Wakeling & Eloise Jenssen
Choreography: Theodore Kosloff
Sound: Harry Lindgren & John Cope
Special Effects: Gordon Jennings, Paul Lerpoe & Devereaux
Jennings
   CAST: Hedy Lamarr (Delilah), Victor Mature (Sam-
son), George Sanders (Saranof Gaza), Angela Lansbury
(Semadar), Henry Wilcoxon (Ahtur), Olive Deering (Miriam),
Fay Holden (Hazel), Julia Faye (Hisham), Rusty [Russ]
Tamblyn (Saul), William Farnum (Tubal), Lane Chandler
(Teresh), Moroni Olsen (Targil), Francis J. McDonald
(Story Teller), Wee Willie Davis (Garmisker), John Miljan
(Lesh Lakish), Arthur Q. Bryan (Fat Philistine Merchant),
Laura Elliott, Jeff York, Bud Moorehouse (Spectators),
Victor Varconi (Lord of Ashdod), John Parrish (Lord of
Gath), Frank Wilcox (Lord of Ekron), Russell Hicks (Lord
of Ashkelon), Boyd Davis (Priest), Fritz Leiber (Lord of
Sharif), Mike Mazurki (Leader of Philistine Soldiers),
Davison Clark (Merchant Prince), George Reeves (Wounded
Messenger), Pedro de Cordoba (Bar Simon), Frank Reicher
(Village Barber), Colin Tapley (Prince), Charles Evans
(Manoah), George Zoritch, Hamil Petroff (Sword Dancers),
Frank Mayo (Master Architect), James Craven (Prince),
Lloyd Whitlock (Chief Scribe), Crauford Kent (Court Astrol-
oger), Harry Woods (Gammad), Stephen Roberts (Bergam
at Feast), Ed Hinton (Makon at Feast), Carl Saxe (Slave),
Nils Asther, Harry Cording (Princes), Charles Meredith
(High Priest), Pierre Watkin (Second Priest), John Miller
(Man with Burro), Lester Sharpe (Saddle Maker), Edgar
Dearing, Hugh Prosser (Tax Collectors), John Merton (As-
sistant Tax Collector), Al Ferguson (Villager), Fred Kohler,
Jr. (Soldier), Tom Tyler (Philistine Captain of Gristmill),
Brahm van den Berg (Temple Dancer), Eric Alden (Courtier),
Robert Kortman (Vendor), Philo McCullough (Merchant), Ted

Hedy Lamarr and Victor Mature in SAMSON AND DELILAH
(Paramount, 1949).

Mapes (Captain Killed by Jawbone), Gertrude Messinger,
Betty Boyd, Dorothy Adams, Betty Farrington, Claire Du
Brey, Greta Granstedt (Women), Byron Foulger, Stanley
Blystone, Crane Whitley, Kenneth Gibson (Men), Charles
Dayton (Midget), Henry Wills (Saran's Charioteer).

Cecil B. DeMille's blockbusting production of the
Samson epic story is, as usual for this producer-director,
big in every way.   DeMille had already produced THE TEN
COMMANDMENTS (q. v.) in 1923 to favorable response and
he would continue to film Biblical spectacles for the rest of
his career.   This version, besides the usual story from the
Book of Judges, has Samson being blinded and destroying
thousands of soldiers with the jawbone of an ass.   Of course,
the main plotline had the strong man (Victor Mature) coming
under the spell of the alluring Delilah (Hedy Lamarr) who
discovers that his strength comes from his hair; she prompt-
ly shaves his head, leaving him powerless.   Deserted by
Delilah and blinded, Samson regains his strength when his
hair grows back.   He destroys the city of the enemy through
his strength and faith, bringing death to the pagans and
eternal salvation to himself.

Besides the top-notch production values which are
common to all DeMille features, SAMSON AND DELILAH
boasted fine performances in the key leading roles, with
Victor Mature just right as the mighty Samson.   Later he
would shine again in the Biblical spectacles, THE ROBE
and its sequel, DEMETRIUS AND THE GLADIATOR (qq. v.).
Hedy Lamarr, perhaps the most beautiful actress ever to
appear on the screen, was perfect as the seductive Delilah,
and George Sanders was his usual suave, evil self as Saranof Gaza, the opponent of Samson and God's word.   As usual in a DeMille epic, the supporting cast was perfect, including George Reeves, who would soon win fame as TV's
"Superman, " and Frank Reicher, best remembered as Captain Englehorn in KING KONG (RKO Radio, 1933) and SON
OF KONG (RKO Radio, 1934).

Variety noted of the film, "It's a fantastic picture
for this era in its size, in its lavishness, in the corniness
of the story telling and in the old-fashioned technique.... "
This was typical of the critical reaction to the feature but
the public loved it and the film made over $11. 5 million
in domestic rentals alone.   In all, SAMSON AND DELILAH
is a very strong production and the best version of the Samson* story yet to appear on film.

---

*It should be noted that the character of Samson has ap-
peared in many non-Biblical motion pic-   (cont. on p. 31)

ADAMO ED EVA (Adam and Eve)
1950
Italy
Lux Film
86 minutes   B/W
Producer: Dino De Laurentiis
Director: Mario Mattoli
Screenplay: Marchesi, Mario Mattoli, Metz
Photography: Aldo Tonti
Music: Pippo Barizizza
Sets: Piero Filippone
  CAST: Macario (Adam), Isa Barizza (Eve); Gianni
Agus, Guglielmo Barnabo, Nerio Bernardi, Riccardo Billi,
Luigi Cimara, Ricky Denver, Grado De Franceschi, Nunzio
Filogamo, Arnoldo Foa, Luisa Friegerio, Lilly Rinaldi,
Mario Riva, Vinicio Sofia, Carlo Tamberlani, Carla Pozzi,
Giuliana Manas.
  A musical-comedy, with a decided emphasis on kid-
ding Italian life and politics, ADAMO ED EVA satirized the
relationship between men and women through the ages, start-
ing with Adam and Eve being tempted by the forbidden fruit
in the Garden of Eden.   One of the film's better sketches was
a take-off on Western movies.
  Long forgotten, this three-decade-old feature is of
interest in that it was produced by Dino De Laurentiis, who
would later helm THE BIBLE (q. v.).

DAVID AND BATHSHEBA
1951
20th Century-Fox
116 minutes   Color
Producer: Darryl F. Zanuck
Director: Henry King
Screenplay: Philip Dunne
Photography: Leon Shamroy

---

tures.   For the most part these were produced in Italy in
the mid-1960s and were in the "sweat, sandals, muscles and
sand" mold.   Their entertainment values were minimal, especially in the badly dubbed versions which appeared in U. S.
grind houses and on television.   Among the titles are SAM-
SON AND THE SEVEN MIRACLES OF THE WORLD (1963),
SAMSON AND THE SLAVE QUEEN (1963), with Samson
teamed with Zorro; SAMSON AND THE MIGHTY CHALLENGE
(1964) and SAMSON VERSUS THE GIANT KINGS (1964).

Walter Talun and Leo Pessin in DAVID AND BATHSHEBA
(20th Century-Fox, 1951).

Editor: Barbara McLain
Music: Alfred Newman
Art Directors: Lyle Wheeler & George Davis
Technical Consultant: Leonard Doss
    CAST: Gregory Peck (David), Susan Hayward (Bath-
sheba), Raymond Massey (Nathan), Kieron Moore (Uriah),
James Robertson Justice (Abishai), Jayne Meadows (Michal),
John Sutton (Ira), Dennis Hoey (Joab), Walter Talun (Goli-
ath), Paula Morgan (Adultress), Francis X. Bushman (King
Saul), Teddy Infuhr (Jonathan), Leo Pessin (David as a Boy),
Gwyneth [Gwen] Verdon (Dancer), Gilbert Barnett (Absalom),
John Burton (Priest), Lumsden Hare (Old Shepherd), George
Zucco (Egyptian Ambassador), Allan Stone (Ammon), Paul
Newlan (Samuel), Holmes Herbert (Jesse), Robert Stephenson,
Harry Carter (Executioners), Richard Michelson, Dick Win-
ters, John Duncan (Jesse's Sons), James Craven (Court An-
nouncer), Shepard Menken (Police Guard), John Dodsworth
(Ahithophel).
    Another in the 1950's series of Biblical spectacles

based far more on fiction than scripture and with more emphasis on lust than gospel. Filmed in Arizona, this colorful outing tells the story of David (Gregory Peck), who forsakes the laws of God when he comes under the spell of the beautiful Bathsheba (Susan Hayward), who is married to Uriah (Kieron Moore). David arranges for Uriah to be killed in battle so he can take Bathsheba as his wife. The Biblical trials and tribulations follow and eventually Bathsheba gives birth to Solomon, the next in line to be king.

Under the skillful direction of Henry King, DAVID AND BATHSHEBA avoided the empty complexities of many Hollywood religious spectacles and instead concentrated on good production values, a literate script and fine performances. Although star Gregory Peck does not care for his overall work in the film, he is quite credible as the lusttorn David, while Susan Hayward is properly alluring as Bathsheba. The supporting cast is excellent, especially James Robertson Justice as Abishal, John Sutton as Ira and silent film star Francis X. Bushman as the aged King Saul. DAVID AND BATHSHEBA was a popular film at the time of its release and it continues to hold up well when viewed today via the small screen.

LA REGINA DI SABA (The Queen of Sheba)
1952
Italy
Oro Film
111 minutes B/W
Producer: Mario Francisci
Director: Pietro Francisci
Screenplay: Raoul De Sarro, Nino Novarese, Pietro Francisci
          & Giorgio Graziosi
Story: Pietro Francisci & Giorgio Graziosi
        CAST: Leonora Ruffo (Balkis, Queen of Sheba), Gino Cervi (King Solomon), Gino Leurini (Prince Rehoboam), Marina Berti (Princess Zymira), Franco Silva (Kabael), Mario Ferrari (High Priest), Isa Pola (Tabuy), Nita Dover (Kinnor), Umberto Silvestri (Issaachar), Dorian Gray (Abner), Franca Tamantini (False Mother), Sulvia Mammi (True Mother).
        The film is set in 1000 B.C. King Solomon (Gino Cervi) sends his son (Gino Leurini) and a friend (Umberto Silvestri) on a dangerous trek to the land of Sheba in order to spy on those who would declare war on Jerusalem. The duo find themselves in the queen's private oasis and Rehoboam,

the son of Solomon, saves the Queen of Sheba (Leonora Ruffo) from a serpent. When they arrive at the palace the king has died and Balkis, the queen, is crowned Sheba's sole ruler. By now she loves Rehoboam but refuses to pledge herself to him until the mountain speaks. When she finds out his true identity, Sheba leads an army on Jerusalem but she is captured by her lover. They escape into the valley of silence where he and the leader of Sheba's army fight over her, with Rehoboam winning. In a landslide the mountain speaks and Sheba and Rehoboam are free to marry.

This Italian production, which had some spectacular battle scenes, took great liberties with the Old Testament story of Solomon and Sheba, although it was "well photographed, competently acted and directed" (Los Angeles Examiner). Lopert Films released the film in the United States in 1953 as QUEEN OF SHEBA.

SINS OF JEZEBEL
1953
Lippert
74 minutes   Color
Producer: Sigmund Neufeld
Director: Reginald LeBorg
Screenplay: Richard Landau
Photography: Gilbert Warrenton
Editor: Carl L. Pierson
Music: Earl Snyder
Art Director: F. Paul Sylos
    CAST: Paulette Goddard (Jezebel), George Nader (Jehu), John Hoyt (Elijah), Eduard Franz (Ahab), John Shelton (Loran), Margia Dean (Deborah), Joe Besser (Yonkel), Ludwig Donath (Nabath), Carmen D'Antonio (Dancer).
    Based on the Book of Kings, SINS OF JEZEBEL told of the life of the sinister Phoenician princess Jezebel (Paulette Goddard), the evil wife of Ahab (Eduard Franz). Speaking through the Prophet Elijah (John Hoyt), who commanded the rains to come from the heavens, God brought about the end of the evil woman.
    Shot in three days at a cost of $100,000, SINS OF JEZEBEL was made to cash in on the then-popular Biblical spectacles being produced. In wide screen and color, with still beautiful movie queen Paulette Goddard in the title role, the film more than met its lower-half of double bill demands.

SLAVES OF BABYLON
1953
Columbia
82 minutes   Color
Producer: Sam Katzman
Director: William Castle
Screenplay: DeVallon Scott
Photography: Henry Freulich
Editor: William A. Lyon
Art Director: Paul Palmentola
Musical Director: Mischa Bakaleinikoff
Special Effects: Jack Erickson
Set Decorator: Sidney Clifford
Assistant Director: Charles S. Gould
Choreographer: Willetta Smith
        CAST: Richard Conte (Nahum), Linda Christian
(Princess Panthea), Maurice Schwartz (Daniel), Terrance
[Terry] Kilburn (Cyrus), Michael Ansara (Belshazzar), Les-
lie Bradley (Nebuchadnezzar), Ruth Storey (Rachel), John
Crawford (General Avil), Ric Roman (Arrioch), Robert Grif-
fith (King Astyages), Beatrice Maude (Cyrus' Mother), Whea-
ton Chambers (Cyrus' Father), Paul Purcell (Overseer),
Julie [Newmar] Newmeyer (Speciality Dancer), Ernestine
Barrier (Princess Mandane).
        Based on stories in the Old Testament, this colorful
outing from the Sam Katzman unit at Columbia appears to be
little seen today.   Artfully directed by William Castle,
SLAVES OF BABYLON is an entertaining little film which
remains true to its Biblical origins and does not deserve
the obscurity it has suffered.
        The story takes place in sixth century B.C. Babylon
with Nebuchadnezzar (Leslie Bradley) destroying Jerusalem
and taking the Israelites back to Babylon as slaves, forcing
them to build the great Temple of Bel Marduk, where they
refuse to worship.   The king is tolerant of this and even
seeks the council of Daniel (Maurice Schwartz), who con-
fides to young warrior Nahum (Richard Conte) that Babylon
will one day fall to a boy shepherd named Cyrus (Terrance
Kilburn), the rightful king of Media.   Nahum goes to Cyrus
and convinces him of his right to the throne.   Nahum leads
an army and wins the kingdom, although in Babylon the
king's evil son, Belshazzar (Michael Ansara), has Daniel
thrown in a den of lions; when he is unharmed, the king believes it is a miracle.   When Cyrus' army attacks Babylon,
Nahum leads them through an opening in a little known un-
derwater gate to the heart of the city and after a fierce
battle, Cyrus becomes the king of Babylon.   The new king

then grants Daniel and Nahum the right to lead their people back to Israel in peace and freedom.

ADAN Y EVA (Adam and Eve)
1956
Mexico
Películas Nacionales
82 minutes   Color
Producer-Director-Screenplay: Alberto Gout
Executive Producer: Francisco Oliveros Del Valle
Photography: Alex Phillips
Editor: Jorge Bustos
Music: Gustavo Cesar Carrion
Set Designer: Manuel Fontanals
Sound: James L. Fields
Assistant Director: Julio Cahero
Production Manager: Alfonso Morones
    CAST: Christiane Martell (Eve), Carlos Baena (Adam), C. Portillo Acosta, P. de Cervantes (Narrators).
    Done totally in pantomime, with spoken narration from the Book of Genesis, ADAN Y EVA (Adam and Eve), a Mexican production, is a serious, reverent attempt to show the story of Creation as told in The Bible.   The film covers the creation of the world, God's creating Adam and then Eve, their happiness in the Garden of Eden, Eve's temptation by the serpent, the fall of man and Adam and Eve's expulsion from the Garden.
    A well-made production, the film was greatly enhanced by Christiane Martell, Miss Universe of 1953, and Carlos Baena in the title roles.   The film, however, was limited in its release appeal because of its frequent nudity, although it was done tastefully and within the framework of the Scriptures.   This aspect of the production, however, confined it to art theatres and grind houses for its United States showings.

THE TEN COMMANDMENTS
1956
Paramount
221 minutes   Color
Producer-Director: Cecil B. DeMille
Associate Producer: Henry Wilcoxon
Screenplay: Aeneas Mackenzie, Jesse L. Lasky Jr.,

Frederic M. Frank & Jack Guriss, from The
Holy Scripture and ancient texts of Josephus,
Eusebius, Philo and The Midrash and the novels
Prince of Egypt by Dorothy Clarke Wilson, Pil-
lar of Fire by Rev. J. H. Ingraham and On
Eagle's Wings by Rev. G. E. Southan
Photography: Loyal Griggs, with J. Peverell Marley, John
Warren & Wallace Kelly
Editor: Anne Bauchens
Music: Elmer Bernstein
Choreography: LeRoy Printz & Ruth Godfrey
Costumes: Edith Head, Ralph Jester, John Jensen, Dorothy
Jeakins & Arnold Freberg
Assistant Directors: Francisco Day, Michael Moore, Ed-
ward Slaven, Daniel McCauley &
Fouard Aref
CAST: Charlton Heston (Moses), Yul Brynner (Rame-
ses), Anne Baxter (Nefertiti), Edward G. Robinson (Dathan),
Yvonne De Carlo (Sephora), Debra Paget (Lilie), John Derek
(Joshua), Sir Cedric Hardwicke (Sethi), Nina Foch (Bithiah),
Martha Scott (Yochabel), Judith Anderson (Mamnet), Vincent
Price (Baka), John Carradine (Aaron), Eduard Franz (Jeth-
ro), Olive Deering (Miriam), Donald Curtis (Mered), Doug-
lass Dumbrille (Jannes), Lawrence Dobkin (Hur Ben Caleb),
Frank De Kova (Abiran), H. B. Warner (Amminadab), Henry
Wilcoxon (Fentau), Julia Faye (Elisheba), Lisa Mitchell,
Noelle Williams, Joanne Merlin, Pat Richard, Joyce Van-
derveen, Diane Hull (Jethro's Daughters), Abbar El Bough-
dadly (Rameses' Charioteer), Fraser Heston (The Infant
Moses), John Miljan (The Blind One), Tommy Duran (Ger-
shou), Francis J. McDonald (Simon), Ian Keith (Rameses I),
Joan Woodbury (Korah's Wife), Ramsay Hill (Korah), Woody
Strode (King of Ethiopia), Dorothy Adams (Hebrew Woman),
Eric Alden (Officer), Henry Brandon (Commander of Hosts),
Touch [Michael] Connors (Amalekite Herder), Henry Corden
(Sheik of Ezion), Edna May Cooper (Court Lady), Kem Dibbs
(Corporal), Fred Kohler Jr. (Foreman), Gail Kobe (Pretty
Slave Girl), John Merton, Amena Mohamed (Architect's As-
sistants), Addison Richards (Fanbearer), Onslow Stevens
(Lugal), Clint Walker (Sardinian Captain), Frank Wilcox
(Wazir), Luis Alberni (Old Hebrew), Michael Ansara, Fred
Coby (Taskmasters), Tony Dante (Libyan Captain), Frank
Darien, Carl Switzer, Edward Earle (Slaves), Franklyn
Farnum (High Officer), John Hurt (Cretan Ambassador),
Nick Hinton (Flagman), Walter Woolf King (Old Man), Em-
mett Lynn (Old Slave), Stanley Price (Slave Carrying Load),
Robert Vaughn (Spearman), Herb Alpert (Drum Player).

Vincent Price and Charlton Heston in THE TEN COMMAND-
MENTS (Paramount, 1956).

Cecil B. DeMille had already made the epitome of religious films with KING OF KINGS (q. v.) (Paramount, 1927) and in the years since he had wanted to remake his 1923 version of THE TEN COMMANDMENTS. As wide screen and color took over the cinema in the 1950s, the producer-director realized he now had the medium to present properly what he knew was to be his final, and he hoped, his greatest epic. The silent version of THE TEN COMMANDMENTS had followed the idiom DeMille had used so successfully during that period, that is telling both ancient and modern stories in the same film, the episodes paralleling each other in plot. With KING OF KINGS, however, and into the sound era DeMille had kept his costumers totally in one period. By the time he was to begin filming his remake of THE TEN COMMANDMENTS DeMille was to the movie-going public the greatest producer of epic melodramas and was expected to turn out a classic in this production--and that is just what he did.

DeMille once said he made his Biblical movies fictional to make his characters appear more human. If this is so, his remake of THE TEN COMMANDMENTS is full of "human" characters because this is one of the most fictional of all films based on The Bible. Although the movie does tell the story of Moses from The Old Testament, as well as being based on a trio of books, THE TEN COMMANDMENTS basically is more than one-half pure fiction.

The story begins with the baby Moses (Fraser Heston) found floating in a basket on the Nile River by an Egyptian queen who raises him in Pharaoh's court. Once he reaches manhood, Moses (Charlton Heston) becomes a prince and the Pharaoh's right-hand manservant. As a result Moses has everything he could want--power, land, wealth and women--but he rejects it all when he learns that he is really a Jew. When Pharaoh hears of his true heritage he casts him out of Egypt and he wanders about the desert for many years, finally marrying a trader's daughter (Yvonne De Carlo). Later Joshua (John Derek) finds Moses and tells him he is "The Deliverer" of his people and that he must return to Egypt and free the Jews from Egyptian rule. Moses climbs to a nearby mountain to meditate and God, in the form of a burning bush, speaks to him and tells him to deliver His chosen people out of Egypt and into the promised land. Moses takes up his staff and returns to Egypt and when the Pharaoh (Yul Brynner) refuses to let his people go he curses the land with plagues. Finally Pharaoh relents and the Exodus from Egypt to Israel begins, with Egyptian troops decimated after the parting of the Red Sea. In the journey through the desert the people lose faith many times and finally God gives Moses The Ten Commandments. Eventually the Jews are led to the promised land, although Moses does not enter it; instead, he goes off into the desert to eternal peace.

Although the general outline of THE TEN COMMAND-MENTS stayed true to the Old Testament accounts of Moses, Hollywood added a great deal of fiction to pad the plot and add the type of glamor Cecil B. DeMille exuded in his films. Among the changes are the details of Moses' early life at Pharaoh's court, the episode with Moses' fiancée (he never had one in Egypt), Pharaoh being Moses' rival since childhood (hardly true considering the deity status of the Egyptian Pharaohs), and the character of Dathan (Edward G. Robinson)--the corrupt "bad guy" of the epic--who never existed.

On the other hand, the film contained splendid examples of DeMille artistry and screen splendor. The scene where God appears to Moses in the form of a burning bush is very beautiful and inspirational, as is the scene where God gives Moses "The Ten Commandments." In the field of special effects, the film proved to be excellent, especially in the parting of the Red Sea (which was actually red jello), the scene where "The Ten Commandments" are burned into the side of a mountain as written with the hand of God, the plagues of Egypt, the burning bush and the earthquake that destroys the orgy of sin near the film's climax. All of these sequences are exceedingly well produced and hold up quite well today, more than two decades since the film's release.

Just as important as the production aspects of the film was its casting. DeMille populated the film with stars, former stars and character actors who had been working with him for decades. Charlton Heston proved himself a first-rate actor in the role of Moses, conveying the difficult part from early manhood to old age with authority. The entire supporting cast was superb, especially Yvonne De Carlo in the vague role of Moses' wife, Yul Brynner as Pharaoh Rameses and John Carradine as Aaron. Among the DeMille veterans in the cast were Henry Wilcoxon, who also served as the film's associate producer, Julia Faye, John Miljan and H. B. Warner, who had given such a brilliant performance as Jesus in DeMille's THE KING OF KINGS, some three decades earlier.

While the critics had their usual mixed feelings about THE TEN COMMANDMENTS, with some dubbing it still "another run of DeMille picture," the moviegoers loved the film and made it a box office sensation. For years the film was in re-release and today its splendor is often rerun via network television. Despite its many fictions, THE TEN COMMANDMENTS is a beautifully-produced motion picture, and if the story strays now and then, the true meaning of The Bible is always there.

THE STORY OF MANKIND
1957
Warner Brothers
100 minutes   Color
Producer-Director: Irwin Allen
Associate Producer: George E. Swink
Screenplay: Irwin Allen & Charles Bennett, from the book
            by Hendrik Van Loon
Photography: Nick Musuraca
Editor: Gene Palmer
Music: Paul Sawtell
Art Director: Art Loel
Assistant Director: Joseph Don Page
Costumes: Marjorie Best
        CAST: Ronald Colman (The Spirit of Man), Hedy Lamarr (Joan of Arc), Groucho Marx (Peter Minuit), Harpo Marx (Isaac Newton), Chico Marx (Monk), Virginia Mayo (Cleopatra), Vincent Price (Satan), Peter Lorre (Nero), Charles Coburn (Hippocrates), Sir Cedric Hardwicke (High Judge), Cesar Romero (Spanish Envoy), John Carradine (Khufu), Dennis Hopper (Napoleon), Marie Wilson (Marie Antoinette), Helmut Dantine (Antony), Edward Everett Horton (Sir Walter Raleigh), Reginald Gardiner (William Shakespeare), Marie Windsor (Josephine), Cathy O'Donnell (Early Christian Woman), Franklin Pangborn (Marquis de Varennes), Melville Cooper (Major Domo), Francis X. Bushman (Moses), Henry Daniell (Bishop of Beauvais), Jim Ameche (Alexander Graham Bell), Dani Grayne (Helen of Troy), Anthony Dexter (Christopher Columbus), Austin Green (Abraham Lincoln), Bobby Watson (Adolf Hitler), Reginald Sheffield (Caesar), Nick Cravat (Apprentice), Alexander Lockwood (Promoter), Melinda Marx (Early Christian Child), Bart Mattson (Cleopatra's Brother), Don Megowan (Early Man), Marvin Miller (Armana), Nancy Miller (Early Woman), Leonard Mudie (Chief Inquisitor), Major Sam Harris (Nobleman), Abraham Sofaer (Indian Chief); George E. Stone, David Bond, Richard Cutting, Toni Gerry, Eden Hartford, Burt Nelson, Tudor Owen, Ziva Rodann, Harry Ruby, William Schallert.
        Hendrik Van Loon's best seller from the 1920s was

brought to the screen by producer-director Irwin Allen (later noted for such TV series as "The Voyage to the Bottom of the Sea," "The Time Tunnel," "Lost in Space" and "Land of the Giants," as well as "disaster" epics like THE TOWER-ING INFERNO) in an effort to make history entertaining as well as informative. The end result was a "sophomoric" (Cue) feature which used a great deal of stock footage from the Warner Brothers library and wrapped it around a number of miscast former stars and character actors playing historical characters. Perhaps the most obviously miscast were Harpo Marx as Sir Isaac Newton and Hedy Lamarr as Joan of Arc. The film was a huge failure and was bombarded by the critics. The Los Angeles Examiner called it an "historical dud" while the Los Angeles Times said it was "amateurishly conceived and acted."

The film begins in the future with mankind in possession of the super-bomb and about to destroy itself unless Heaven intervenes. In a trial before the Heavenly Tribunal, the Spirit of Man (Ronald Colman) defends mankind and its deeds against the prosecutor, The Devil (Vincent Price), who claims mankind should be allowed to destroy itself. Thus the history of the world unfolds in order for the judges to make a decision. In Biblical terms, the film touches on religion only on two occasions: Moses (Francis X. Bushman) is seen receiving The Ten Commandments in a well staged sequence, and later the Roman Emperor Nero (Peter Lorre) is shown in his persecution of early Christians. These were vignettes and, like the rest of the sequences in the fast-moving feature, were quite brief.

STVORENI SVETA (The Creation of the World)
1958
Czechoslovakia
90 minutes   Color
Director-Screenplay: Eduard Hofman
Music: Jan Rychlik
Art Director: Jean Effel

The Devil appears in this low-budget animated feature on Genesis, which was based on a series of French booklets on the subject by Jean Effel, who served as the film's art director. Although never released in the United States, this Communist-country production apparently used the topic of religion to get laughs, and not for its spiritual aspects.

DAVID ED GOLIA (David and Goliath)
1959
Italian
ANSA Cinematografica
95 minutes   Color
Executive Producer: Emimmo Salvi
Directors: Richard Pottier & Ferdinando Baldi
Screenplay: Umberto Scrapelli, Gino Mancini, Emimmo
          Salvi & Ambrogio Malteni
Photography: Adalberto Albertini & Carlo Fiore
Editor: Franco Fraticelli
Music: Carlo Innocenzi
Art Director: Oscar D'Amico
Choreography: Carla Renalli
Assistant Director: Gianfranco Baldanello
Makeup: Gugliemo Bonatti
          CAST: Ivo Payer (David), Orson Welles (King Saul),
Pierre Cressoy (Jonathan), Eleanora Rossi Drago (Maab),
Edward Hilton (Prophet Samuel), Massimo Serato (Abner),
Furio Meniconi (King Asrod), Dante Maggio (Cret), Kronos
(Goliath), Giulia Rubini (Michal), Umberto Fiz (Lazar),
Luigi Tosi (Benjamin), Ugo Sasso (Huro); Carlo D'Angelo,
Gabriele Tinti, Ileana Donelli, Carla Foscair, Fabrizio
Capucci, Roberto Miali, Renato Terra, Emma Baron.
          Issued in the United States in 1961 as DAVID AND
GOLIATH by Allied Artists, this dubbed costumer was
filmed in Jerusalem and Yugoslavia.   It told how power-
mad King Saul (Orson Welles) was denounced by the
Prophet Samuel (Edward Hilton), who chose young shepherd
David (Ivo Payer) to lead the Israelis.   Wanting to trap the
youth, Saul's evil advisor Abner (Massimo Serato) has David
go to the enemy Philistines asking for a truce.   There King
Asrod (Furio Meniconi) agrees to the truce if David will do
battle with the giant Philistine Goliath (Kronos).   When
David slays Goliath he comes home to his people in triumph
and Abner tries to kill him, but King Saul kills his advisor
to save the youth and then offers David the hand of his
daughter Michal (Giulia Rubini).
          This overly dramatic costume melodrama suffered
from poor dubbing in its U.S. release as well as from a
bloated and overly hammy performance from Orson Welles
as King Saul.   The result was a very brief theatrical release for the feature before it was shunted off to television.

GIUDITTA E OLOFERNE (Judith and Holofernes)
1959

Italy-France
Vic Films/CEC
94 minutes   Color
Director: Signor Cerchio
Screenplay: Fernando Cerchio, Damino Damiani, Gian Paolo
                    Callegri & Guildo Malatesta
         CAST: Massimo Girotti (Holofernes), Isabelle Corey
(Judith), Renato Baldini (Arbar), Yvette Masson (Rispa),
Gianni Rizzo (Ozia), Enzo Doria (Daniel).
         Taken from "The Lost Books of the Bible, " this
film tells of the Jewish girl Judith (Isabelle Corey) who
tries to save her people from the pagan conqueror general
Holofernes (Massimo Girotti), who abolishes their religion
and forces the people to worship a statue or be imprisoned.
Judith disguises herself as a courtesan and becomes a favorite of the Assyrian general, whose head she cuts off and
takes back to her people, giving them the courage to rebel
against the invaders.
         Universal released the film in the United States in
1962 as HEAD OF A TYRANT, minus eleven minutes of its
original running time. Isabelle Corey proved charming in
the title role as Judith but her presence is all that distinguishes this version of the story, which was done much better by D. W. Griffith in 1914 in JUDITH OF BETHULIA
(q. v.).

NOAH'S ARK
1959
Warner Brothers
1 reel   Color
Producer: Walt Disney
Animator: Bill Justice
         The story of Noah, his ark and the great flood were
retold in this brief one-reeler from Walt Disney Productions.
Animator Bill Justice used stick figures in making this short,
which was nominated for an Academy Award.

SOLOMON AND SHEBA
1959
United Artists
139 minutes   Color
Producer: Ted Richmond
Director: King Vidor

Screenplay: Anthony Veiller, Paul Dudley & George Bruce
Story: Crane Wilbur
Photography: Freddie Young
Editor: John Ludwig
Music: Mario Nascimbene
Art Directors: Richard Day & Alfred Sweeney
Choreography: Jaroslav Berger
Special Effects: Alex Weldon
Sound: F. C. Hughesdon & Aubrey Lewis
    CAST: Yul Brynner (Solomon), Gina Lollobrigida
(Sheba), George Sanders (Abonijah), Marisa Pavan (Abishag),
David Farrar (Pharaoh), John Crawford (Joab), Laurence
Naismith (Hezrei), Jose Nieto (Ahab), Alejandro Rey (Sittar),
Harry Andrews (Baltor), Julio Perra (Zadok), Mauruchi Fres-
no (Bathsheba), William Devlin (Nathan), Felix De Pomes
(Egyptian General), Jean Anderson (Takyan), Jack Guillim
(Josiah), Finlay Currie (King David).
    Advertised as "The Mightiest Motion Picture Ever
Created," SOLOMON AND SHEBA was a $6 million epic
that seemed doomed from the start. Star Tyrone Power
died while on location filming in Spain and his scenes were
hastily reshot with Yul Brynner, who had scored so well as
Rameses in THE TEN COMMANDMENTS (q. v.) three years
before. Full of banal dialogue, tame orgy scenes and poorly
conceived romance, the film turned out to be "an animated
comic strip utilizing live actors" (Saturday Review).
    The story told of how the Egyptian Pharaoh (David
Farrar) hoped to defeat his enemy, Israeli king Solomon
(Yul Brynner), by having his ally, the beautiful Sheba (Gina
Lollobrigida), seduce him. The two fall in love, however,
and the barbarian queen persuades Solomon to let her perform pagan rites in a sacred temple, which is destroyed by
a lightning bolt, killing Solomon's adopted sister (Marisa
Pavan). This tribulation causes Sheba to vow to return to
her homeland with Solomon's religion if he is spared in the
upcoming battle with the Egyptians.

THE CREATION OF WOMAN
1960
India
16 minutes   Color
Producer: Ismail Merchant
    The story of Creation is retold with the focus on how
God created Eve, the first woman.

ESTHER E IL RE (Esther and the King)
1960
United States-Italy
20th Century-Fox/Galatea
110 minutes   Color
Producer-Director: Raoul Walsh
Screenplay: Raoul Walsh & Michael Elkins
Photography: Mario Bava
Editor: Jerry Webb
Music: Francesco Lavagnino & Robert Nicolosi
Art Directors: G. Giovanni & Massimo Tavazzi
             CAST: Joan Collins (Esther), Richard Egan (King Ahasuerus), Denis O'Dea (Mordecai), Georgio Fantoni (Haman), Rik Battaglia (Simon), Renato Baldini (Klydrathes), Gabriele Tinti (Samuel), Rosalba Neri (Zeresh), Robert Buchanan (Hegai), Daniela Rocca (Queen Vashti), Folco Lulli (Tobiah).

Veteran Hollywood director Raoul Walsh produced and directed this costumer in Italy and the result was a sadly mediocre and boring production.   Sexy Joan Collins was terribly miscast in the title role and Richard Egan was plainly bored in his role as the Persian king.   Filmed in Eastmancolor De Luxe and CinemaScope, ESTHER AND THE KING was one of the reasons television was so popular in the early 1960s.

Taking place in Persia in 400 B.C., the film told of the ambitious Judean maiden Esther (Joan Collins) who marries the Persian king (Richard Egan) after he finds out that his first wife had been unfaithful.   The girl then tries to use her influence to stop his persecution of her people. Palace intrigues and attempted murder were included in the backdrop of this story, which culminated in a battle between the people of Judea and the soldiers of a conspirator.   Unfortunately the battle scenes were poorly conceived and lackluster in presentation.   TV Movies correctly dubbed this film a "cardboard costumer."

GIUSEPPE VENDUTO DEI FRATELLI (Joseph Sold By His
        Brothers)
1960
Italy
Donati & Carpentieri Films-Cosmopolis Film-Jolly Film
103 minutes   Color
Producers: Ermanno Donati & Luigi Carpentieri
Directors: Luciano Ricci & Irving Rapper

Screenplay: Guglielmo Santangelo, Oreste Biancoli, Ennio
             De Concini & Guy Elmes
Photography: Riccardo Pallottini
Editor: Mario Serandrei
Music: Mario Nascimbene
Art Director: Oscar D'Amico
Costumes: Maria De Matteis
        CAST: Geoffrey Horne (Joseph), Robert Morley
(Potiphar), Belinda Lee (Henet), Finlay Currie (Jacob), Vera
Silenti (Asenath), Mario Girotti (Benjamin), Carlo Giustini
(Reuben), Arturo Dominici (Rekmira), Robert Rietty (Phar-
aoh), Julian Brooks (Chief Baker), Mimo Billi (Chief Butler),
Marietto (Benjamin as a Child), Marco Guglielmi (Judah),
Dante De Paolo (Simeon), Charles Borromel (Dan), Helmut
Schneider (Zebulun), Loris Bazzocchi (Issachar), Antonio
Sergurini (Gad), Mario Mariza (Asher), Tonko Sarcevic
(Levi).
        This lavish production tells the story of Joseph
(Geoffrey Horne), the favorite of the fourteen sons of Jacob
(Finlay Currie), who is sold into slavery by his brothers in
Egypt so he will not get their father's wealth.   In slavery
he saves the life of his master (Robert Morley) and becomes
a favorite because of accurate dream predictions.   When he
rebuffs the advances of his master's pretty young wife (Belinda Lee) he comes into disfavor but soon becomes a con-
fidant of the Pharaoh (Robert Rietty) because of his ability
to foretell future events.   He accurately predicts seven
years of prosperity and seven years of famine for Egypt
and because he has advised Pharaoh to store grain for the
famine he is rewarded with a post as a powerful official.
When his brothers come to Pharaoh's court in search of
food to buy, Joseph tells them who he is and he forgives
them for selling him into slavery.
        Despite the grand looking sets, this dubbed costumer
is a tedious effort hampered by terrible acting and juvenile
dialogue.   This dubbed version was issued in the United
States in 1962 as THE STORY OF JOSEPH AND HIS BRETH-
REN by Colorama Features/Capitol Films.   It is also called
THE STORY OF JOSEPH and was released in Great Britain
as SOLD INTO EGYPT.

THE PRIVATE LIVES OF ADAM AND EVE
1960
Universal
86 minutes   B/W & Color

Producer: Red Doff
Directors: Albert Zugsmith & Mickey Rooney
Screenplay: George Kennett and Robert Hill, from a story
by George Kennett
Photography: Philip Lathrop
Editor: Eddie Broussard
Music: Van Alexander
Art Directors: Alexander Golitzen & Richard Riedel
Makeup: Bud Westmore
CAST: Mickey Rooney (Nick Lewis/The Devil),
Mamie Van Doren (Evie Simms/Eve), Fay Spain (Lil Lewis/
Lilith), Mel Torme (Hal Sanders), Martin Milner (Ad
Simms/Adam), Tuesday Weld (Vangie Harper), Paul Anka
(Pinkie Parker), Cecil Kellaway (Doc Baylor), Ziva Rodann
(Passiona), June Wilkinson, Theona Bryant, Phillipa Fallon,
Barbara Walden, Toni Covington (Devil's Familiars), Nancy
Root, Donna Lynne, Sharon Wiley, Miki Kato, Andrea Smith,
Buni Bacon, Stella Garcia (Satan's Sinners).
This so-called romantic comedy appeared to be a
cross between The Old Testament's Garden of Eden story
and John Steinbeck's The Wayward Bus. Its plotline found
a busload of passengers on their way to Reno stranded in
an old church during a storm, with one of them reading
from The Bible and several passengers having the same
dream--The Devil (Mickey Rooney) sends a sexy girl (Fay
Spain) to the Garden of Eden to tempt Adam (Martin Milner)
while Eve (Mamie Van Doren) eats of the forbidden fruit before Adam can be tempted.
With sequences in Spectacolor, THE PRIVATE LIVES
OF ADAM AND EVE was basically a flat comedy with a few
funny moments. The so-called humor in the film, however,
was exceedingly forced, especially Mickey Rooney's performance as the Devil, as well as the serpent in the Garden.
The cast itself was an odd assortment of players and the
public generally avoided this so-called farce. It should be
noted that co-director Albert Zugsmith, who had produced
some fairly good features at Universal in the 1950s (e. g. ,
TOUCH OF EVIL [1957]), reached the apex of his career as
a director with this, his first directorial outing. After that
his career nosedived with exploitation items like SEX KIT-
TENS GO TO COLLEGE (Allied Artists, 1960), DOG EAT
DOG (Ajay/Unione, 1964) and RAPIST (Famous Players,
1973).

A STORY OF DAVID
1960

MARDEP Productions A. G.
95 minutes   Color
Producer: George Patcher
Director: Bob McNaught
Screenplay: Gerry Day & Terence Maple
    CAST: Jeff Chandler (David), Barbara Shelley (Abigail), Basil Sydney (Saul), David Knight (Jonathan), Donald Pleasence (Nabal), Peter Arne (Doeg), Angela Browne (Michal); Richard O'Sullivan, Robert Brown, David Davies, Martin Wyldeck, John Van Eyssen, Zena Marshall, Charles Carson, Alec Mango, Peter Madden, Peter Hempson.

Originally produced as an ABC-TV special called "David the Outlaw," this Israeli-made feature was exhibited in theatres in the United States and Great Britain under the title A STORY OF DAVID.   For its British release the film ran 104 minutes, when issued there by Fox, but for its U. S. issuance the film was cut by nine minutes.   Today the film appears on U. S. television via American International.

The often-filmed story told of Saul (Basil Sydney), king of Israel, being jealous of young warrior-shepherd David (Jeff Chandler), who receives greater acclamation from the people after their return from defeating the Philistines, their traditional enemy, and David's slaying of the giant Goliath.   Doeg (Peter Arne), chief herdsman of the kingdom, takes advantage of Saul's rage to poison his mind against David by telling him David is after the king's throne. When Saul finds David leaving his daughter's (Angela Browne) quarters, the king hurls a spear at him but impales his own shadow.   David flees and takes shelter with herdsman Nabal (Donald Pleasence), who turns him in to the king.   That night David enters Saul's tent and disarms the king, who asks for his forgiveness.   Not trusting Saul, David looks for a sign from God and when a mountain goat appears and goes into the mountains (although there are no mountain goats in the region), David takes this as the sign and gathers his men and Abigail (Barbara Shelley), the unwilling bride of Nabal, and they follow the goat's path to freedom.

Movies on TV (1977) said of this pedestrian drama, "Better than usual production, but generally undistinguished, slow moving."   It should be noted that star Jeff Chandler was too old for the part of Young David, although he handled the chore in his usual good fashion.   John Mountjoy wrote in his essay, "The Cinema Looks at God" in Film Review 1968-69 (1968), that the film "was a sort of Biblical Western notable in that it almost forgot sex and sadism."

THE STORY OF RUTH
1960
20th Century-Fox
132 minutes Color
Producer: Samuel G. Engel
Director: Henry Koster
Screenplay: Norman Crowin
Photography: Arthur E. Arling
Editor: Jack W. Holmes
      CAST: Elana Eden (Ruth), Stuart Whitman (Boaz),
Tom Tryon (Mahlon), Peggy Wood (Naomi), Viveca Lindfors
(Eleilat), Jeff Morrow (Tob), Thayer David (Hedak), Les
Tremayne (Elimelech), Eduard Franz (Jehoan), Leo Fuchs
(Sochin), Lili Velantz (Kera), John Gabriel (Chilion), Ziva
Rodann (Oraph), Basil Ruysdael (Shammah), John Banner
(King of Moah), Adelina Pedroza (Iduma), Daphne Einhorn
(Tebah), Sara Taft (Eska), Jean Inness (Hagah), Berry
Kroeger (Huphim), Jon Silo (Tacher); Don Diamond, Chrystine
Jordan, Kelton Garwood, Charles Wagenheim, Ralph Moody,
Ben Astar, Charles Horvath, Robert Adler, Anthony Jochim,
Stassa Damacus, Doris Wise, Victor Buono, Inez Pedroza.
      This is an adaptation of the Book of Ruth with liber-
ties taken with the Biblical text, although those liberties do
enhance somewhat the dramatic content of the film, which is
far too long at 132 minutes. Further hampering the proceedings is the casting of inexperienced Elana Eden in the
title role and a supporting cast that seems only to be going
through its paces, except for Peggy Wood, who is quite
good as Ruth's mother-in-law.
      THE STORY OF RUTH tells of the ex-high priestess,
Ruth (Elana Eden), who denounces her pagan gods when she
marries a Judean (Tom Tryon) and finds comfort in his God.
When she is widowed she is accused of idolatry but is cleared
of the charge by Boaz (Stuart Whitman), a friend of her late
spouse. In many respects an interesting and intelligent film,
the feature was another of those 1960s' Biblical epics which
did not capture the fancy of the movie-going public.

SODOMA E GOMORRA (Sodom and Gomorrah)
1961
Italy-France
Titanus/S. N. Pathé/20th Century-Fox
154 minutes Color
Producer: Goffredo Lombardo
Directors: Robert Aldrich & Sergio Leone

Screenplay: Hugo Butler & Giorgio Prosperi
Photography: Silvano Ippoliti, Mario Moutouri & Cyril
Knowles
Editor: Peter Tanner
Music: Miklos Rozsa
Makeup: Euclide Santoll
Choreography: Archie Savage
Special Effects: Lee Zavits, Serge Urbisaglia & Wally
Veevers
Set Decorators: Gino Brosio & Emilio D'Andria
Prolog/Main Titles: Maurice Binder
Assistant Director: Gus Agosti
Art Director: Ken Adams
Second Unit Director: Oscar Randolph
Costumes: Giancarlo Bartolini Salimbani
CAST: Stewart Granger (Lot), Pier Angeli (Ildith),
Stanley Baker (Astaroth), Rossana Podesta (Shuah), Anouk
Aimée (Queen Bera), Claudio Mori (Maleb), Rik Battaglia
(Melchir), Giacomo Rossi Stuart (Ishmael), Feodor Chalia-
pin (Alabios), Aldo Silvani (Nacor), Enzo Fiermonte (Eber),
Scilla Gabel (Tamar), Antonio De Teffe (Captain), Massimo
Pietrobon (Isaac), Andrea Tagliabue (Eber's Son), Francesco
Tensi (Old Man), Mitzuko Takara (Orpha), Liana Del Balzo
(Hebrew Woman), Alice & Ellen Kessler (Dancers), Mimmo
Palmara (Mimmo).

This laborious costume spectacle attempted to tell the
story of Lot and his family fleeing the twin cities of sin before they were destroyed by the wrath of God. The English
version was directed by Robert Aldrich while the Italian one
was helmed by Sergio Leone, soon to win fame for his violent "Spaghetti Westerns." The talents of either director
were not much in evidence in this lumbering story of Lot
(Stewart Granger) leading a band of Hebrews to the twin
cities ruled over by a power-mad queen (Anouk Aimée). All
of the evils of the cities, including plenty of simulated or-
gies, were included and the plot culminated with two angels
freeing Lot from the queen's prison and leading him and his
family to safety, with Lot's wife turning into a pillar of salt
as God destroys the evil cities.

Unfortunately Hollywood fiction was heavily used in
this film and its overall sensationalism more than overshad-
owed the finest aspect of the film, its performances. Stewart Granger, especially, was quite good in the difficult role
of Lot, and co-stars Pier Angeli, Stanley Baker, Rossana
Podesta and Anouk Aimée also rose above the mundane script
and glossy production values, although Ms. Aimée was shack-
led with one of the most ludicrous lines ever delivered in

films when she intoned, "Welcome, sodomites. "
The film was issued in the United States as SODOM AND GOMORRAH but its success was minimal.

ADAM AND EVE
1962
Czechoslovakia
90 minutes   Color
Producer-Director: Dusan Merek
The Creation story from the Book of Genesis, centering on Adam and Eve, was depicted in this animated film. The finale also had the world destroyed by a bomb in the future.

JOSEPH AND HIS BRETHREN
1962
Israel
65 minutes   Color
Producer-Director: Alina & Yoram Gross
This puppet feature, using the process of animation, tells the story of Joseph, who was sold into slavery in Egypt by his jealous brothers.

I PATRIARCHI DELLA BIBBIA (The Patriarchs of the Bible)
1963
Italy
San Paolo Film
Color
Director: Marcello Baldi
Screenplay: Giuseppe Mangione & Ottavio Jemma
Photography: Marcello Masciocchi
Music: Ted Uselli & Gino Marinuzzi Jr.
CAST: John Douglas, Judy Parker, Fosco Giachetti.
Another in the series of Italian spectacles from the 1960s which did not get much release outside its homeland, I PATRIARCHI DELLA BIBBIA told the stories of such Old Testament figures as Adam and Joseph, including the Creation and the Deluge.

IL VECCHIO TESTAMENTO (The Old Testament)
1963
Italy
Cineproduzione/Filmar
120 minutes   Color
Director: Gianfranco Parolini
   CAST: Brad Harris, Margaret Taylor, John Heston,
Mara Lane, Susan Paget, Philippe Hersent, Jacques Berthier,
Enzo Doria, Isarco Revaioli, Jay Stewart, Carlo Tamberlani,
Ingrizio Duco.
   Another colorful spectacle from Italy, this Biblical
drama told the Apocrypha tale of the victory of the Hebrews
over the Syrians in 150 B.C.   Opening in Jerusalem, the
film finds the Syrians trying to place a pagan god in the
Jews' temple, which causes a revolt.   The Hebrews, fear-
ing retribution, flee to Jericho under the leadership of priest
Matatia and his five sons, the Maccabees.   Matatia, however, dies in the desert and his sons lead their people to
the mountains.   They join forces with the Arabs to rout the
Syrians, and with the aid of a thunderbolt from heaven they
enter the enemy's stronghold and take it, restoring peace.
   Nicely produced, with spectacular battle scenes, THE
OLD TESTAMENT is another in the long string of Italian
films which failed to get international release.   A poorly
dubbed, and often hacked, version has been issued to U.S.
television via Four Star/Picturmedia as THE OLD TESTA-
MENT.

SAUL E DAVIDE (Saul and David)
1964
Italy-Spain
San Paolo Film Roma/Madrid
150 minutes   Color
Producer: Emilio Cordero
Director: Marcello Baldi
Screenplay: Emilio Cordero, Marcello Baldi & Tonino
            Guerra
Music: Teo Usuelli
   CASE: Norman Wooland (Saul), Gianni Garko (David);
Luz Marquez, Elisa Cegani, Virgilio Teixeira, Paolo Goz-
lino, Carlos Casaravilla, J. Anthony Mayans.
   Samuel, the last of the great prophets of Israel,
grows old and the tribe's elders force him to name a suc-
cessor.   He choses Saul.   After Saul's first victories in
war, discontent arises and Samuel realizes that God has
transferred His protection to one more worthy because of

Saul's disobedience. When shepherd boy David slays the giant Philistine Goliath with a sling, Saul takes David into his house, but he suspects that the youth is the one God has chosen to succeed him and he soon wants to free himself of the young man. Due to Saul's persecutions, David flees but returns and saves Saul's life and the king ends his distrust of him. When Saul and his son Jonathan are killed in battle with the Philistines, David is chosen as his successor, fulfilling Saul's final wish.

Another in the string of Italian spectacles retelling Old Testament stories, SAUL E DAVIDE was over-long and not particularly appealing to mid-1960s audiences. In fact, unlike other epics of its ilk, the feature apparently was never issued in the U.S. theatrically, although a dubbed version is available to television, under the title SAUL AND DAVID. The film's plot was derived from the First Book of Samuel in the Old Testament.

I GRANDI CONDOTTIERI (The Great Leaders)
1965
Italy-Spain
San Paolo Film/San Pablo Films
110 minutes   Color
Producer: Marcello Baldi
Director: Franz Perez Dolz
Screenplay: Ottavio Jemma, Flavio Nicholina, Marcello
             Baldi & Tonino Guerra
Photography: Marcello Masciocchi
Music: Ted Usuelli
     CAST: Fernando Rey (Gideon); Anton Geesink, Ivo Garrani, Rosalba Neri, Luz Marquez, Paolo Gozlino, Maruchi Fresno, Giorgio Cerioni, Ana Maria Noe, Jose Jaspe.

An Italian-Spanish co-production, this feature was released in Italy in 1965 as I GRANDI CONDOTTIERI (The Great Leaders) and the next year in Spain as LOS JUECES DE LA BIBLIA (The Judges of the Bible). A two-part film, it told the Old Testament stories of Gideon and Samson.

The first part of the film told of Gideon (Fernando Rey), a 40-year-old peasant who is chosen by the Lord to save the tribe of Israel from the Midianites. He is victorious in saving his people but cannot bring himself to kill the captured leader of the enemy, realizing that the victory was not his but God's. Next the story of Samson is retold, complete with his affair with Delilah, the loss of his strength when his head is shaved, his being blinded and reduced to slavery, and his final burst of strength when he calls on the Lord for help and causes the collapse of the Philistines' temple, bringing about the enemy's destruction.

Filmed on a good sized budget and in lavish color, this spectacle apparently was not released outside Europe. Rather fine at times, the film suffers from having been done before, and usually done better. Although some of the performances are good, especially that of international star Fernando Rey, the overall level of the production is mediocre and the scenes where Delilah seduces Samson are overdone to such a degree that they are hokey. Perhaps the highlight of the film is Samson's destruction of the temple at the finale.

This film was also called SAMSON AND GIDEON.

LA BIBBIA (The Bible)
1966
United States-Italy
20th Century-Fox
177 minutes   Color
Producer: Dino De Laurentiis
Directors: John Huston & Ernest Haas
Screenplay: Christopher Fry, with Jonathan Griffin, Ivo
            Perilli & Vittorio Bonicelli
Photography: Giuseppe Rotunno
Editor: Ralph Kemplen
Music: Toshiro Mayuzumi
Art Director: Mario Chiari
Makeup: Alberto De Rossi
Special Effects: Augie Lohman
      CAST: Michael Parks (Adam), Ulia Bergryd (Eve), Richard Harris (Cain), Stephen Boyd (Nemrod), George G. Scott (Abraham), Ava Gardner (Sarah), Franco Nero (Abel), Peter O'Toole (The Angel), John Huston (Noah/Narrator/ Voice of God), David Warner (Voice of Adam), Pupella Maggio (Noah's Wife), Cabriele Ferzetti (Lot), Eleonora Rossi Draggo (Lot's Wife), Roberto Rietti (Eliezzar), Zoe Sallis (Agar), Adriana Ambesi, Grazia Maria Spina (Lot's Daughters); Claudie Lange, Alberto Lucantoni, Luciana Conversi.

Released in the United States and Great Britain as THE BIBLE ... IN THE BEGINNING, this epic film was produced by Dino De Laurentiis, who had planned to film the entire Old Testament when he announced plans for this

George C. Scott and Alberto Lucantoni in THE BIBLE (20th Century-Fox, 1966).

super-production in the early 1960s.   By 1965 the film was running over 20 hours and was not completed.   When the picture was finally issued the next year it was down to three hours' running time and, as the title indicated, covered only the first twenty-two chapters of Genesis.   The result was a film that was decidedly uneven.   F. Maurice Speed, writing in Film Review 1968-69 (1969), called the film one "done on a vast scale with extremely good taste" while in retrospect Leonard Maltin's TV Movies (1978) called the film a "bomb," and added, "Definitely one time you should read the book instead."

Beginning with the Creation, the film covers Adam and Eve, Cain and Abel, Noah's Ark, The Flood, the Tower of Babel, the story of Abraham up to the sacrifice of Isaac, and the destruction of Sodom and Gomorrah.   Perhaps due to the swift coverage of these events, the film moves quickly and never drags, as is often the problem with Biblical epics.

Visually satisfying was the opening "Creation Sequence" which led to the portions with Adam (Michael Parks) and Eve (Ulia Bergryd) in the Garden of Eden.   An excellent effect in this sequence was the Devil appearing to Eve in the form of a serpent.   Next came the sequence where Cain (Richard Harris) kills his brother Abel (Franco Nero), and then Noah (John Huston) and the flood are shown, the flood sequences being exceptionally well handled.   Next came the story of Abraham (George C. Scott), and the film culminated in the destruction of Sodom and Gomorrah, another superbly handled sequence.   The special effects and second unit work in the film were quite good, as evidenced by the portion of the film which detailed Noah's descendants building the Tower of Babel.

Besides its good production values, the film also was well acted, with George C. Scott and Ava Gardner standing out in the cast in their roles as Abraham and Sarah, while Richard Harris gave a brutal, but fine, performance as Cain.   Director John Huston gave himself three roles in the film: Noah, the voice of God and the film's narrator.   Huston certainly looked the part of Noah and he was a competent narrator, although it was a bit presumptuous to grant himself also the part of the voice of God.   This is perhaps not surprising, coming from a man who basically squandered the massive talents once evident in such screen classics as THE MALTESE FALCON (Warner Brothers, 1941) and THE TREASURE OF SIERRA MADRE (Warner Brothers, 1948).

All in all, THE BIBLE ... IN THE BEGINNING was a pictorially satisfying film which many found inspirational.

Sadly, the film was not the box office power it was expected to be and Dino De Laurentiis' plans for filming the rest of the Old Testament were shelved.

JOSEPH THE DREAMER
1967
Israel
Color
Producer: Yoram Gross
    Yoram Gross, who co-produced the puppet-film JOSEPH AND HIS BRETHREN (q. v.) in 1962, remade the story of Joseph in this version, still another puppet film.

MAGOO AT SEA
1967
UPA
112 minutes   Color
Music: Charles Brandt
    CAST: Jim Backus (Voice of Mr. Quincy Magoo); Marvin Miller, Howard Morris, Julie Bennett, Shepard Menkin, Joe Gardner, Paul Frees (Voices).
    MAGOO AT SEA is a feature-length cartoon culled from "The Famous Adventures of Mr. Magoo" series telecast on NBC-TV during the 1964-65 season.   In the series Mr. Magoo served as the host and story teller and the cartoon character took on the guise of assorted characters of historical significance.   For this outing, which was issued to television as a feature in 1967, Mr. Magoo played Captain Kidd, hunted Moby Dick, adapted Treasure Island, and did his own interpretation of the story of Noah from The Old Testament.
    The sequence about Noah and the ark is especially well done.   It is aimed at juvenile viewers but it proves fun for adults as well.

LA CREACION (The Creation)
1968
Spain
Movinter
11 minutes   Color
Director: Antonio Morales

Childlike drawings detail the Creation story of Adam and Eve from the Book of Genesis in this color short from Spain.

EL PECO DE ADAN Y EVA (The Sin of Adam and Eve)
1968
Mexico
Azteca
Color
Producer-Director-Screenplay: Miguel Zacharias
     CAST: Jorge Rivero (Adam), Candy Wilson (Eve).
     Telling the story of Adam (Jorge Rivero) and Eve (Candy Wilson) in the Garden of Eden, EL PECO DE ADAN Y EVA has a most complicated release history. Shown in its homeland of Mexico in 1968, the film was finally issued in the United States in 1971 by New World Pictures under the title THE SIN OF ADAM AND EVE. The next year Woolner Brothers acquired distribution of the feature, and by now star Jorge Rivero had become George Rivero. Later that year Crest Films issued the picture in the Los Angeles area and Jorge Rivero was now George Rivers and producer-director-writer Miguel Zacharias was redubbed Michael Zachary. In 1976, eight years after its initial release, the color feature was acquired by Dimension Pictures which released it in the South.

THE JOYS OF JEZEBEL
1970
P. S. Films
75 minutes   Color
Producer-Director: A. P. Stootsberry
Screenplay: Maurice Smith
Photography: Dwayne Rayven
Editor: Mark Perri
Music: Vic Lane
Art Director: Earl Marshall
Assistant Director: Tony Rand
Production Coordinator: James Brand
Production Manager: Bethel Buckalew
Makeup: Ray Sebastian
     CAST: Christine Murray (Jezebel), Christopher Stone (Lucifer), Johnny Rocco (Joshua), Dixie Donovan (Rachel), Angela Graves (Ruth), Jay Edwards (Jeremiah), Woody Lee

(Solomon), Jess White (Goliath), La La (Lust), Geets Romo (Sol), Alice Friedland (Sarah), Ron Smith (Isaac), Feleshia Manning (Esther), Sherise Roland (Eve), Jackie Owens (Goliath's Girl), Bonnie Cooper (Solomon's Girl), Paul Austin, Sidney Cliff (Donkeymen), Terry Tassione, Tony Caccardo, Snoopy, Daniel Grant (Pit Men), Betty Avin, Johanne Thomas, Lynne, Jeanette Mills, Monica Williams, Ruth Liben, Casey Larrain (Pit Girls).

THE JOYS OF JEZEBEL is another example of the seemingly endless XXX-rated feature films designed for the pornography trade. A parody, the film told of the princess Jezebel (Christine Murray) who is betrayed and killed by Joshua (Johnny Rocco). In hell she makes a pact with Lucifer (Christopher Stone) to send him the virgin Rachel (Dixie Donovan) so that she can get revenge for her murder.

A whole gamut of Old Testament characters appear in the film, with Goliath (Jess White) being thrown into a pit of nymphs; Solomon (Woody Lee), who is credited as "the world's first dirty old man," seducing Eve (Sherise Roland); and pornographic visions of Ruth, Rachel, Sarah, Isaac and assorted other Biblical characters. One sequence even has a scorned Ruth (Angela Graves) going to Rachel for "sisterly comfort."

The film, also known as THE JOY OF JESABELLE and JEZEBEL, was reissued in 1975.

BIBLE
1974
Poolemar
84 minutes   Color
Producer: Marvin Shulman
Director-Screenplay-Photography: Wakefield Poole
Editors: Joseph Nelson & Peter Schneckenburger
Sound: Aaron Nathanson
   CAST: Bo White (Adam), Caprice Couselle (Eve), Georgina Spelvin (Bathsheba), Nicholas Flamel (David), Robert Benes (Uriah), Nancy Wachter (Handmaiden), Brahm van Zetten (Samson), Gloria Grant (Delilah), Bonnie Mathis (Mary), Dennis Wayne (Angel).

An erotic dramatization of various episodes from The Old Testament, BIBLE was not a successful film, perhaps because it was not hardcore enough for the XXX-rated trade nor softcore enough for the grindhouses. Certainly this film had no appeal to a mass audience, and certainly it was avoided by the devoutly faithful.

Among the stories told erotically in the X-rated feature was the story of Adam and Eve, filmed in the Virgin Islands; the story of Samson and Delilah, with a supporting cast of midgets; and the affair between David and Bathsheba, the latter portrayed by Georgina Spelvin, the star of such hardcore features as THE DEVIL IN MISS JONES (Marvin, 1973) and R-rated exploitation items such as GIRLS FOR RENT (Independent-International, 1975).

BIBLE was also released as IN THE BEGINNING and had a variety of working titles including WAKEFIELD POOLE'S BIBLE, B. C. SCANDALS and WAKEFIELD POOLE'S SCANDALS.

THE STORY OF JACOB AND JOSEPH
1974
ABC-TV/Columbia-Screen Gems
120 minutes   Color
Producer: Mildred Freed Alberg
Director: Michael Cacoyannis
Script: Ernest Kinoy
Photography: Ted Moore & Austin Dempster
Editor: Kevin Connor
Art Director: Kuli Sander
Music: Mikis Theodorakis
Costumes: Judy Moorcroft
Consultant: Dr. David Noel Freedman
CAST: Keith Michell (Jacob), Tony Lo Bianco (Joseph), Colleen Dewhurst (Rebekah), Herschel Bernardi (Laban), Harry Andrews (Isaac), Alan Bates (Narrator), Julian Glover (Esau), Yoseph Shiloah (Pharaoh), Yossi Grabber (Butler), Yona Elian (Rachel), Rachel Shore (Potiphar's Wife), Amnon Meskin (Baker), Bennes Maarden (Potiphar), Yehuda Efroni (Reuben), Shmuel Atzmon (Judah).

The first telefeature produced from a Biblical source, THE STORY OF JACOB AND JOSEPH told the story of Jacob (Keith Michell) and his birthright and the story of Joseph (Tony Lo Bianco) being sold into slavery by his brothers. Both accounts were narrated by Alan Bates and the film was telecast on ABC-TV on April 7, 1974.

Taken from the Old Testament, the story tells how Jacob and Joseph, the twin sons of Isaac (Harry Andrews) and Rebekah (Colleen Dewhurst), vie for their birthright and how Joseph is sold into slavery in Egypt by his brothers. There he becomes a favorite of Pharaoh (Yoseph Shiloah) because of his ability to predict the future through dreams.

When famine forces Jacob into Egypt to buy food for his family, he finds his brother and they are reunited. This led the way for the migration of the Jews to Egypt, four centuries before Moses.

Writing in Films in Review, Jack Edmund Nolan said the telefeature "wrought great drama from its near-documentary approach and ... is probably the feature film most faithful to the Bible as a source."

MOSES THE LAWGIVER
1975
United States-Italy
RAI Television/ITC/ATV
360 minutes   Color
Producer: Vicenzo Labella
Director: Gianfranco De Bosio
Screenplay: Anthony Burgess, Vittorio Bonicello, Bernardino
             Zappani & Gianfranco De Bosio
Photography: Marcello Gatti
Editor: Alberto Balleti
Music: Ennio Morricone
Second Unit Director-Special Effects: Mario Bava
Art Director: Pier Luigi Basile
Songs & Dances: Dov Seltzer
Choreography: Oshra El Kayam
Costumes: Enrico Sabbatini
        CAST: Burt Lancaster (Moses), Anthony Quayle (Aaron), Ingrid Thulin (Miriam), Will Lancaster (Young Moses), Irene Papas (Zipporah), Laurent Terzieff (Pharaoh Mernephta), Yousef Shiloah (Dathan), Aharon Ipale (Joshua), Shmuel Rodensky (Jethro), Richard Johnson (Narrator), Mario Ferrari (Rameses II), Mariangela Melato (Egyptian Princess), Simonetta Stefanelli (Cotbi), Melba Englander (Mernephta's Wife), Antonio Piovanelli (Koreb), Marina Berti (Eliseba); Paul Muller, Jose Quaglio, Umberto Raho, John Francis Lane, Paul Verani, Jacques Herlin, Giancarlo Badese, Cosimo Cinieri, Renato Chiantoni, Didi Lukof, Enzo Fieramonte, Andrea Aureli, Percy Hogan, Fausto DiBella, Galia Kohn, Umberto Rabo, Dina Doronne, Marco Steiner, Yossi Warjansky, Almos Tapshir, Haim Bashi, Haim Banai.
        CBS-TV telecast MOSES THE LAWGIVER as a six-part mini-series in 1975 (June 21, 28, July 5, 12, 26, August 2) to very favorable ratings.   Filmed in the summer of 1973 on location in Jerusalem and the Negev (where the

Burt Lancaster in MOSES THE LAWGIVER (Avco-Embassy, 1975).

company found itself briefly trapped during the Arab-Israeli War), the film goes into great detail in telling the story of Moses, with little fiction involved. The screenwriters did a fine job in adapting the Old Testament story of Moses and the film chronicles his birth, calling, the plagues, journey through the desert and the many miracles Moses performed through God's will.

In the early portions of the film, Will Lancaster played the Young Moses while in the bulk of the telefeature his father, Burt Lancaster, played the lawgiver at the age of 120. Both father and son were quite good, with Burt Lancaster particularly powerful as the elder Moses. Anthony Quayle was outstanding as Aaron.

Despite its attempt to present an accurate portrait of Moses, the film did not meet with critical praise. Variety noted, "[The film] makes a stab at realism through location sites but generally skims over religious-historical aspects as digest of Exodus. Figures lack genuine depth thanks to episodic approach. As drama, film fails to generate dramatic values, or most important, involvement."

The six-hour telefeature was re-edited for theatrical release in the United States in 1976 by Avco-Embassy, but the compact version failed to garner much release. Sir Lew Grade, who supplied the funds for this production, apparently sold the project to television in the hope that this would stimulate box office trade when the film finally hit the theatres. The ploy was not successful.

MOSES UND ARON (Moses and Aaron)
1975
West Germany
Janus-Film
110 minutes   Color
Directors-Screenplay: Jean-Marie Straub & Daniele Straub-
                         Huillet
Photography: Ugo Piccone
Music: Arnold Schoenberg
        CAST: Gunther Reich, Louis Devos, Eva Caspo,
Roger Lucas.

Arnold Schoenberg's three-act opera, MOSES UND ARON, was brought to the screen in its native land in 1975, some forty-five years after it was first started. Taking place on Mt. Sinai in Palestine in Biblical times, the opera recreated the Hebrews' situation after their exodus from Egypt, and their search for the Promised Land under the leadership of Moses.

The opera was first performed in 1951 and the next year it was presented in English by the BBC of London. The first complete performance of the opera in concert (the third act was unfinished) took place in 1954. Although a well made production, this screen version was not widely distributed outside West Germany due to the language barrier.

IN SEARCH OF NOAH'S ARK
1976
Sunn Classics Pictures
95 minutes Color
Producer: Charles E. Sellier Jr.
Director: James L. Conway
Screenplay: James L. Conway & Charles E. Sellier Jr.,
      from the book by David Balsinger
Photography: George Stapleford
Editor: Sharon Miller
      CAST: Vern Adix (Noah).

Billed as a docu-drama, IN SEARCH OF NOAH'S ARK is a speculation film which claims that the Ark built by Noah to save civilization during the Great Flood is embedded in the ice and snow of Mt. Ararat in Turkey, just as it is stated in The Bible.

The story of Noah (Vern Adix) and the Flood is enacted by a cast of little-known players, with seventy-one speaking parts plus stand-ins, as well as thirty different kinds of animals. A geographical profile of Mt. Ararat is presented, showing the sedimentary deposits and salt clusters which suggest that a flood did take place in the area. The story of Noah is further substantiated by archaeological studies, historical surveys, reconstructions, scientific tests and eyewitness accounts. The latter include records of expeditions to the site of the Ark, from 700 B.C. to the present. These include the examination of timber discoveries from the Ark by Sir James Bryce and Fernand Navarra, as well as aerial photographs which do show "something" quite large and craft-like buried in the ice of Mt. Ararat. The film concludes with interviews with authorities and professors, as well as actual footage from several of the expeditions.

While the feature does not really answer any of the questions it poses, the film is an interesting one, although cheaply made, and its manner of handling the subject makes it fun to speculate on "what might be."

Vern Adix in IN SEARCH OF NOAH'S ARK (Sunn Classics, 1976).

THE STORY OF DAVID
1976
ABC-TV/Columbia
200 minutes   Color
Producer: Mildred Freed Alberg
Script: Ernest Kinoy
Photography: John Coquilon
Editor: Sidney Katz
Music: Laurence Rosenthal
Consultant: Dr. David Noel Freedman

Part One--DAVID AND KING SAUL
Directors: Alex Segal & David Lowell Rich
Art Director: Kuli Sander
    CAST: Timothy Bottoms (David), Anthony Quayle
(King Saul), Norman Rodway (Joab), Odeb Teumi (Jonathan),
Mark Dignam (Samuel), Yehuda Effroni (Abner), Tony Tar-
ruella (Goliath), Ahuva Yuval (Abigail), Irit Benzer (Young
Michal), Avram Ben-Yosef (Ahimelech), Yakar Sernach
(Abiathar), Ilan Dar (Eliab), Koya Reuben (Shammah), David
Topaz (Abinadab), Ori Levy (Gaza).

Part Two--DAVID THE KING
Director: David Lowell Rich
Art Directors: Kuli Sander & Fernando Gonzalez
    CAST: Keith Michell (King David), Jane Seymour
(Bathsheba), Susan Hampshire (Michal), Norman Rodway
(Joab), Brian Blessed (Abner), Barry Morse (Jehosephat),
David Collings (Nathan), Nelson Modlin (Absalom), Terrance
Hardiman (Uriah), Janette Sterke (Abigail), David Nielson
(Amnon), Eric Chapman (Seriah).
    Made for television and telecast in two parts (on
April 9 and April 11, 1976) this well made feature was
filmed in Israel and Spain by producer Mildred Freed Al-
berg, who had previously done THE STORY OF JACOB
AND JOSEPH (q. v.).
    The first section of the telefeature told how shepherd
boy David (Timothy Bottoms) had the courage to slay the
giant Goliath (Tony Tarruella) and win the hand of King
Saul's (Anthony Quayle) daughter, Michal (Irit Benzer).
David also had to soothe Saul with his harp-playing but the
king proved to be moody with fits of anger and he soon
grew jealous of David and saw him as a threat to this
throne.   Part two of the drama focused on David (Keith
Michell) as the king of Israel, succeeding Saul, and his
adulterous affair with the tempting Bathsheba (Jane Sey-
mour).

Timothy Bottoms in THE STORY OF DAVID (ABC-TV, 1976).

TV Guide called the film "a vivid, well-acted Biblical drama" and, indeed, it was a well-produced, inspirational project in which the true meaning of the Biblical stories was presented.

GREATEST HEROES OF THE BIBLE
November 19, 1978-May 22, 1979
NBC-TV/Schick Sunn Classic Productions
8½ hours   Color
Producers: Bill Carnford & Jim Simmons
Executive Producer: Charles E. Sellier, Jr.
Director: James L. Conway
Script: Stephen Lord, Brian Russell & S. S. Schweitzer
Photography: Paul Hipp
Editor: O. Nicholas Brown
Art Director: Paul Staheli
Music: Bob Summers
Sound: Rod Sutton
    Schick Sunn Classic Productions of Salt Lake City, Utah, a company which had produced such genre exploitation items as IN SEARCH OF NOAH'S ARK, BEYOND AND BACK, and IN SEARCH OF HISTORIC JESUS (qq. v.), teamed with NBC-TV to make this eight-part telefeature based on the Old Testament.   Filmed in Arizona, the mini-series turned out to be a high quality production, well made and finely acted, with fast-paced scripts and a fairly accurate inter-pretation of the Scriptures. *
    The following is a listing of the individual segments of the telefilm, broadcast dates, cast and character names. It should be noted that Peter Mark Richman provided the voice of God in the first four parts of the mini-series, with Victor Jory serving as narrator on the final four segments.

"David and Goliath" November 19, 1978
    CAST: Roger Kern (David), Ted Cassidy (Goliath), Hugh O'Brian (Abner), John Dehner (Debuknar); Jeff Corey, Michael Ruud, Dan Travanti, John LaZar, Teck Murdock.

"Samson and Delilah" November 19, 1978
    CAST: Ann Turkel (Delilah), John Beck (Samson),

---

*NBC-TV telecast the first group of the mini-series' seg-ments during National Bible Week, marking the first time a television network recognized this event.

John Schuck (Jair), Victor Jory (Horaz), James Olson (Polah); Ann Doran, Charles Siebert, Vincent Caristi, Steve DeFrance, David Chambers, Kristen Curry.

"Noah and the Deluge" November 19 & 20, 1978
   CAST: Lew Ayres (Noah), Eve Plumb (Lilla), Rita Gam (Xantha), Jay Hammer (Ham), Ed Lauter (Ularat), William Adler (Japheth), Sam Weisman (Shem); Judith Marie Bergan, Lauren Frost, Mark Lenard, Robert Emhardt, Raymond Singer.

"Joshua and the Battle of Jericho" November 20, 1978
   CAST: Robert Culp (Joshua), Cameron Mitchell (Assurabi), Sydney Lassick (King Agadiz), John Doucette (Reuben), Sondra Gurrie (Rahab), Royal Dano (Gad), Brad David (Galadan), John Hansen (Joash); Irving Forbush, Rand Bridges, Brian Erickson, Jon Lormer, William Daniels.

"Moses" November 20 & 21, 1978
   CAST: John Marley (Moses), Anne Francis (Zipporah), Frank Gorshin (Ocran), Robert Alda (Vizier), Julia Adams (Queen), Joseph Campanella (Pharaoh), Lloyd Bochner (Imhotep), Ron Rifkin (Beseleel), Al Ruscio (Aaron); Bernard Behrens, Robert Carricart, John McLiam, Shane Otis.

"The Judgment of Solomon" November 21, 1978
   CAST: Tom Hallick (Solomon), John Carradine (King David), John Saxon (Adonijah), Carol Lawrence (Bathsheba), John Hoyt (Nathan), Tyne Daly (Abishag), Steven Keats (Bennaiah), Kevin Dobson (Joab), Robert Carricart (Hesed); Bill Quinn, Richard Jamison, Gene Dynarski, Tiger Thompson, Lisa Allen.

"Daniel in the Lion's Den" November 22, 1978
   CAST: David Birney (Daniel), Robert Vaughn (Darius), Dean Stockwell (Hissar), Nehemiah Persoff (Malimar), Sherry Jackson (Joanna); Andrew Bloch, Harvey Solin.

"Joseph and His Brothers" November 22, 1978
   CAST: Sam Bottoms (Joseph), Albert Salmi (HarGatep), Bernie Kopell (Potiphar), Barry Nelson (Pharaoh), Carol Rossen (Nairubi), Harvey Jason (Reuben), Walter Brooke (Jacob); Sorrell Booke, John Larraquette, Karia Salem, Joshua Bryant, Steve Tannen.

"Jacob's Challenge" March 18, 1979
   CAST: Barry Williams (Jacob), Peter Fox (Esau),

June Lockhart (Rebekah), Stephen Elliott (Isaac), Tanya Roberts (Bachemath), Hed Redford (Perua).

"The Story of The Ten Commandments"   May 8, 1979
    CAST: John Marley (Moses), Richard Mulligan (Aaron), Khristoffer Tabori (Eleazar), Anson Williams (Nabar), Lorrie Mahaffey (Sira), Granville Van Dusen (Joshua).

"The Tower of Babel"   May 15, 1979
    CAST: Vincent Edwards (Amathar), Richard Basehart (Johtan), Ron Palillo (Hevet), Erin Moran (Tova), Dana Elcar (Ranol), Cliff Emich (Mardon).

"Sodom and Gomorrah"   May 22, 1979
    CAST: Ed Ames (Lot), Gene Barry (Abraham), Rick Jason (Darghir), Dorothy Malone (Nagar), Julie Parrish (Shebelah), David Opatoshu (Hasdrugar), Peter Mark Richman (King Thagon).

PART II

THE FILMS OF THE NEW TESTAMENT

LA PASSION (The Passion)
1897
France
Lear
5 minutes B/W
        LA PASSION, from France, was the first film to
chronicle the life of Jesus Christ and probably is the first
motion picture to be based on any portion of The Bible. It
presented a brief version of "The Passion Play," an old
church program about the "passion" or "life" of Christ.
Like most early silent films, this one is no longer extant.
        Many more versions of "The Passion Play" were to
follow, both from Europe and the United States. For years
these films were shown in Catholic churches for their educational value but such showings were banned in 1912 by
Papal decree.

LA PASSION (OBERAMMERGAU PASSION PLAY)
1897
France
Lumière
B/W
Director: H. Hurd
        The life of Jesus Christ was presented in this film-
ing of "The Passion Play," made in Bavaria and presenting
the Oberammergau version of the perennial "La Passion."

THE PASSION PLAY
1897

Austria
Klaw & Erlanger
B/W
Producers: Mark Klaw & Abraham Erlanger
Director: W. W. "Doc" Freeman
     Even at this early date in the infancy of the motion picture, this version of "The Passion Play" was considered just another entry in such presentations. Filmed on location in Horitz in Bohemia, it was actually just a photographed folk procession which was crudely made and poorly received.

THE PASSION PLAY
1898
Lubin
B/W
Producer: Sigmund Lubin
     Sigmund Lubin produced this early United States entry into the "Passion Play" series, this time filming the perennial story on a backlot in Philadelphia. Although it was crudely produced, the short film proved to be a successful beginning for Lubin, who was soon to develop one of the filmdom's major production companies.

LA PASSION (The Passion)
1898
France
Gaum
B/W
     Another early French silent film version of "The Passion Play."

THE PASSION PLAY
1898
Hollaman
2100 feet B/W
Producers: Rich G. Hollaman & Albert G. Eaves
Director: L. J. Vincent
Screenplay: Salmi Morse
Photography: William C. Paley
     CAST: Frank Russell (Christus), Frank Gaylor

(Judas), Fred Strong (Pontius Pilate).

This surprisingly long, for its period, two-reeler was one of the first American attempts to film "The Passion Play" on the life of Jesus Christ. More surprisingly, the names of the makers, technicians and actors have been preserved. The film was shot in 24 scenes on the roof of New York City's Grand Central Palace and it was not sub-titled as a narrator was present for each of its performances. The film was generally successful wherever it was exhibited.

LE CHRIST MARCHANT SUR LES FLOTS (Christ Walking on
    Water)
1899
France
Méliès
620 feet B/W
Producer: George Méliès
    The wizard of early French cinema, producer George Méliès, used his famous trick-photography to "dazzle" audiences by showing Jesus Christ walking on water. The techniques Méliès employed in his short films at the turn of the century were in themselves "miracles" for that time period. This is one of the first films to be made from The Bible without using "The Passion Play" theme.

LE JUIF ERRANT (The Wandering Jew)
1904
France
Star
200 feet B/W
Director: George Méliès
    Eugène Sue's novel, Le Juif Errant (The Wandering Jew), was the basis for this early French film directed by special effects wizard George Méliès. Like the novel, it told of the medieval legend of the Jerusalem shopkeeper who refused to let Jesus Christ rest at his door while on His way to Calvary, and thus is doomed to wander the world forever.

LA PASSION DE NOTRE-SEIGNEUR JESUS CHRIST (The Life
    and Passion of Jesus Christ)

1905
France
Pathé
22122 B/W
Directors: Ferdinand Zecca & Lucien Nonguet
     Still another version of "The Passion Play" from
France, this version ran a lengthy (for its time) two reels.
Co-director Ferdinand Zecca previously made another Bib-
lical film, SAMSON AND DELILAH (q. v.) in 1903, one he
would remake five years later.

LA VIE DU CHRIST (The Life of Christ)
1906
France
Gaum
2320 feet B/W
Directors: Alice Guy, Victor Jasset & George Hatot

LA PASSION DE JESUS (The Life of Jesus)
1907
France
Pathé
5 minutes B/W
Director: Segundo De Chomon
     Two more films from France on "The Passion Play"
theme, the former quite long for its time at two reels,
while the latter, at one-half reel, had a much more common length for pre-1910 films.

BEN-HUR
1907
Kalem
1 reel B/W
Director: Sidney Olcott
     This little-known film was the first of three versions
of the Lew Wallace novel. It is important in cinema history
in that it resulted in the first lawsuit against a motion picture company for the violation of a literary copyright. The
case was in court for four years before the Kalem Company
agreed to pay $25,000 for the copyright violation, thus es-
tablishing the premise of motion picture rights to books and
plays.
     The film itself, however, was hardly worth all the

hassle. When it was issued it was advertised as "Sixteen magnificent scenes with illustrated titles, positively the most superb motion-picture spectacle ever made. " Actually all the one-reeler contained was some interior shots along with a filming of a chariot race, which was a live attraction at a fireworks display at Sheepshead Bay. The religious motif was hardly in evidence in this brief outing, with the chariot race dominating the footage, as, ironically, it would do in the two spectacle remakes.

THE LIFE OF CHRIST
1907
2164 feet   B/W
    The first American version of the life of Christ, using "The Passion Play" formula.

JERUSALEM IN THE TIME OF CHRIST
1908
Kalem
1200 feet   B/W
    Quite long for its time, JERUSALEM IN THE TIME OF CHRIST was basically an historical documentary. It contained two scenes set in 70 B. C. , seven scenes depicting the life of Jesus Christ and two scenes set in 65 and 70 A. D.

SALOME
1908
Vitagraph
710 feet   B/W
Director: J. Stuart Blackton
Screenplay: Liebler, from Oscar Wilde's play.
    CAST: Florence Lawrence (Salome); Maurice Costello.
    The first of many film versions of the story of Biblical seductress, Salome, this film starred popular early screen players Florence Lawrence and Maurice Costello. An adaptation of Oscar Wilde's play, this long-lost item predates the screen version of the play done in 1923 (q. v.) by Nazimova.

THE STAR OF BETHLEHEM
1908
Edison
905 feet B/W
An early American short detailing the birth of Jesus Christ in Bethlehem, this film was intended for the Easter film trade. The film should not be confused with Thanhouser's THE STAR OF BETHLEHEM (q.v.) issued in 1912.

LA VIE LA PASSION DE JESUS CHRIST (The Life and Passion of Jesus Christ)
1908
France
Pathé
3114 feet B/W
CAST: Monsieur Normand (Jesus Christ), Madame Moreau (Virgin Mary).
This is a remake of the 1905 film of the same title, again detailing a French version of "The Passion Play." The film was reissued in 1914 as LIFE OF OUR SAVIOUR (q.v.) and in 1921 new footage was added and it was falsely billed as an "all new motion picture" under the title BEHOLD THE MAN (q.v.).

THE BIRTH OF JESUS
1909
France
Color
An early short from France, this film told of the events surrounding the birth of The Saviour. It was also one of the earliest films to be made in color--the process of that time being to hand-tint each frame of film for the color effect.

THE KISS OF JUDAS
1909
France
Film d'Art
676 feet B/W
CAST: M. Lambert, M. Sully.
An early French short, this film told of the events at The Last Supper and up to the time of Judas' suicide.

THE PASSION PLAY
1909
Great Britain
Gaumont
2200 feet   Color
     Great Britain entered "The Passion Play" production
series with this six-reeler on the subject.   The thing which
distinguishes this outing from others from Europe and the
United States is that it was in color.   Each frame of the
film was hand-colored, the method of making color films then.

HEROD AND THE NEWBORN KING
1910
France
Gaumont
B/W
     One of a series of early silent short films from
France recreating portions of The Bible, HEROD AND THE
NEWBORN KING told the events surrounding the birth of
Jesus Christ and how the Infant and Joseph and Mary were
forced to flee into Egypt to escape the death edict issued
against The Saviour by King Herod.   It is interesting to note
that a much later film, DESERT DESPERADOES (RKO Radio,
1959), told a modern-day story with the Flight into Egypt as
its background, although Jesus was not shown in this version.

RESURRECTION OF LAZARUS
1910
France
Eclair
645 feet   B/W
     Not much is known about this lost film, which tells
the story of the miracle of the raising of Lazarus from the
tomb by Christ.   Records indicate that this French production was made on location in Palestine.

JESUS
1911
B/W
     CAST: Jacques Guilhene.
     Little is known about this film.   Outside of its title,
release year and star, the film, and all information about

it, seems to be lost to the ages. It perhaps is one of the series of French films of the period on Biblical subjects.

THE MIRACLE
1911
France
Eclipse
1040 feet B/W
    An import from France, and set in a mythical kingdom, THE MIRACLE showed Jesus Christ restoring life to a baby, a prince who was killed by a pretender to his throne.
    THE MIRACLE was a reproduction of the Reinhardt pantomime which had originally been presented at the London Olympia. Variety reported that it was "probably the finest exhibition of the 'Celluloid drama' ever conceived. In some respects it is superior to the original pantomime spectacle, in that the paths of the performers--or characters--may be followed more minutely and with greater detail than is possible in the original, due to the possibility of showing the scenic progression with the unfolding of the plot. "

THE MYSTERIOUS STRANGER
1911
France
Eclipse
610 feet B/W
    In this French import, Jesus Christ appears as a stranger in modern times and returns life to the dead daughter of a repentant farmer, the girl having been struck by lightning.
    This film should not be confused with a non-religious film of the same title, which was released in 1913 by Essanay and starred Bryant Washburn.

FROM THE MANGER TO THE CROSS, or JESUS OF
        NAZARETH
1912
Kalem
6 reels B/W
Director: Sidney Olcott

Robert Henderson Bland, Alice Hollister, Jack Clark and
Sidney Olcott in FROM THE MANGER TO THE CROSS
(Kalem, 1912).

Screenplay: Gene Gautier
Photography: George K. Hollister
Sets: Dr. Schick
    CAST: Robert Henderson Bland (Jesus Christ), Gene
Gautier (Virgin Mary), Jack Clark (John the Beloved Disci-
ple), Robert G. Vignola (Judas), Percy Dyer (Jesus as a
Boy), Alice Hollister (Mary Magdalene), Helen Lindroth
(Martha), J. P. McGowan (Andrew), Sydney Baber (Lazarus),
Sidney Olcott (Blind Man).
    FROM THE MANGER TO THE CROSS, subtitled
JESUS OF NAZARETH, is the first important religious film
produced by a United States film company. It is also one of
the first films to be shot entirely outside its home studio and
was one of the first movies to be made on location. In fact,
the producers of the film announced that "wherever possible
each scene is to be enacted in the exact location as pointed
out by leading authorities." The film was shot in the Holy
Land in 1912, with the Egyptian sequences done the year before in that country. For interiors a special studio was
built in Jerusalem.

Some $100,000 was spent in the production of FROM
THE MANGER TO THE CROSS, making it one of the most
expensive projects of its time for the film industry. The
film, however, grossed over $1 million and proved to be
the most successful film made by the Kalem Company.

Popular actress Gene Gautier, who enacted the role
of the Virgin Mary, wrote the original screenplay for the
production, which covered the life of Christ from birth to
the Crucifixion. A five-act drama, the film employed forty-
two actors for its principal roles along with hundreds of local people as extras, as well as camels. A total of three
months was spent in filming the production.

FROM THE MANGER TO THE CROSS begins with the
birth of Jesus in the city of Bethlehem and proceeds to the
flight to Egypt and Jesus' boyhood in Nazareth. From there
it proceeds to the ministry of Jesus, including various miracles such as the raising of Lazarus. Next came the events
during the last week in the life of Jesus and the film culminated with the Crucifixion and the Resurrection.

British actor Robert Henderson Bland enacted the role
of Jesus Christ and he gave great dignity to the part. Bland
became so engrossed in the part that he later wrote two
books about the making of the film, From the Manger to the
Cross (1922) and Actor-Soldier-Poet (1939). His performance as Jesus Christ ranks along with those of H. B. Warner, Robert Wilson and Max von Sydow as being among the
best portrayals of the Saviour on film.

On October 3, 1912 the film was given a special
showing at London's Queen's Hall and afterward Cardinal
Bourne commented, "A new art has been turned to a noble
use with wonderful success." For years afterward the
movie enjoyed great success and it was not until Cecil B.
DeMille filmed THE KING OF KINGS in 1927 that a better
version of the story appeared. Seen today, FROM THE
MANGER TO THE CROSS still holds up very well and the
movie must rank as one of the most important motion pictures ever made about a religious subject.

THE ILLUMINATION
1912
Vitagraph
1000 feet B/W
CAST: Helen Gardner (Sabina), Rosemary Theby
(Ruth), Harry Northrup (Maximus), Tom Powers (Joseph),
Wallace Reid (Centurion); Charles Kent, Hal Reid, Rose

Tapley.

THE ILLUMINATION tells the story of two married couples in Jerusalem at the time of Jesus Christ, one a Roman couple, the other Jewish. One spouse from each couple is affected by the teachings of Jesus Christ while the other partners are not affected until they visit the tomb and find He has risen. In this moving film, Jesus Christ is shown only as a light moving across the faces of onlookers--thus giving the film its title.

SATAN
1912
Italy
Ambrosia
6800 feet B/W
Director: Luigi Maggi
Screenplay: Guido Volante

CAST: Maria Bonnard, Rina Alby, Mary Cleo Tarlarina, Antonio Grisanti.

SATAN was a four-part film in which The Devil was shown in four phases of history, the second part being the life of Jesus Christ. The film was based on the epic poems "Paradise Lost" by John Milton and "The Messiah" by Friedrich Klopstock. It was also called THE DREAM OF HUMANITY and SATANA.

SAVED BY DIVINE PROVIDENCE
1912
Pathé
B/W

Another lost film from the cinema's infancy, this American Pathé production was set in modern times and it told of a mother who finds her lost son through a vision of Jesus Christ.

THE STAR OF BETHLEHEM
1912
Thanhouser
Three Reels B/W
Director-Screenplay: Theodore Marston

CAST: William Russell, Florence LaBadie, Harry

Benham, Marguerite Snow, James Cruze.

The story of the events leading up to the birth of Christ are detailed in this Thanhouser release. The story has an angel (the Angel Gabriel in a suit of armor) telling three shepherds to follow the Star of Bethlehem to locate the Saviour of mankind, who has just been born in a stable.

Unlike most early silent films, this movie still exists and a print of it rests in the paper print collection of The Library of Congress. Its condition, however, would make it difficult viewing, as noted in Kemp L. Niver's Motion Pictures from the Library of Congress Paper Print Collection 1894-1912 (1967): "As the film exists at present, it is difficult to follow the story line since the so-called tableau form was used for all the scenes, which show good production values although their short length does not permit a flow of connected ideas."

THE CARPENTER
1913
Vitagraph
1000 feet B/W
Director: Wilfred North
Screenplay: Marguerite Bersch
CAST: Earle Williams (Harry Faulkner); Lillian Walker, Charles Kent, E. K. Lincoln, Ned Finley, Mrs. Mary Maurice, Herbert L. Barry, Niles Welch.

A Civil War melodrama in which a family is torn apart by being on opposite sides of the conflict, THE CARPENTER had a brief sequence in which Jesus Christ appears as a stranger who enters the family home and brings peace to its members.

THE CRIMSON CROSS
1913
France
Eclair
3 Reels B/W
A most interesting film from France, THE CRIMSON CROSS looked at the mysteries of the Rosary in the context of religious intolerance. The film opens in Puritan New England, where a Spanish sea captain comes to port with his goods. There he meets the daughter of a merchant and explains to her the fifteen mysteries of the Rosary and its

five transcendent mysteries and what they stand for.

The major portion of the final two reels of the film reverts to Biblical times showing The Annunciation, Visitation, Nativity, Presentation in the Temple, Finding of the Child in the Temple, Agony in the Garden, Scourging, Crowning with Thorns, Way of the Cross, Crucifixion, The Resurrection, Ascension, Descent of the Holy Ghost, Assumption and Coronation of Mary.

The finale of the three-reeler reverts back to Puritan times with a fight ensuing between the crew of the Spanish ship and the Puritans, and the captain dying of his wounds but comforted by the Rosary. The end finds the Puritan father forgiving his daughter for her association with the Catholic captain.

Reporting on THE CRIMSON CROSS, The Moving Picture World said "while in it there is much that is very finely done ... there are one or two scenes in it that are undeniably crude."

A DAUGHTER OF THE HILLS
1913
Famous Players
3 reels B/W
Director-Screenplay: J. Searle Dawley
      CAST: House Peters, Laura Sawyer, Mr. Nares, Wellington A. Playter, Frank Van Buren.

This drama relates the story of how St. Paul converts a gladiator and his wife to Christianity in ancient Rome.

L'EBRO ERRANTE (The Wandering Jew)
1913
Italy
Roma
4600 Feet B/W
      An Italian adaptation of the novel The Wandering Jew by Eugène Sue about the merchant in Jerusalem who would not show kindness to Christ by letting Him rest at his door on the way to Calvary, and was thus doomed to wander the world forever. Another Italian film, MOROK (Pasquali Films, 1917), was also supposedly based on Eugène Sue's novel.

QUO VADIS
1913
Italy
Cines Film Company
8 reels B/W
Director: Enrico Guazzoni
	Henryk Sienkiewicz' novel has been the basis for
three spectacle films produced in Italy. The book is based
on the tradition that St. Peter wanted to leave Rome because of the persecution of Christians by Nero, and was
met by Jesus Christ who told him that if he left His people
He would return and be crucified again, this time in Rome.
	This initial version of QUO VADIS is a major movie
in the history of the cinema. It was imported into the
United States by George Kleine, a leader of the Motion Picture Patents Company, and it was the longest film shown in
this country up to that time. As a result of its tremendous
popularity, it paved the way for the feature-length movies
we know today.
	QUO VADIS was remade in a silent version in 1925
and in a sound color version in 1951 (both versions q. v.).

THE THREE WISE MEN
1913
Selig
1000 feet B/W
Producer: Colin Campbell
Screenplay: Anthony McGuire
	CAST: Thomas Santschi (Sidney Roger), Wheeler
Oakman (Harry Wild), Wallace Brownlow, William Hutchin-
son, Eddie James (The Three Wise Men), Frank Clark (The
Devil), Frederick W. Huntley (Jesus Christ), William Seiter
(Joseph), Eddie James (Mike O'Platters), Bessie Eyton
(Mary Marshall/Mary).
	THE THREE WISE MEN was billed as a "charming
little miracle play" in which a wealthy Broadway rounder
(Thomas Santschi) is transported from Broadway, via a
dream, to a lonely desert, there to meditate upon the holy
truths of a pamphlet a Salvation Army girl (Bessie Eyton)
has given him. Three wise men (Wallace Brownlow, William Hutchinson, Eddie James) come out of the east on
camels and the young man follows them under the guiding
star of Bethlehem to their destination, the birthplace of
Christ (Frederick W. Huntley), but he is refused admission
to the lonely stable until he cleanses his soul. Then the
man awakens from his dream, finding a new life through

the great lesson of the ages.

The film was based on two paintings: "The First Christmas" and "Behold, I Stand at the Door and Knock." The star of the film, Thomas Santschi, would become famous the next year when he engaged in his famous fight sequence with William Farnum in THE SPOILERS (Universal, 1914).

THE BIRTH OF OUR SAVIOUR
1914
Edison
1000 feet   B/W
Director: Charles Brabin
Screenplay: DeWitt L. Pelton
CAST: Carlton King (Joseph), Gertrude McCoy (Mary), Harry Linson, Charles Sutton, Harry Eytinge (The Three Wise Men), Frank McGlynn (Herod).

Released just six days before Christmas in 1914, THE BIRTH OF OUR SAVIOUR recounted the events surrounding the birth of Jesus Christ and the Flight to Egypt.

The story begins in Nazareth where the maiden Mary (Gertrude McCoy) is chosen as the bride of the carpenter Joseph (Carlton King) and tells how the angel Gabriel comes to her and says she will bring forth a son, the Saviour. Next is recounted how Mary and Joseph must journey to Bethlehem to be included in the area census; there Mary gives birth to Jesus in a manger.   The visit of the Three Wise Men is shown, as is King Herod's (Frank McGlynn) order to kill all the babes in the area in hopes the Saviour might perish.   An angel warns Joseph of the peril and he and Mary and the Infant journey to the land of Egypt, where the Christ Child will be safe.

THE LAST SUPPER
1914
American Film Manufacturing Company
2000 feet   B/W
Director-Screenplay: Lorimer Johnstone
CAST: Sydney Ayres (Jesus Christ), Jack Richardson (Judas), Harry Von Meter (John), Vivian Rich (The Girl Who Loves), Caroline Cooke (The Worldly Woman), Louise Lester (Woman of Poverty), Charlotte Burton (The Girl Who Does Not Think), Violette Neitz (Foolish Girl), Edith Borella

(Woman of the Slums).
    Released in the spring of 1914, this two-reeler de-
picted scenes from the life of Jesus Christ (Sydney Ayres)
in the last days, including His walking on water and the
final supper with His disciples.

MARY MAGDALENE
1914
Kennedy Films
    This early silent film told a rather complicated story
about the life of courtesan Mary Magdalene, who became a
devout follower of Jesus Christ.   According to the film,
Mary Magdalene had two principal lovers, Syrius Superbus
and Judas.   She meets Roman noble Canis Proculus and
they fall in love, but while he is away Mary sees Christ
and is overcome by His magnetism.   Influenced by Portia,
the wife of Syrius and a follower of Jesus, Mary forsakes
her sinful life and becomes a believer in Christ.   When
Judas finds out that Mary plans to follow Christ to Jerusalem, he and Syrius follow and the latter writes Canis
that Mary has been unfaithful.   Judas then becomes a follower of Christ to be near Mary, who is, he believes, in
love with Jesus.   When Canis arrives in Jerusalem, Mary
tells him she cannot be his wife until he believes in Jesus.
Meanwhile Syrius and Judas betray Christ by obtaining a
warrant for his arrest from Pilate and they ally themselves
with Caiaphas in denouncing the Saviour.   Mary enlists
Canis' aid in stopping the injustice but he can do nothing.
When Syrius tries to persuade Mary to run away with him
in order to save Jesus from the crowd, she refuses and
the angry Syrius tells the crowd she is a follower of the
Nazarene.   Just as she is about to be killed by the mob,
Canis and his soldiers arrive and save her.   Canis then
tells Mary he believes that Christ led him to her and that
he now believes in the Saviour.   The story ends with the
hanging of Judas and the progress of Canis and Mary up
the hill of Calvary where the three crosses show at the
top of the hill.
    Although a lost film, the plot synopsis of MARY
MAGDALENE shows that screen writers, even in the earliest days of films, took great liberties with the Scriptures
in order to dramatize their movies.   Although the character of Mary Magdalene appears in practically all feature
films about the last days of Jesus it was not until 1959
that another film was made that dealt principally with the
character.   It was the Italian feature LA SPADE E LA

CROCE (q. v.), released in the United States as MARY MAGDALENE, starring Yvonne De Carlo in the title role.

LA PASSION (The Life of Our Saviour)
1914
France
Pathé
7 reels B/W
          CAST: Monsieur Moreau (St. Joseph), M. Normand (Jesus Christ), M. Jacquinet (Judas Iscariot), Madame Moreau (Virgin Mary), Le Petit Brand (The Boy Christ).
          This film had been shown before as LA VIE LA PASSION DE JESUS CHRIST (q. v.) in 1908 but it was expanded and issued in this version in 1914 with an added attraction: the film was now hand-colored, both the old and new footage. The film was to see further life when portions of it were interpolated with still more new American footage for BE-HOLD THE MAN (q. v.) in 1921.

THE TRIUMPH OF AN EMPEROR
1914
Italy
Savoia
5 reels B/W
          CAST: Arturo Garzes (Constantine), D. Lombardi (Maximian), F. Bonino (Mascentius), A. Durelli (Licinius), M. Mariani (St. Maternus), A. Costamagna (Fausta), M. Jacobini (Constantine's Sister), E. Garrone (Elvius Brutus), J. Bay (Sainte Helene), M. Tarabini (St. Viktor).
          Imported from Italy and released in the United States by the World Film Corporation, THE TRIUMPH OF AN EM-PEROR took place three hundred years after the birth of Christ and its scenes were laid in Milan, Rome and in Gaul. The story told of the Emperor Constantine (Arturo Garzes) and how he fought other emperors to give full liberty to Christianity. In one scene Constantine has a vision of the Cross in the heavens, and in another Jesus Christ appears to him in his tent and tells him to emblazon the cross on the shields and banners of his army and that this will bring victory. *

---

*Nearly a half-century later the Italian-made feature CON-STANTINE IL GRANDE (Jonia Films, 1961) (cont. on p. 90)

The Moving Picture World called this film a "beautiful picture offering ... [and] a wonderful production of the film art in all respects. "

CIVILIZATION
1916
Triangle
10 reels   B/W
Producer: Thomas H. Ince
Associate Producer: J. Parker Read
Directors: Raymond B. West & Reginald Barker
Screenplay: C. Gardner Sullivan
Photography: Irvin Willat & Dal Clawson
Editor: LeRoy Stone
    CAST: Herschel Mayall (King of Wredpyrd), Lola May (Queen Eugenie), Howard Hickman (Count Ferdinand), Enid Markey (Kathryn Haldemann), George Fisher (Jesus Christ), J. Frank Burke (Luther Rolf), Charles K. French (Prime Minister), J. Barney Sherry (Blacksmith), Jerome Storm, Ethel Ullman (Blacksmith's Children), Kate Bruce (A Mother), Lillian Read (Young Child); Alice Terry, Claire DuBrey, Gertrude Claire, Fannie Midgely, Natalie Talmadge.
    In a Graustarkian kingdom, the ruler (Herschel Mayall) declares war on a neighbor.   His hopes rest with an inventor (Howard Hickman) whose fiancée (Enid Markey) is a leader in the women's peace movement.   She converts her lover to the cause and he refuses to sink a passenger ship carrying contraband.   During a mutiny on his submarine he becomes ill and encounters the spirit of Christ (George Fisher).   Later Christ takes over the king's body and leads him into the battlefield to see the hell of war.   As a result the king changes his mind and declares peace.
    CIVILIZATION was a pacifist feature made at a time when there was great fever for the United States to go to war in Europe to oppose the Axis powers.   President Woodrow Wilson personally attached great significance to the feature in an effort to stave off United States involvement in World

---

retold the story with the Emperor Constantine (Cornel Wilde) seeing a vision of the Cross bearing the inscription "By This Sign Conquer. "   The character of Jesus Christ, however, did not appear in the feature, which was issued in the United States in 1962 by Avco-Embassy as CONSTANTINE AND THE CROSS.

War I.

The film, which cost $100,000 and grossed eight times that amount, again showed Jesus Christ maligned and persecuted in His efforts to restore peace to the world.

In retrospect, Jack Spear wrote of the film in Films in Review, "[It] was an overpraised film whose role in the peace movement has been constantly magnified.... The picture suffered from an implausible story ... and was pseudo-religious, poorly motivated and lacking in sincerity."

CIVILIZATION was reissued with a soundtrack in 1931, in a tinted version that was reduced to six reels in running time.

INTOLERANCE
1916
Wark Releasing Company
14 reels B/W
Producer-Director-Screenplay: D. W. Griffith
Photography: G. W. Bitzer
Editors: Rose & James Smith
Music: D. W. Griffith & Joseph Carl Breil
Sets: Frank Wortman
Property Master: Ralph De Lacy
Assistant Directors: Arthur Berthelon, Allan Dwan, Erich
        von Stroheim, Christy Cabanne, Tod Browning, Jack
        Conway, George Nicholls, Lloyd Ingraham
        CAST: "Of All Ages": Lillian Gish (Woman Who
Rocks the Cradle).
"The Modern Story": Mae Marsh, Fred Turner,
Robert Harron, Sam De Grasse, Vera Lewis, Miriam Cooper, Walter Long, Tully Marshall, Tom Wilson, Ralph Lewis, Lloyd Ingraham, Barney Bernard, Rev. A. W. McClure, Max Davidson, Monte Blue, Jennie Lee, Marguerite Marsh, Edward Dillon, Clyde Hopkins, William Brown, Alberta Lee, Mary Alden, Pearl Ellmore, Lucille Brown, Luray Huntley, Mrs. Arthur Mackly.
"The Judean Story": Howard Gaye (Jesus Christ), Olga Grey (Mary Magdalene), Lillian Langdon (Virgin Mary), Bessie Love (Bride of Cana), George Walsh (Bridegroom), Gunther von Ritzau, Erich von Stroheim (Pharisees).
"The French Story": Margery Wilson, Eugene Pallette, Spottiswoode Aiken, Maxwell Stanley, Josephine Crowell, Ruth Handforth, Georgia Pearce [Constance Talmadge], N. E. Lawrence, Joseph Henaberry, Morris Levy, Howard Gaye, Louis Romaine.

Erich von Stroheim and Gunther von Ritzau in INTOLERANCE (Wark Releasing, 1916).

"The Babylonian Story": Constance Talmadge, Elmer Clifton, Alfred Paget, Seena Owen, Carl Stockdale, Elmo Lincoln, George Seigmann, Tully Marshall, George Fawcett, Kate Bruce, Loyola O'Connor, James Curley, Howard Scott, Alma Rubins, Ruth Darling, Margaret Moony, Mildred Harris, Pauline Starke, Winifred Westover, Grace Wilson, Lotte Clifton, Ah Singh, Ranji Singh, Ed Bruno, James Burns, Martin Landry, Wallace Reid, Charles Eagle Eye, William Dark Cloud, Charles Von Cortlandt, Jack Cosgrove.
INTOLERANCE is D. W. Griffith's superspectacle, a film so far ahead of its time that even today audiences have trouble conceiving its magnitude. Made as an edict against man's inhumanity to man, the film interpolated four separate stories, three from history and one modern-day melodrama, to tell its tale. Of the four stories, "The Judean Story," which presented three episodes from the life of Christ (Howard Gaye), was the least well conceived, although the sequences were beautifully filmed and quite inspirational. Griffith's recreation of Judea is superb and Howard Gaye's

performance as Jesus is quite good. The three episodes shown from Christ's life were the miracle at Cana, Christ's mercy toward the adulterous woman and the Crucifixion, the latter two from the Fourth Gospel. Basically, D. W. Griffith showed Jesus Christ as a victim of intolerance.

Although the Judean sequence took up only a small portion of this three-hour epic, Griffith ran into problems when he filmed the Crucifixion portion. According to an article in Variety (April 7, 1916),* the B'nai Brith, the most powerful Hebrew society in the United States at the time, brought pressure to bear on Griffith to omit the sequences which showed the Jews crucifying Christ. For the sequence, Griffith had hired all the orthodox Hebrews he could find in Los Angeles. According to the article, the pressure proved too much for Griffith, who burned the negative of the scene in the presence of the B'nai Brith committee which was talking to him on the matter. He later reshot the sequence, showing Roman soldiers nailing Christ to the Cross.

A point of interest is that Howard Gaye was also featured in "The French Story" sequence in the role of Cardinal Lorraine.

CHRISTUS
1917
Italy
Cines/Historic Features
6 reels B/W
Director: Count Giulio Antamoro
CAST: Giovanni Pasquali (Jesus Christ), Lyda Gys (Virgin Mary).

Most aspects of Christ's life are presented in this Italian production, including His walking on water, rejecting temptation, angels and His Resurrection. This hour-long feature was made in Egypt with Lord Kitchener providing the extras and camels for the production, which was based on scenes from famous paintings.

Supposedly the Cines company made several films about Christ around 1914, but this is the only title to surface.

---

*The short article is reprinted in The Kindergarten of the Movies: A History of the Fine Arts Company by Anthony Slide (Scarecrow Press, 1980).

THE PASSING OF THE THIRD FLOOR BACK
1917
Great Britain
Ideal
6 reels B/W
Director: Herbert Brenon
    CAST: James Forbes-Robertson (Walter Walturdow);
Molly Pearson, Ketty Galanta, Auguste Haviland, Ben Gra-
ham, Grace Stephens.
    Based on Jerome K. Jerome's popular play, this si-
lent feature told of a stranger who comes to a rooming house
full of unhappy people and brings peace of mind to them all.
It is assumed that the stranger is Jesus Christ. The play
had been a popular stage vehicle for James Forbes-
Robertson, who recreated the title role in this film, which
was issued in the United States in 1918 by First National.
A sound version (q. v.) was made in 1936 starring Conrad
Veidt.

SALOME
1918
Fox
6 reels B/W
Director: J. Gordon Edwards
Screenplay: Adrian Johnson
    CAST: Theda Bara (Salome), G. Raymond Nye (King
Herod), Albert Roscoe (John the Baptist), Bertram Grassby
(Prince David), Herbert Heyes (Sejanus), Genevieve Blinn
(Queen Marian), Vera Doria (Naomi), Alfred Fremont (Galla).
    SALOME was the thirty-first film to star popular
screen vamp Theda Bara and it caused a furor with churches
and religious groups because of its presentation of the Biblical story. The plot had dancer Salome (Theda Bara) in-
stigating the downfall of King Herod's (G. Raymond Nye)
wife (Genevieve Blinn) and lusting after John the Baptist
(Albert Roscoe). He rejects her, and she demands his head
on a silver platter.
    Not only was the story a bit overdone for the period,
but Miss Bara's attire (or lack of same), plus her seductive
dance of the seven veils, was certainly reason enough to
raise the ire of many religious groups and theatre patrons.
    Director J. Gordon Edwards helmed this and twenty-
one other Theda Bara Fox starrers (she made thirty-nine
features for the studio) and he later directed two other religious spectacles for Fox, THE QUEEN OF SHEBA (q. v.)
in 1921 and THE SHEPHERD KING (q. v.) in 1923.

THE ETERNAL MAGDALENE
1919
Goldwyn
5 reels B/W
Director: Arthur Hopkins
Photography: Philip Rosen
 CAST: Margaret Marsh (Elizabeth Bradshaw), Charles Dalton (Elijah Bradshaw), Charles Trowbridge (Paul
Bradshaw), Donald Gallaher (Macy), Maud Cooling (Mrs.
Bradshaw), Vernon Steele (Preacher), Maxine Elliott (The
Eternal Magdalene).
 Based on Robert H. McLaughlin's popular stage success, this film told of a preacher (Charles Dalton) who
casts out his own daughter (Margaret Marsh) on the eve of
a series of revival meetings because she has become preg-
nant out of wedlock. Exhausted, he falls into a deep sleep
and is transported back to Biblical times. He meets The
Eternal Magdalene (Maxine Elliott) who shows him the real
evils of his "reform" work and how it has driven good people into sinful ways. Awakening from his dream, the man
asks his daughter to stay, and then finds out that she and
her lover are secretly married.
 Existing stills from this feature tend to indicate that
the character of Jesus Christ made a fleeting appearance in
the film.

THE GREAT REDEEMER
1920
Metro
5 reels B/W
Producer: Maurice Tourneur
Director: Clarence Brown
Screenplay: Jules Furtham & Jack (John) Gilbert
Story: H. H. Van Loan
Photography: Charles J. Van Enger
Art Director: Floyd Mueller
Assistant Director: Charles Dorian
Chief Electrician: Freddie Carpenter
 CAST: House Peters (Dan Mallory), Marjorie Daw
(The Girl), Jack MacDonald (Sheriff), Joseph Singleton
(Murderer).
 A cowboy artist (House Peters) is jailed and spends
his time making drawings on his cell wall, including one of
the Crucifixion. During the night the moon is uncovered by
a cloud and the rays of light fall on the picture, making it

come alive. A murderer (Joseph Singleton) in a cell across the block sees the apparition of Jesus Christ appearing from the sketch on the wall and calls for a priest; he spends the rest of the night in confession. The next day he goes peacefully to his death.

THE GREAT REDEEMER was the first picture directed by Clarence Brown and it was co-adapted to the screen by Jack Gilbert, who later became a famous silent screen lover under the name of John Gilbert. The film was so successful that it was the first picture produced by Metro to play on Broadway.

BEHOLD THE MAN
1921
America/France
Pathé/Selwyn
6 reels B/W (with color sequences in Pathécolor)
Director: Spencer Gordon Bennet
Screenplay: Harding O. Martin
Titles: Arthur F. Warde
Art Director: Maryan F. Broada
CAST: H. O. Pettibone (The Father), Sybil Sheridan (The Mother), Richard Ross (The Son), Violet Axzelle (The Daughter).

A mother in the present day (1921) tells her children the story of Jesus Christ, from the Annunciation to the Ascension. The story excludes many parts of His life. The only new footage in this film were the modern-day sequences directed by Spencer Gordon Bennet, who would later become a noted director of silent and sound serials. The footage about Christ came from the 1908 French film, LA VIE LA PASSION DE JESUS CHRIST (q. v.) which had been reissued in 1914 in color and retitled LIFE OF OUR SAVIOUR or THE PASSION (q. v.). The whole effort was obviously a patchwork job produced to cash in on the availability of color footage about the life of Jesus Christ.

BLADE AM SATANS BOG (Leaves from Satan's Book)
1921
Denmark
Nordisk Films
Director: Carl Theodore Dreyer
Screenplay: Elgar Hjer & Carl Theodore Dreyer, from the

novel by Marie Corelli
Photography: George Schneevoigt
Art Directors: Carl Theodore Dreyer, Axel Bruun & Jens
        G. Lund
    CAST: Helge Nissen, Halvard Hoff, Jacob Texiere,
Erling Hanson, Ebon Strandin, Tenna Kraft, Clara Pontoppidan,
Hallander Helleman, Carlo Wieth, Karina Bell, Elith Pio.

Carl Theodore Dreyer's artistic horror film from
Denmark was a four-part feature dealing with Satan taking
over the souls of four people in various times in history.
One segment dealt with Satan's involvement in the life of
Jesus Christ. The film was based on the novel by Marie
Corelli. The same book was later used by D. W. Griffith
as the basis of his feature THE SORROWS OF SATAN (Paramount, 1925) but Jesus Christ was not involved in that
film's plotline.

DER STERN VON BETHLEHEM (The Star of Bethlehem)
1921
Germany
B/W
Director: Lotte Reiniger
German director Lotte Reiniger, credited as one of
the inventors of the silhouette film, made this version of
the events surrounding the birth of Jesus Christ, in her
native Germany. The feature was made in the animated
silhouette format. Thirty-five years later she remade the
film in color in Great Britain as THE STAR OF BETHLE-
HEM (q. v.).

CRUSADE OF THE INNOCENT
1922
Popular Film Company
5 reels B/W
An exploitation item, this feature told a story involv-
ing leprosy, seduction, syphilis, murder, cruelty and final
redemption, with closeups of Jesus Christ* being used in all

---

*Another feature of the period, THE SERVANT IN THE
HOUSE (Federated Film Exchange of America, 1921), was
based on a 1908 play about religious corruption, and one of
the characters in the story bore a striking resemblance to
Jesus Christ.

the film's art titles.   Little else is known about this lost
states' rights release.

I. N. R. I.   (Jesus of Nazareth, King of the Jews)
1923
Germany
Neumann
70 minutes   B/W
Producer: Hans Neumann
Director-Screenplay: Robert Wiene
Photography: Reimar Kuntze, Axel Gaatkjair & Ludwig
                    Lippert
          CAST: Asta Nielsen (Mary Magdalene), Gregori
Chmara (Jesus Christ), Henny Porten (Virgin Mary), Alex-
ander Cranof (Judas); Werner Krauss, Emanuel Reicher,
Heinrich von Twardowski, Alexander Granach.
          The life of Jesus Christ unfolds in this film as it is
told by a priest to a prisoner who is about to be executed.
The film, shot mostly in Palestine, was made as a vehicle
for popular Danish star Asta Nielsen, who portrayed Mary
Magdalene, while her husband, Gregori Chmara, played
Christ.
          In 1934 the film was released in the United States
with an English narrated soundtrack and retitled CROWN OF
THORNS.   It was shown on a states' rights basis and many
theatres used it that year as a Holy Week presentation.

SALOME
1923
George H. Wiley, Inc.
6 reels   B/W
Producer-Director: Malcolm Strauss
          CAST: Diana Allen (Salome); Vincent Coleman,
Christine Winthrop.
          This poverty-row version of SALOME has the title
character (Diana Allen) at odds with her step-mother, Queen
Herodias, over the love of an Egyptian prince who visits
King Herod's court.   When Herod promises Salome any wish
if she will dance for him, the girl plans to ask for the
prince's release from prison, where he was placed by Herodias after he spurned her.   Herodias, however, threatens to
have the prince killed if Salome does not ask Herod for the
death of The Wanderer (another name for John the Baptist),

who has also been imprisoned. Salome does so, later rescues the prince and they flee into the desert.

Another retelling of the well-known Biblical story of
Salome and her dance of the seven veils, this version took
great liberties with the original tale. Interestingly, The
Bible does not actually name the girl. The name "Salome"
is given in the history written by Josephus, a Jew who lived
in the area. Ironically, Josephus' history is questioned by
many authorities as the scribe nowhere mentions Jesus
Christ, except in one document which is said to be a fraud.

SALOME
1923
Allied
6 reels   B/W
Producer: Nazimova
Director: Charles Bryant
Screenplay: Peter M. Winters, from the play by Oscar
              Wilde
Photography: Charles Van Enger
Set Designer & Costumes: Natacha Rambova
Musical Arrangements: Ulderico Marcelli
       CAST: Nazimova (Salome), Rose Dione (Herodias),
Mitchell Lewis (Herod), Nigel de Brulier (Jokasnan), Earl
Schenck (Young Syrian), Arthur Jasmine (Page), Frederic
Peters (Naaman), Louis Dumar (Tigellinus).

       Stage star Nazimova produced this highly arty version
of Oscar Wilde's 1894 play, the film telling how dancer
Salome (Nazimova) becomes enraged at being rebuffed by
Jokasnan (Nigel de Brulier) and how she dances for King
Herod (Mitchell Lewis) in order to get her wish of the man's
head delivered on a silver platter. When her request is
granted, Salome kisses the head and the act so disgusts
Herod that he has her killed.

       The exotic sets and costumes for SALOME were
based on Aubrey Beardsley designs and were brought to the
screen by Natacha Rambova, better known at the time as
Mrs. Rudolph Valentino. While it is a beautifully designed
and photographed feature which won praise from a few high-
brow critics, the film was literally snubbed by the movie-
going public. Photoplay warned its readers that the feature
was "a hot house orchid of decadent passion ... this is
bizarre stuff."

THE WANDERING JEW
1923
Great Britain
Stoll
8 reels   B/W
Director: Maurice Elvey
Screenplay: Alicia Ramsey, from the play by E. Temple
          Thurston
Photography: John Cox
Art Director: Walter M. Murton
          CAST: Matheson Lang, Hutin Britton, Malvina Long-
fellow, Isabel Elsom, Florence Sanders, Shayle Gardner,
Hubert Carter, Jerrold Robertshaw, Winifred Izard, Fred
Raynham, Lewis Gilbert, Hector Abbas, Lionel D'Aragon,
Gordon Hopkirk.
          Unlike three early silent films on the subject, this
version of THE WANDERING JEW was based on the play by
E. Temple Thurston and not on the Eugène Sue novel.   Still
the story was the same, telling of the Jerusalem merchant
who would not give sanctuary to Christ on His way to Calvary and was then doomed to roam the world forever.   The
character of Jesus Christ was not seen in this production
which director Maurice Elvey remade in 1933 (q. v.).

THE PASSION PLAY
1924
Germany
Gospel
45 minutes   B/W
Director: Dimitri Buchowetzki
Screenplay: Berhnard Gotthart, inspired by the painting
          "The Last Supper" by Leonardo Da Vinci
          CAST: Adolph Fassnacht (Jesus Christ), George
Fassnacht (Judas).
          A German version of "The Passion Play," but this
time with a twist: the film is based on the painting by
Leonardo Da Vinci, "The Last Supper."   Da Vinci painted
Christ's final meal set in a glorious mansion and this image
(portrayed as such in this film) has stuck in the public mind
through the ages.   In truth, however, Christ and His disciples ate The Last Supper in either a cavern or in the woods.
          Today this silent feature has some historical impor-
tance, other than being a recreation of the Da Vinci painting, in that it was a filming of The Passion Play of Freiburg,
Germany, in which members of the Fassnacht family had appeared for generations.

BEN-HUR
1925
Metro-Goldwyn-Mayer
12 reels B/W and Color
Producers: Louis B. Mayer, Samuel Goldwyn & Irving Thalberg
Directors: Fred Niblo and Ferdinand P. Earle
Screenplay: Bess Meredyth and Carey Wilson, from the
               novel by Lew Wallace
Titles: Katharine Hilliker & H. H. Caldwell
Adaptation: June Mathis
Photography: Rene Guissart, Percy Hilburn, Karl Struss,
               Clyde De Vinne, E. Burton Greene, George
               Meehan & Paul Eagles
Editor: Lloyd Nosler
Assistant Editors: Basil Wrangell, William Holmes, Harry
               Reynolds & Ben Lewis
Music Score: William Axt & David Mendoza
Second Unit Director: B. Reeves Eason
Sets: Cedric Gibbons, Horace Jackson & Arnold Gillespie
Art Effects: Ferdinand P. Earle
Assistant Director: Charles Stallings
Production Manager: Harry Edington
Production Assistants: Silas Clegg, Alfred Raboch & Wil-
               liam Wyler
Wardrobe: Herman J. Kaufmann
Traveling Mattes: Frank D. Williams

Carmel Myers
and
Francis X. Bushman
in
BEN-HUR
(MGM, 1925)

CAST: Ramon Novarro (Ben-Hur), Francis X. Bushman (Messala), May McAvoy (Esther), Betty Bronson (Virgin Mary), Claire McDowell (Princess of Hur), Katherine Key (Tirzah), Carmel Myers (Iras), Nigel de Brulier (Simonides), Mitchell Lewis (Sheik Ilderim), Leo White (Samballat), Frank Currier (Ames), Charles Belcher (Balthasar), Dale Fuller (Amrad), Winter Hall (Joseph).

General Lew Wallace's all-time best seller, Ben Hur, A Tale of the Christ, was first published in 1880 and around the turn of the century became a perennial stage vehicle. In 1907 Kalem made a film version of BEN-HUR (q. v.), but it was not until 1923 that Metro began making this version, which was to be the ultimate in screen spectacle. Director Charles Brabin began the picture in Italy with George Walsh cast in the title role. After nearly two years the studio hired director Fred Niblo to helm the production and Ramon Novarro replaced George Walsh in the lead. The finished product, released late in 1925 with a pricetag of $4 million, proved to be a blockbuster and it grossed over $9 million at the box office. The film was reissued in 1931 in an abbreviated version with sound effects.

Set in Jerusalem, the story tells how Ben-Hur (Ramon Novarro), of the Jewish House of Hur, is befriended by Roman Centurion Messala (Francis X. Bushman), but is betrayed when the Roman finds out he is a Jew. To please the governor, Messala arrests the entire family and causes a general to be killed. Ben-Hur is sentenced to be a galley slave and is driven into the desert; there he meets Jesus Christ, who gives him new hope. When he saves the life of the ship's captain, Ben-Hur is befriended by the man and becomes wealthy as a charioteer. He defeats Messala in a combat race. Back in Jerusalem, Jesus is crucified and Ben-Hur's leprous mother (Claire McDowall) and sister (Katherine Key) are converted to Christianity and are cured. Ben-Hur and his family are then reunited and return to their palace.

Jesus Christ's presence in BEN-HUR is mainly indicated by the use of His hands. After the actual production was finished by Fred Niblo, a Nativity sequence, filmed in color, with Betty Bronson as the Virgin Mary, was added and was directed by Ferdinand P. Earle, who also did the art effects for the film. Niblo refused to be associated with this scene.

Although showing the parallels between the lives of Christ and the fictional Ben-Hur and their few meetings, the silent BEN-HUR is best remembered as one of the movies' most spectacular productions. Although basically a dull story, it was finely acted and its chariot race sequences are considered to be some of the most exciting footage ever placed on film; the sequence being staged by "B" Western director B. Reeves "Breezy" Eason. In discussing the film in retrospect, Kevin Brownlow wrote in The Parade's Gone By (1968), "Undoubtedly one of the best epics ever made, the original has retained its impressiveness. The performances are remote and theatrical, but their dignity ideally fits the sagaesque quality of the story.... BEN-HUR carries almost as powerful an impact today as it did on its release."

M-G-M remade the film in 1959 and the remake proved just as successful as the original film, although it was not as good. Ironically, the remake was directed by William Wyler, who had worked on the original for one day, as an assistant director on some of the crowd scenes for the chariot race.

THE MAN NOBODY KNOWS
1925
Pictorial Clubs
6 reels B/W
Director-Photography: Errett LeRoy Kenepp
Screenplay: Bruce Barton, from his novel
Music: Alexander Savine
        Bruce Barton wrote the book The Man Nobody Knows: A Discovery of Jesus Christ in 1925 and it was an immediate sensation. Barton quickly adapted the book for this film, which was produced in Palestine and issued in the United States on a states' rights basis; it had little success.
        The film used professional actors to tell the story of Jesus Christ and it interpolated scenes of the places in the Holy Land where He lived and preached. Music was used for the film with arrangements of hymns and oratorios.

QUO VADIS
1925
Italy
First National
B/W
Producers: Gabrielle d'Annuzio & George Jacoby
Director: Arturo Ambrosio
        CAST: Emil Jannings (Nero), Lillian Hall Davis

(Lygia), Andre Habay (Petronius); Elena Di Sangro, Elga Brink, Rina de Liguoro, Alphonse Fryland, Bruto Castellani, Gino Viotti, R. Van Riel.

A remake of the 1913 (q. v.) version of QUO VADIS, this version of the novel by Henryk Sienkiewicz was imported into the United States by First National and it was shown in two parts with an intermission. Like the book, it told how Jesus Christ appeared before St. Peter and told him to fight to keep Christianity in ancient Rome. The first part of the film showed the events leading up to the burning of Rome, while the second half detailed Emperor Nero's (Emil Jannings) persecution of the Christians.

Although a large-scale spectacle, this version had its faults, as voiced by the New York Times: "The whole production is excellent as a spectacle, but is too tedious in many sequences to be good entertainment." A third version of the film followed in 1951 (q. v.).

SPARROWS
1926
United Artists
9 reels B/W
Director: William Beaudine
Screenplay: Tom McNamara, Carl Harbaugh and Earle
             Browne
Titles: George Marion, Jr.
Adaptation: C. Gardner Sullivan
Story: Winifred Dunn
Photography: Charles Rosher, Karl Kruss & Hal Mohr
Art Director: Harry Oliver
Electrical Effects: William S. Johnson
        CAST: Mary Pickford (Mama Mollie), Gustav von Seyffertitz (Grimes), Roy Stewart (Richard Wayne), Mary Louise Miller (Doris Wayne), Charlotte Mineau (Mrs. Grimes), Spec O'Donnell (Ambrose Grimes), Lloyd Whitlock (Burley), A. L. Schaeffer (Confederate), Mark Hamilton (Hog Buyer), Monty O'Grady (Splutters), Muriel McCormac, Billy "Red" Jones, Cammilla Johnson, Mary McLane, Billy Butts, Jack Lavine, Florence Rogan, Seesel Ann Johnson, Sylvia Bernard (The Sparrows).

        An evil man (Gustav von Seyffertitz) and his family run a farm for unwanted children near a swamp. The children are treated brutally but are somewhat protected by the eldest (Mary Pickford) who tells the smaller children that God will protect them as He does His sparrows. When a

child (Mary Louise Miller) is kidnapped and the police look
for her, the man orders his brutal son (Spec O'Donnell) to
throw her into the swamp. The older girl rescues her and
tries to escape with the other children through the dangerous
swamp as they are being hunted by their guardian and his
son.

SPARROWS was a popular Mary Pickford vehicle and
in one sequence Jesus Christ appears to take a dead baby
from Mary Pickford's arms.

THE WANDERER
1926
Paramount
9 reels B/W
Director: Raoul Walsh
Screenplay: James T. O'Donahue, from the play by Maurice
            V. Samuels
Photography: Victor Milner
Art Director: Lawrence W. Hitt
    CAST: Greta Nissen (Tisha), William Collier, Jr.
(Jether), Ernest Torrence (Tola), Wallace Beery (Pharis),
Tyrone Power [Sr.] (Jesse), Kathryn Hill (Naomi), Kathlyn
Williams (Huldah), George Rigas (Gaal), Holmes Herbert
(Prophet), Snitz Edwards (Jeweler).
    A Famous Players-Lasky production, THE WANDERER
told the Biblical tale of the Prodigal son. The plot had
shepherd Jether (William Collier, Jr.) being lured to Babylon by Tisha (Greta Nissen), a priestess of the goddess
Ishtar. There he spends his share of his father's wealth
on her, and when he ends up broke she rejects him. A
prophet's prediction of the destruction of the city comes to
pass at a feast for Ishtar but Jether is saved and returns
home to his family where he is honored, both for his safe
return and because he did not reject God.
    THE WANDERER was shown with tinted sequences
and Photoplay reported it was "a spectacularly beautiful production."

THE KING OF KINGS
1927
Producers Distributing Corporation (PDC)
15 reels B/W and Color
Producer-Director: Cecil B. DeMille

George Siegmann, Victor Varconi and H. B. Warner in
THE KING OF KINGS (Paramount, 1927).

Screenplay: Jeannie MacPherson
Photography: Peverell Marley
Assistant Cameramen: Fred Westerberg & Jacob A.
                               Badaracco
Editors: Ann Bauchens & Harold McLernon
Associate Editor: Clifford Howard
Art Directors: Mitchell Leisen & Anton Grot
Assistant Director: Frank Urson
Second Assistant Directors: William J. Cowen & Roy Burns
Costumes: Earl Luick & Gwen Wakeling
Makeup: Fred C. Ryle
Technical Engineers: Paul Sprunck & Norman Osunn
Research: Elizabeth McGaffee
        CAST: H. B. Warner (Jesus Christ), Dorothy Cum-
ming (Mary the Mother), Ernest Torrence (Peter), Joseph
Schildkraut (Judas), Joseph Striker (John), Robert Edeson
(Matthew), Jacqueline Logan (Mary Magdalene), William Boyd

(Simon of Cyrene), Julia Faye (Martha), Alan Brooks (Satan),
Sidney D'Albrook (Thomas), David Imboden (Andrew), Charles
Belcher (Phillip), Clayton Packard (Bartholomew), Robert
Ellsworth (Simon), Charles Requa (James the Less), John T.
Prince (Thaddeus), Rudolph Schildkraut (Caiaphas), Sam De
Grasse (The Pharisee), Carson Ferguson (The Scribe), Vic-
tor Varconi (Pontius Pilate), Mizuel Coleman (Prosculia),
Montagu Love (Roman Centurion), M. Moore (Mark), Theo-
dore Kosloff (Malchus), George Siegmann (Barabbas), Jose-
phine Norman (Mary of Bethany), Kenneth Thomson (Laza-
rus), Viola Lowe (Woman Taken in Adultery), Muriel McCor-
mac (Blind Girl), Clarence Burton (Dysamac), James Mason
(Gestas), May Robson (Gestas' Mother), Dot Farley (Caia-
phas' Servant), Hector Sarno (Galilean Carpenter), Leon
Holmes (Imbecile Boy), Jack Padgen (Captain of Roman
Guard), Robert St. Angelo, Redman Finley, James Dime,
Richard Alexander, Budd Fine, William De Boar, Robert
McKee, Tom London, Edward Schaeffer, Peter Norris, Dick
Richards (Roman Soldiers), James Farley (Executioner),
Otto Lederer (Eber), Bryant Washburn (Young Roman),
Lionel Belmore (Roman Noble), Monte Collins (Rich Judean),
Luca Flamma (Gallant of Galilee), Sojin (Prince of Persia),
Andre Cheron (Wealthy Merchant), William Costello (Baby-
lonian Noble), Sally Rand (Mary Magdalene's Slave), Noble
Johnson (Charioteer); Ed Brady, Joe Bonomo, Lucille Brown,
Fred Cavens, Charles Clary, Sidney Franklin, David Dunbar,
Julia Swayne Gordon, Brandon Hurst, Theodore Lorch,
James Marcus, George F. Marion, Edward Piel, Charles
Sellon, Walter Shumway, Charles Stevens, Carl Stockdale,
Josef Swickard, Charles West.

Cecil B. DeMille's silent version of THE KING OF
KINGS was regarded for decades as the finest telling of the
story of Jesus Christ on film. One of this book's authors
(Michael R. Pitts) regards it as the best religious film ever
made in Hollywood. Since its release the feature has been
seen by over a half-billion people and it has been subtitled
in two dozen languages. As recently as two decades ago
some 600 prints of the film were available during Lent and
even today, more than a half-century after the film's release, THE KING OF KINGS is still used by many television
stations as their special Easter presentation. The picture
has also been screened in remote regions of the world by
Paulist Fathers and missionaries have carried prints of it
up the Ganges and Congo rivers. If there was ever a truly
international religious film, then the 1927 version of THE
KING OF KINGS is it.

Copyrighted at 18 reels, the film was a 15-reeler

(13, 500 feet) when road-shown in 1927 and it was cut to 11 reels for its general release.   Although filmed in black and white, the opening and closing scenes were in two-color Technicolor, although all prints in use today are entirely in black and white.   THE KING OF KINGS does not cover the boyhood of Christ (H. B. Warner) but begins with His casting out of the seven deadly sins from Mary Magdalene (Jacqueline Logan) and then presents episodes from the life of Christ, including the Passion.

H. B. Warner's performance as Christ is one of the finest ever put on film.   He gives a quiet, yet very masculine, portrayal of The Saviour and his work is truly inspirational.   A fine character actor, Warner continued on in films for another three decades, although this feature was certainly the apex of his distinguished career.   Ironically, in 1956, he also appeared in Cecil B. DeMille's THE TEN COMMANDMENTS (q. v.) for Paramount.

The supporting cast of the feature is also excellent and even the bit roles were cast to perfection.   Among the supporting players were William Boyd as Simon of Cyrene (he later became famous as "Hopalong Cassidy"), and Joseph Schildkraut (as Judas), who years later was featured in THE GREATEST STORY EVER TOLD (United Artists, 1965) (q.v.). It is ironic that in this film, Schildkraut's father, Rudolph Schildkraut, portrayed Caiaphas.   Thus father and son were cast by DeMille as the two men most responsible for the Crucifixion.   Victor Varconi also gave a fine performance as Pontius Pilate, as did Jacqueline Logan as Mary Magdalene.

An interesting aspect of the film's plot was filmed but not included in the feature.   The sequence showing a love relationship between Judas and Mary Magdalene was deleted, although the inference to such a situation does remain in the released version.

THE KING OF KINGS is a monumental effort and Cecil B. DeMille always considered it his finest film. Practically every other version of the story of Christ pales in comparison.   Perhaps Will Rogers best summed up the greatness of the movie when he said, "There will never be a greater picture because there is no greater subject."

JESUS OF NAZARETH
1928
Ideal Pictures
5700 feet   B/W

Editor-Titles: Jean Conover
    CAST: Philip Van Loan (Jesus Christ), Anna Lehr
(Virgin Mary), Charles McCaffrey (Pontius Pilate).
    Coming at the end of the silent film era, this poverty-
row feature attempted to film every single aspect of the life
of Jesus Christ. Unfortunately the film did not have the
budget to accomplish this monumental feat and the end result was a poor quality feature which did not get wide showings. A half-century later the idea, with the same title,
was done right when it was produced for television.

MOTHERHOOD: LIFE'S GREATEST MIRACLE
1928
States Cinema Corporation
6 reels B/W
Screenplay: Lita Lawrence
    CAST: George E. Patton, Adelaide M. Chase.
    Opening with sequences of Jesus Christ in the man-
ger, this film then switched to paralleling modern stories
about a pair of poor and wealthy couples and how their con-
trasting life styles are affected by approaching motherhood.
    Made by Blue Ray Productions in 1925, the film was
not distributed for three years.

THE PASSION PLAY
1928
Passion Play Committee
B/W
    The durable "Passion Play" resurfaced again in this
feature film, made toward the end of the silent film era.
Although the film had theatrical distribution, it was mainly
made for church and educational showings.

THE PASSION PLAY
1930
B/W
    "The Last Supper" was interpolated into this version
of the perennial "Passion Play." Ironically this feature was
made as a silent film, although it was made well into the
sound era. The film received no theatrical showings; instead, it opted for church and educational playdates.

It should be noted that during the sound era the number of film versions of "The Passion Play" continued to match those from the silent days. From this point forward, however, these productions tended to be national in origin; that is, they were produced by Catholic countries on both sides of the Atlantic and were played in the individual countries' theatres with little release outside these countries. These "Passion Play" outings were mainly filmed from the 1930s into the 1950s.

OBERAMMERGAU PASSION PLAY
circa 1930s
Screen Art Sales Company
B/W

Billed as "The World's Best and Only Passion Play," this states' rights release was apparently filmed in the 1920s and issued to theatres and churches a decade later with a soundtrack. Besides a narration the soundtrack includes sacred songs by the Roxy Chorus and organist Emil Velazco.

The feature, an actual filming of the Oberammergau version of the Passion Play in Europe, was billed as the first talking picture version of the perennial Passion. Advertising for the production claimed that special talking picture equipment was used for it, along with a special projectionist who traveled with the feature. The film was issued in 35mm for theatrical showings and 16mm for churches.

DESTINATION UNKNOWN
1933
Universal
65 minutes   B/W
Director: Tay Garnett
Screenplay: Thomas Buckingham
Photography: Edward Snyder
Editor: Milton Carruth

CAST: Pat O'Brien (Matt Brennan), Ralph Bellamy (The Stowaway), Alan Hale (Lundstrom), Russell Hopton (Georgie), Tom Brown (Johnny), Betty Compson (Ruby Smith), Noel Madison (Maxie), Stanley Fields (Gattallo), Rollo Lloyd (Dr. Fran), Willard Robertson (Joe Shane), Charles Middleton (Turk), Richard Alexander (Alex), Forrester Harvey (Ring), George Rigas (Tauru).

A stranger (Ralph Bellamy) appears on a ship that is stranded on the Pacific Ocean with no wind, and brings peace to those on board. When the ship is wrecked, the stranger saves the crew and passengers and then disappears.

This well-done programmer implies that the stranger is Jesus Christ and the miracle of the changing of salt water into fresh water is shown. The film is quite similar to STRANGE CARGO (q. v.), which also featured silent film star Betty Compson.

THE WANDERING JEW
1933
Great Britain
Twickenham
111 minutes   B/W
Producer: Julius Hagen
Director: Maurice Elvey
Screenplay: H. Fowler Mear, from the play by E. Temple
             Thurston
Photography: Sydney Blythe
       CAST: Conrad Veidt (Matathias); Marie Ney, Cicely Gates, Basil Gill, Anne Grey, Dennis Hoey, Jack Livesey, Bertram Wallis, Joan Maude, John Stuart, Arnold Lucy, Peggy Ashcroft, Francis L. Sullivan, Felix Aylmer, Ivor Barnard, Abraham Sofaer.

       Veteran British director Maurice Elvey remade his 1923 (q. v.) version of this film* and it retained the traditional storyline about the storekeeper in Jerusalem who is forced to wander the world alone after refusing to let Christ rest at his doorstep along the journey to Cavalry. As in the earlier version, the character of Jesus Christ was not seen in this film.

       Conrad Veidt, who played the title role, would star in THE PASSING OF THE THIRD FLOOR BACK (q. v.) three years later.

ECCE HOMO (Behold the Man)
1935

_____
*A Yiddish film, THE WANDERING JEW (Jewish-American Film Art, 1933), with Jacob Ben-Ami, was not based on either the play or the novel.

France
Transat Films
105 minutes   B/W
Producer-Director: Julien Duvivier
Screenplay: Julien Duvivier & Joseph Raymond [Chanoine
          Reymond]
Photography: G. J. Kruger
Music: Jacques Ibert
          CAST: Robert Le Vigan (Jesus Christ), Jean Gabin
(Pontius Pilate), Harry Baur (Herod), Juliette Verneuil (Virgin Mary), Edwige Verneuil (Claudia); Andre Bacque, Charles
Granval, Hubert Prelier, Lucas Gridoux, Van Daele.
          A programmer made in France by noted producer-
director Julien Duvivier, ECCE HOMO is a nicely photo-
graphed film concerned with the Holy Week events from
Palm Sunday until Easter.   Among the events dramatized
in this photoplay are Christ's (Robert Le Vigan) entry into
Jerusalem, the driving of the merchants from the Temple,
Jesus' betrayal by Judas Iscariot, the Last Supper, Christ
in the Garden of Gethsemane, His trials before the high
priests, Pilate and Herod, the scourging by the Roman soldiers, the march to Calvary, the Crucifixion and the Resurrection.
          In addition to fine direction and photography, the film
boasted excellent performances, especially those of unknown
Robert Le Vigan as Christ, French film idol Jean Gabin as
Pilate, and Harry Baur as King Herod.
          Film Daily called ECCE HOMO "an extraordinary
picture" and added, "the sweep of the production is tremendous."   The trade paper concluded, "Everybody connected
with the production of this picture can feel justly proud.
Director Duvivier has contributed a mighty theme with a
technique that is sweepingly effective and at the same time
dramatically powerful in its simplicity, sensitivity and handling of details.   The musical score in itself is an achievement, catching every slightest mood of the picture with a
magic all its own."
          The film, the first all-talking film made on the life
of Christ, was road-shown in the United States in 1937 as
GOLGOTHA by the Golgotha Corporation.   This dubbed version was 97 minutes in length.

THE LAST DAYS OF POMPEII
1935
RKO Radio

Basil Rathbone, John Wood and Preston Foster in THE LAST
DAYS OF POMPEII (RKO Radio, 1935).

90 minutes B/W
Producer: Merian C. Cooper
Director: Ernest B. Schoedsack
Screenplay: Ruth Rose & Boris Ingster
Story: James A. Creelman & Melville Baker
Photography: Eddie Linden Jr. & Ray Hunt
Editor: Archie Harschek
Music: Roy Webb
Special Effects: Vernon Walker & Harry Redmond
        CAST: Preston Foster (Marcus), Basil Rathbone
(Pontius Pilate), Alan Hale (Burbix), John Wood (Flavius as
a Man), Louis Calhern (Prefect), David Holt (Flavius as a
Boy), Dorothy Wilson (Clodia), Wyrley Birch (Leaster),
Gloria Shea (Julia), Frank Conroy (Gaius), William V. Mong
(Cleon), Edward Van Sloan (Calvus), Zeffie Tilbury (Wise

Woman).

A blacksmith, Marcus (Preston Foster), in Pompeii becomes an arena gladiator when his wife and baby are killed by a nobleman's chariot. Becoming a champion interested only in wealth, Marcus adopts Flavius (David Holt), the small son of a gladiator killed in the arena. He grows close to the boy and after being wounded in combat Marcus turns to slave trading. A wise woman (Zeffie Tilbury) advises Marcus to take the boy to see "the greatest man in Judea," who he assumes is Pontius Pilate (Basil Rathbone). Pilate hires Marcus to steal horses for him but the boy is hurt and is taken to Jesus Christ, who heals him. When Marcus leaves Jerusalem he sees Christ sentenced to die on the Cross but he does not try to save Him from the mob. Years later Marcus is head of the arena in Pompeii but the grown Flavius (John Wood) opposes the slaughter of slaves by the gladiators and leads a revolt. When Flavius is captured among the slaves, Marcus orders the games stopped, and when Mount Vesuvius erupts he dies in order to save Flavius and the slaves. As he dies, Jesus Christ appears and blesses Marcus.

THE LAST DAYS OF POMPEII is an entertaining costumer which is somewhat dated today. Most interesting Biblically in the film is Basil Rathbone's portrayal of Pilate as a haughty aristocrat. Jesus Christ is seen only as a shadow when curing the little boy, and from a distance carrying the Cross to Calvary. At the finale He is shown as a transparent figure blessing the dying Marcus.

THE PASSING OF THE THIRD FLOOR BACK
1936
Great Britain
Gaumont-British
90 minutes   B/W
Associate Producer: Ivor Montagu
Director: Berthold Vietrel
Screenplay: Michael Hogan & Alma Reville, from the story
              and play by Jerome K. Jerome
Photography: C. Courant
Editor: D. N. Twist
Music: Louis Lory
        CAST: Conrad Veidt (The Stranger); Anna Lee, Rene Ray, Frank Cellier, Mary Clare, Beatrix Lehmann, John Turnbull, Cathleen Nesbitt, Ronald Ward, Jack Livesey, Sara Allgood.

Conrad Veidt, who had previously starred in the sound remake of THE WANDERING JEW (q. v.), played the title role in this melodrama from Jerome K. Jerome's popular play. Veidt played the stranger who comes to a boardinghouse and brings peace to all those who meet him; the stranger is presumed to be Jesus Christ.

TRIUMPH
1937
Great Britain
World Commonwealth Films
B/W
This little known British feature showed scenes from the lives of many famous persons such as Socrates, Leonardo da Vinci and Abraham Lincoln. Also included in the film were the lives of Jesus Christ and St. Francis of Assisi. The film was well acted by a cast of professional or semi-professional actors, but it appears to have received little release outside its debut in London late in 1937. TRIUMPH received no recorded United States playdates.

PRINCE OF PEACE
1939
Great Britain
GB Instructional
23 minutes B/W
Director: Donald Carter
      CAST: Pamela Kelino (Mary).
A short telling the story of the birth of Jesus Christ from the Book of Luke in The New Testament.

STRANGE CARGO
1940
Metro-Goldwyn-Mayer
105 minutes B/W
Producer: Joseph L. Mankiewicz
Director: Frank Borzage
Screenplay: Lawrence Hazard, from the novel Not Too Nar-
            row, Not Too Deep by Richard Sale
Photography: Robert Planck
Editor: Robert J. Kern

Music: Franz Waxman
Art Director: Cedric Gibbons
     CAST: Clark Gable (Andre Verna), Joan Crawford (Julie), Ian Hunter (Cambreau), Peter Lorre (Cochon), Paul Lukas (Hessler), Albert Dekker (Moll), Eduardo Ciannelli (Floubert), Victor Varconi (Telez), John Aldredge (Dufend), Frederic Worlock (Grideau), Paul Fix (Benet), Bernard Nedell (Marfeu), Francis McDonald (Mosseng), Betty Compson (Suzanne), Charles Judels (Renard), Jack Mulhall (Djinning), Dewey Robinson (George), Harry Cording, Richard Alexander, Bud Fine, James Pierce, Hal Wynant (Guards), Gene Coogan (Convict), Art Miles, Bud O'Connor (Subordinates), Eddie Foster, Frank Lackteen, Harry Semels (Convicts), Stanley Andrews (Constable), William Edmunds (Watchman).

     STRANGE CARGO is an interesting film that has little to do with religion, although one of its main characters, Cambreau (Ian Hunter), is supposed to be Jesus Christ in a modern-day setting.

     The plot concerns a group of eight convicts on Devil's Island who escape and trek through the jungle, where they meet another escaped convict (Clark Gable) and his trollop girlfriend (Joan Crawford). The convict wrests control of the group from Moll (Albert Dekker), a brutal killer, and they land on a deserted island where they meet Cambreau. The stranger knows all about the prisoners' past lives, performs a few miracles and does his best to reform the lot. The group of sinners soon comes under the spell of this man and he changes the course of their lives.

THE GREAT COMMANDMENT
1941
20th Century-Fox
82 minutes   B/W
Producer: John T. Coyle
Associate Producer: Rev. James K. Friedrich
Director: Irving Pichel
Screenplay: Dana Burnet
Photography: Charles Boyle
Editor: Ralph Dixon
     CAST: John Beal (Joel), Maurice Moscovitch (Lamech), Albert Dekker (Longinus), Marjorie Cooley (Tamar), Warren McCollum (Zadok), Lloyd Corrigan (Jemuel), Ian Wolfe (Tax Collector), Olaf Hytten (Nathan), Anthony Marlowe (Singer), Lester Scharff, Albert Spehr (Zealots), Marc

Loebell (Judas), Harold Minjir (Andrew), Earl Gunn (Wounded Man), George Rosener (Merchant), Irving Pichel (Voice of Jesus Christ), John Merton (Under Officer), Percy Evans, Stanley Price (Elders), D'Arcy Corrigan (Blind Man), Max Davidson (Old Man).

The title of this feature refers to charity and it tells the story of pacifist Jews in Jerusalem at the time of Christ who oppose Roman rule and whose leader (John Beal) goes against his own family when he accepts Jesus Christ as his saviour. Taking place in 30 A.D., it tells the story of the Jewish Revolt against the Romans and how Christ and His Disciples spread the gospel at that time. Jesus is not seen in the film but is represented by a friendly voice speaking parables.

Produced by Cathedral Films in 1939, this film was one of the first features to be made by a totally religious production company with a professional Hollywood cast. The film was intended for theatrical release but it was purchased by 20th Century-Fox who planned to remake the feature as a vehicle for contract star Tyrone Power. When that project failed to materialize, the studio issued the feature nationally in 1941.

Reviews for THE GREAT COMMANDMENT were decidedly mixed. Time magazine said the film had a "wonderful nerve-quivering eerie power," while the Los Angeles Times commented that it was "a superlative film which is probably the finest, most consistent, impressive and appealing story of Christ's time that has ever been made." The Hollywood Reporter thought "it has frequent touches of true greatness" but the New York Times said it was a "poorly done costume drama" that "has good intentions but fails them totally."

It is interesting to note that the voice of Jesus Christ in the film was supplied by director Irving Pichel; his contribution was one of the highlights of the feature. Pichel used his voice quite effectively on the film's soundtrack, and its trailing across the countryside as the Disciples brought forth the gospel was one of the most powerful portions of the movie. Pichel, who had a varied career as both an actor and director, would again work for Cathedral Films when he directed DAY OF TRIUMPH (q.v.) in 1953, which was his final film. He also directed another religious theatrical feature film, MARTIN LUTHER (DeRochemont, 1953), which was selected as one of the ten best films of 1953 by the New York Times.

THE LAWTON STORY
1949
Hallmark
125 minutes B/W & Cinecolor
Producer: Kroger Babb
Directors: William Beaudine & Harold Daniels
Screenplay: Mildred A. Horn
Screen Treatment: Milton Raison
Story: Scott Darling
Original Pageant Story: Rev. A. Mark Wallock
Photography: Henry Sharp, Wallace Chewning & Edward
                Movius
Editor: Richard Currier
        CAST: Ginger Prince (Ginger), Forrest Taylor (Uncle Mark), Ferris Taylor (Uncle Jonathan), Millard Coody (Jesus Christ), Gwyn Shipman (Jane), Darlene Bridges (Virgin Mary), Willa Pearl Curtis (Herself), A. S. Fisher (Simon Peter), Hazel Lee Becker (Mary Magdalene), Maude Eburne (Henrietta); William Ruhl, Russell Whitman, Lydia McKim, Billy Lord.
        Set in modern-day Lawton, Oklahoma, the film told the story of the town's annual Oklahoma Passion Play, which was started in 1926 by Rev. A. Mark Wallock, minister of the Lawton Congregational Church. The film is divided into two portions, separated by an intermission. The first half tells of the town's preparations for the Passion Play presentation and its effects on the community and its people. The second portion is the actual presentation of the Passion Play staged in a large mountain amphitheatre outside the town and enacted by the community's 3,000 inhabitants. This portion of the feature was shot in Cinecolor.
        The feature was reissued in 1951 as PRINCE OF PEACE and it is also known as THE LAWTON STORY OF THE PRINCE OF PEACE.

THE TRIUMPHANT HOUR
1950
Family Theatre
58 minutes B/W
Producer: Rev. Patrick Payton
Director: Frank McDonald
Screenplay: James D. Roche
        CAST: Don Ameche, Ann Blyth, Jack Haley, Bob Hope, Ruth Hussey, Rita Johnson, Fibber McGee & Molly, Roddy McDowall, Pat O'Brien, Jane Wyatt, Sarah Allgood,

Jerry Colonna, Pedro De Cordoba, The Dionne Quintuplets, James Gleason, Ann Jamison, Nan Harriman, Gilbert Russell.

THE TRIUMPHANT HOUR, one of the first motion pictures to be made specifically for television, is an Easter drama of the meditations of the five Glorious Mysteries of the Rosary. Among the incidents included in the drama are the Resurrection of Christ, His appearance to the Apostles, the Ascension, the Descent of the Holy Ghost, the Assumption of Mary and the Coronation in Heaven. All these scenes are related to the recitation of the various decades of the Rosary by Hollywood stars, some of whose families (i. e., Bob Hope, Jerry Colonna, Jack Haley, Pat O'Brien, Roddy McDowall) also appear. A quartet of song solos also make up the drama, including Ann Blyth rendering "Come Holy Ghost."

The Boston Post called the film "a solemn and stirring re-enactment of the glorious resurrection of Christ ... one of the most inspiring observances of Easter ever presented." Unfortunately this early telefeature was made in black and white and as a result does not get the exposure today that it really deserves.

DER FALLENDE STERN (The Fallen Star)
1951
West Germany
NDF Distributors
Director: Harald Braun
Screenplay: Harald Braun & Herbert Witt
Photography: Richard Angst
Music: Werner Eisbrenner
    CAST: Dieter Borsche, Paul Dahlke, Werner Krauss, Bernard Wicki.

DER FALLENDE STERN's plotline had Jesus Christ and The Devil at odds over the soul of a woman. The film was full of hard-to-understand symbolism and was not a popular item outside its native country.

QUO VADIS
1951
United States-Italy
Metro-Goldwyn-Mayer
171 minutes   Color

Producer: Sam Zimbalist
Director: Mervyn LeRoy
Screenplay: John Lee Mahin, S. N. Behrman & Sonya Le-
 vien, from the novel by Henryk Sienkiewicz
Photography: Robert Surtees & William V. Small
Editor: Robert E. Winters
Assistant Directors: William A. Horning, Cedric Gibbons &
 Edward Cargagno
 CAST: Robert Taylor (Marcus Vinicius), Deborah
Kerr (Lygia), Leo Genn (Petronius), Peter Ustinov (Nero),
Patricia Laffan (Poppaea), Finlay Currie (Peter), Abraham
Sofaer (Paul), Marina Berti (Unice), Buddy Baer (Ursus),
Felix Aylmer (Platius), Nora Swinburne (Pomponia), Ralph
Truman (Tigellinus), Norman Wooland (Nerva), Peter Miles
(Nazarius), Geoffrey Dunn (Terpnos), Nicholas Hannen (Sen-
eca), S. A. Clarke-Smith (Phaon), Rosalie Crutchley (Acte),
John Ruddock (Chilo), Arthur Walge (Croton), Elspeth March
(Miriam), Strelsa Brown (Rufia), Alfred Varelli (Lucan),
Roberto Ottaviano (Flavius), William Tubbo (Alexander),
Pietro Tordi (Galba), Lia De Leo (Pedicurist), Enzo Stuarti,
Sophia Loren, Elizabeth Taylor (Extras).
 Filmed in wide screen and Technicolor, this third
version of QUO VADIS was a huge spectacle film which re-
counted the persecution of the Christian martyrs in Ancient
Rome. In this version, however, Jesus Christ is not seen
although He does appear in spirit early in the proceedings,
with His words being spoken through a boy who is with St.
Peter (Finlay Currie). Also, in its initial stages, the film
presents scenes from the life of Christ, during a sermon
delivered by St. Peter.

THE WESTMINSTER PASSION PLAY-BEHOLD THE MAN
1951
Great Britain
Film Reports/Companions of the Cross
75 minutes B/W
Producers: Susan Dallison & Fred T. Swan
Director: Walter Rilla
Screenplay: Walter Rilla & Walter Meyjes, based on the
 play Ecce Homo by Walter Meyjes & Charles
 P. Carr
 CAST: Charles P. Carr (Jesus Christ), Walter
Meyjes (Narrator).
 "The Passion Play" has been done many times before,
but this British feature was the Westminster version, based

on the play by Walter Meyjes, who narrated the film, and
Charles P. Carr, who portrayed Jesus Christ. To evaluate
the film critically would be unfair, as it was a church project and not meant to be a professional film, although it was
co-adapted to the screen and directed by Walter Rilla, a
noted actor-writer-director and father of film director Wolf
Rilla. The film is very unassuming, but serves its purpose
for what it was meant to be--inspirational.

I BEHELD HIS GLORY
1952
Cathedral Films
55 minutes   B/W
Producer: Rev. James K. Friedrich
Director: John T. Coyle
Screenplay: Arthur T. Harman
Story: Rev. John Evans
Photography: Freddie West
Editor: Thomas Neff
        CAST: Robert Wilson (Jesus Christ), George Mac-
ready (Cornelius), Lowell Gilmore (Pilate), James Flavin
(Longinus), Grandon Rhoades (Eltheas), Thomas Charles-
worth (Thomas), Morris Ankrum (Peter), I. Stanford Jolley
(Dismas), Virginia Wave (Mary of Magdala).
        Cornelius (George Macready), a Roman Centurion,
arrives in the village of Far-isha in search of Eltheas
(Grandon Rhoads), a kinsman of the disciple Thomas (Thomas Charlesworth). There the Centurion tells Eltheas the
story of Jesus Christ (Robert Wilson) as he witnessed it
himself. He tells Eltheas and his family how he was detailed to duty in Jerusalem during the last part of the great
Jewish Passover Feast and how he heard of Jesus from his
old comrade, Centurion Longinus (James Flavin). He tells
of the entry of Jesus into Jerusalem and of His cleansing
the Temple of the money changers. He goes on to tell of
the Passover Supper and the betrayal of Jesus by Judas,
the arrest of Jesus and His trial before Sanhedrin, His appearance before the Roman Procurator Pilate (Lowell Gilmore) and how the priesthood incited the crowd against
Christ. Cornelius recites how Pilate is forced by the
priesthood to turn Christ over to the crowd in deference to
the thief Barabbas. As a soldier of Rome, Cornelius then
had to carry out the sentence of death for Christ. He wit-
nesses the Crucifixion and, later, while guarding Christ's
tomb, sees a blinding flash of light, hears a rumble as of

Morris Ankrum (left, with beard) and Robert Wilson (standing) in I BEHELD HIS GLORY (Cathedral Films, 1952).

an earthquake; then the soldiers find the stone rolled away and the tomb empty. The Centurion then recounted how he searched out Thomas and was told of the Resurrection. Cornelius concluded his recitation by saying, "I will tell this story all the days of my life, so none that hear me can doubt, for I, also, a Centurion of Rome, Beheld His Glory. "

Made for distribution to churches, I BEHELD HIS GLORY is also available for television showings as well as 16mm rental. The film was well produced and was enacted by a group of well-seasoned Hollywood character actors, although the role of Jesus Christ went to non-professional actor Robert Wilson, who bore a striking resemblance to the endless array of portraits of Christ painted throughout the ages since His Resurrection. Wilson was so fine in the role that he repeated it in Cathedral Films' DAY OF TRIUMPH (q. v.), which was released theatrically. In that feature Lowell Gilmore also repeated his role of Pontius Pilate.

Many viewers have found I BEHELD HIS GLORY to be a profound and moving religious experience. The

approach of having the last days of Christ told as seen
through the eyes of another person was also used in the
feature film, POWER OF THE RESURRECTION (q. v.).

ST. MATTHEW PASSION
1952
Austria
Erma Films of Vienna
120 minutes B/W
Producer-Director: Ernst Marischka
Editor: Robert Flaherty
Music Director: Herbert von Karajan
    American film documentary pioneer Robert Flaherty,
who made such classics as NANOOK OF THE NORTH (1920),
MOANA (1926), TABU (1929) and MAN OF ARAN (1934),
conceived and edited this feature, which proved to be his
final production before his death in 1951.   There are no
actors in this feature, which presents the Passion Play
events, from the Last Supper to the entombment, in famous
paintings from the 14th to the 18th centuries, including the
works of Da Vinci, Masaccio, Caravaggio, Van Eyck, Velas-
quez, Cranach, Reni, Rubens, Raphael, Bosch and Titian.
As the musical background for the film Johann Sebastian
Bach's oratorio, "The Gospel According to St. Matthew,"
was performed by soloists Elisabeth Schwartzkopf, Karl
Schmitt Walter, Hans Braun, Elisabeth Hoengen, Walter
Ludwig and the Choir of the Viennese Singverein and the
Vienna Boys' Choir.
    In reviewing this documentary, the New York Times
said, it "is more formidable as a musical recording than
as a piece of motion-picture art ... it is without true dy-
namic quality and represents no achievement in the creative
use of the screen."   The film was issued in the United
States by Academy Productions.

THE ROBE
1953
20th Century-Fox
135 minutes Color
Producer: Frank Rosa
Director: Henry Koster
Screenplay: Philip Dunne, from the novel by Lloyd C.
           Douglas

Adaptation: Gina Kaus
Photography: Leon Shamroy
Editor: Barbara McLean
Art Directors: Lyle Wheeler & George W. Davis
Music: Alfred Newman
      CAST: Richard Burton (Marcellus Gallio), Jean Simmons (Diana), Victor Mature (Demetrius), Michael Rennie (Peter), Jay Robinson (Caligula), Dean Jagger (Justus), Torin Thatcher (Senator Gallio), Richard Boone (Pontius Pilate), Betta St. John (Miriam), Jeff Morrow (Paulus), Ernest Thesiger (Emperor Tiberius), Dawn Addams (Junia), Leon Askin (Abidor), Helen Beverley (Rebecca), Frank Pulaski (Quintus), David Leonard (Marcipor), Michael Ansara (Judas), Jay Novello (Tiro), Nicholas Koster (Jonathan), Francis Pierlot (Dodinius), Emmett Lynn (Nathan), Thomas Browne Henry (Marius), Sally Corner (Cornelia), Rosalind Ivan (Julai), Anthony Eustrel (Sarpeadon), Pamela Robinson (Lucia), George E. Stone (Gracchus), Marc Snow (Auctioneer), Mae Marsh (Woman), George Keymas (Slave), John Doucette (Ship's Mate), Ford Rainey, Sam Gilman (Ships' Captains), Cameron Mitchell (Voice of Jesus Christ); Frank De Kova, Harry Shearer, Arthur Page, Peter Reynolds, Virginia Lee, George Melford, Eleanor Moore, Irene Dewetrion, Dan Ferniel, Leo Curley, George Robotham, Alex Pope, Jean & Joan Corbett, Gloria Saunders, Percy Helton, Ed Mundy, Anthony Jochim, Van Des Autels, Roy Gordon, Hayden Roarke, Ben Astar.
      THE ROBE is an impressive motion picture and the first feature to be filmed in CinemaScope. It was very popular with moviegoers and grossed $17.5 million in domestic rentals.
      A fictional story, the film told of the "magical powers" of the robe that Jesus Christ wore on His way to Calvary. The crux of the plotline centered on Marcellus (Richard Burton), a Roman official charged with crucifying Jesus Christ, and his Greek slave, Demetrius (Victor Mature), a convert to Christ. When, after the Crucifixion, Marcellus puts on the robe worn by Christ, he becomes obsessed with it and Christianity.
      Jesus Christ is seen twice in the film, first riding into Jerusalem on Palm Sunday and later on the Cross. His face is not shown on either occasion but His voice is heard, the dubbing being done by Cameron Mitchell.
      THE ROBE, from Lloyd C. Douglas' 1942 novel, proved so popular that Victor Mature again played the Greek slave in DEMETRIUS AND THE GLADIATORS (q.v.).

Charles Laughton, Rita Hayworth and Stewart Granger in
SALOME (Columbia, 1953).

SALOME
1953
Columbia
105 minutes   Color
Producer: Buddy Adler
Associate Producer: Earl Bellamy
Director: William Dieterle
Screenplay: Harry Kleiner
Story: Harry Kleiner & Jesse L. Lasky, Jr.
Photography: Charles Lang
Editor: Viola Lawrence
Music: George Duning
Dances: Daniele Amfithentrof
Musical Director: Morris Stoloff
Orchestrations: Arthur Morton
Chorales: Robert Wagner Chorale
Choreography: Valerie Buttis
Men's Costumes: Emile Santiago
Gowns: Jean Louis
Technicolor Consultant: Francis Cugat

Technical Consultant: Millard Sheets
Art Director: John Meehan
Set Decorator: William Kiernan
Makeup: Clay Hamilton
Sound Engineer: Lodge Cunningham
        CAST: Rita Hayworth (Princess Salome), Stewart
Granger (Commander Claudius), Charles Laughton (King
Herod), Judith Anderson (Queen Herodias), Sir Cedric Hard-
wicke (Caesar Tiberius), Alan Badel (John the Baptist),
Basil Sydney (Pontius Pilate), Maurice Schwartz (Ezra),
Rex Reason (Marcellus Fabius), Arnold Moss (Micha), Rob-
ert Warwick (Courier), Carmen D'Antonio (Salome's Ser-
vant), Michael Granger (Captain Quintas), Karl Davis (Slave
Master), Sujata & Asoka (Oriental Dancers), Joe Shilling,
David Wold, Ray Beltram, Joe Sawaya, Anton Northpole,
Franz Roehor, William McCormick (Advisors), Eduardo
Cansino (Roman Guard), Mickey Simpson (Herod's Guard
Captain), Barry Brooks, Bruce Cameron, John Crawford,
Tristram Coffin (Guards), Lou Nova (Executioner), Fred
Letuli, John Woodd (Sword Dancers), William Spaeth (Fire
Eater), Duke Johnson (Juggler), Alel Pina, Jerry Pina,
Henry Pina, Henry Escalante, Gilbert Maques, Miguel
Gutierez, Ramiro Rivas, Ruben T. Rivas, Richard Rivas,
Hector Urtiaga (Acrobats), Earl Brown, Bud Cokes (Gali-
lean Soldiers), George Khoury, Leonard George (Assassins),
Eva Hyde (Herodias' Servant), Charles Wagenheim (Simon),
Leslie Denison (Court Attendant), Henry dar Boggia, Michael
Couzzi, Babker Ben Ali, Don De Leo, John Parrish, Eddy
Fields, Robert Garabedion, Sam Scar (Politicians), Michael
Mark (Old Farmer), David Leonard, Maurice Samuels, Ralph
Moody (Old Scholars), Guy Kingsford, Carleton Young (Offi-
cers), Paul Hoffman (Sailmaster), Stanley Waxman (Patrician),
Saul Martell (Dissenting Scholar), Jack Low, Bert Rose,
Tom Hernandez (Townsmen), Trevor Ward (Blind Man),
Fred Berest, Rick Vallin, George Keymas (Soldiers), Roque
Barry (Slave), Italia De Nublia, David Ahdar, Charles Sol-
dani, Dimac Sotello, William Wilkerson, Mario Lamm, Tina
Menard (Converts).
        The perennial screen vehicle, SALOME, subtitled
"The Dance of the Seven Veils," was revived again, this
time as a vehicle for the aging, but still beautiful, screen
siren Rita Hayworth. The story, however, proved hack-
neyed and the cast of leading players did little to help matters. Rita Hayworth was quite seductive in the role, so
much so that she created a protest from women's groups.
Stewart Granger was passive as Claudius while Charles
Laughton as Herod and Judith Anderson as his wife literally

chewed up the scenery in their hammy performances. The
familiar plot remained: Salome dances the seven veils for
Herod in order to see John the Baptist (Alan Badel) killed
for preferring Christianity to her. The end, however,
added the fiction of Salome's conversion to Christianity.
    The critics detested this color spectacle. The Lon-
don Daily Sketch wrote, "This shameful film should be
scrapped because it is nothing more than a shameless per-
version of the Bible and a blot on Hollywood's record."
Years later Gene Ringgold commented, in The Films of
Rita Hayworth (1974), "the screenplay ... was not only
historically dubious, it was dramatically boring and com-
pletely void of the special kind of vulgarity which always
made Cecil B. DeMille's biblical spectacles engrossing
films, if not enlightening experiences."
    Jesus Christ is seen twice in SALOME, both times
from the back, and the film closes with His delivery of the
Sermon on the Mount.

DAY OF TRIUMPH
1954
Century Films
110 minutes   Color
Producer: Rev. James K. Friedrich
Associate Producer: Spencer H. Lees
Directors: Irving Pichel & John T. Coyle
Screenplay: Arthur T. Horman
Photography: Ray June
Editor: Thomas Neff
Music: Daniele Amfitheatrof
Makeup: Larry Butterworth
    CAST: Robert Wilson (Jesus Christ), Joanne Dru
(Mary of Magdala), Lee J. Cobb (Zadok), Touch [Michael]
Connors (Andrew), James Griffith (Judas), Lowell Gilmore
(Pilate), Tyler McVey (Peter), Ralph Freud (Caiaphas);
John Stevenson, Toni Gerry, Everett Glass, Anthony Warde,
Peter Whitney, The Roger Wagner Chorale.
    The head of Cathedral Films, Rev. James K. Fried-
rich, produced DAY OF TRIUMPH for distribution to
churches in 1952 but the color production proved so fine
that Century Films issued it to theatres in 1954 and it had
considerable popularity. Having previously presented portions of Christ's life in I BEHELD HIS GLORY (1952) (q. v.),
Friedrich set out to again tell the story of the Saviour, but
this time within the framework of a fictional plot. The

Robert Wilson, who portrayed Jesus Christ in I BEHELD
HIS GLORY (Cathedral Films, 1952) and DAY OF TRIUMPH
(Century Films, 1954), and in Cathedral Films' sound film-
strips, "Story of Jesus" and "The Passion Story."

story revolved around a secret group in Jerusalem, of which Judas (James Griffith) was a member, wanting to use Jesus (Robert Wilson) to start a revolt against the ruling Romans. The film contained action, pageantry, suspense and the interplay of human emotions while remaining true to the Scriptures; as a result it was praised by Protestant, Catholic and Jewish clergy.

Made at a cost of $600,000, this finely photographed and acted feature recreated the Sermon on the Mount, Mary of Magdala (Joanne Dru) becoming a follower of Christ, the raising of Lazarus, Jesus' entry into Jerusalem on Palm Sunday, the purging from the Temple of the money changers by Jesus, the judgment of Christ by Pilate, the Crucifixion and the Resurrection. The film also concluded that Judas committed suicide because of the shame he felt for causing Christ's Crucifixion after trying to involve Him in the revolt led by Zadok (Lee J. Cobb).

One of the most striking things about the film, which was shot mostly in the Vasquez Rocks area of California, was the performance of Robert Wilson in the role of Jesus Christ. He brought a quiet sense of honesty to the role, one he had already done in I BEHELD HIS GLORY the year before. Life magazine said of Wilson: "In his makeup [he] bears a striking resemblance to the traditional concept of the Saviour." Perhaps due to this resemblance, Wilson has played Christ on film more than any other actor. Besides his starring roles in the two features for Cathedral Films he has also portrayed Christ in that company's sound filmstrip series, "Story of Jesus" and "The Passion Story."

DAY OF TRIUMPH was later re-edited to 90 minutes in length and today a 30-minute version of the highlights of the feature is also available.

DEMETRIUS AND THE GLADIATORS
1954
20th Century-Fox
101 minutes   Color
Producer: Frank Ross
Director: Delmer Daves
Screenplay: Philip Dunne
Photography: Milton Krasner
Editors: Dorothy Spencer & Robert Fritch
Music: Franz Waxman & Alfred Newman
Art Directors: Lyle Wheeler & George W. Davis
Choreography: Stephen Papich

Assistant Director: William Eckhart

CAST: Victor Mature (Demetrius), Susan Hayward (Messalina), Michael Rennie (Peter the Fisherman), Debra Paget (Lucia), Anne Bancroft (Paula), Jay Robinson (Emperor Caligula), Barry Jones (Claudius), William Marshall (Glydon), Richard Egan (Dardanius), Ernest Borgnine (Strabo), Charles Evans (Cassius Chaerea), Everett Glass (Kaeso), Karl Davis (Macro), Jeff York (Albus), Carmen de Lavallade (Slave Girl), John Cliff (Varus), Barbara James, Willetta Smith (Dancers), Selmer Jackson (Senator), Douglas Brooks (Cousin), Fred Graham (Decurion), Dayton Lummis (Magistrate), George Eldredge (Chamberlain), Paul Richards (Prisoner), Ray Spiker, Gilbert Perkins, Paul Stander, Jim Winkler, Lyle Fox, Dick Sands, Woody Strode (Gladiators), Paul "Tiny" Newlan (Potter), Allan Kramer (Clerk), Paul Kruger (Courtier); and Richard Burton, Jean Simmons and the voice of Cameron Mitchell from THE ROBE (q. v.).

This film was a direct sequel to THE ROBE (q. v.) and told the story of the Greek slave Demetrius (Victor Mature), now free, and of how he loses and then finds again his faith in God. The story of the robe that Christ wore to Calvary is also continued from the first film, with Peter (Michael Rennie) giving the robe to Demetrius, who hides it with a potter while the mad Roman emperor Caligula (Jay Robinson) searches for it because he believes it will give him eternal youth.

The film follows Demetrius as he is sent to gladiators' school in Rome and then becomes a favorite of Messalina (Susan Hayward), the wayward wife of Claudius (Barry Jones), the uncle of Caligula. When he thinks God has not saved the girl he loves from death, Demetrius renounces his faith and becomes Messalina's lover, but when he finds his real love with the robe it restores his faith. When Caligula is killed by his own soldiers, Claudius becomes emperor and promises to stop persecuting Christians.

A colorful film made in CinemaScope, DEMETRIUS AND THE GLADIATORS proved to be a good sequel to THE ROBE and it grossed over $4 million in the United States alone. Performances in the film were especially good, with Victor Mature solidly repeating the title role while Susan Hayward was alluring as Messalina, priestess of the goddess Isis. The supporting cast was also strong, especially Michael Rennie's quiet underplaying of Peter the Fisherman and Jay Robinson's mad Caligula, both roles repeated from the first film. Also good were Barry Jones as Claudius, William Marshall as the Nubian who befriends Demetrius, and Ernest Borgnine as the master of the gladiators' school.

The finale of THE ROBE, with Richard Burton as Marcellus Gallio and Jean Simmons as Diana going to their deaths because of their conversion to Christ, opens this film. In another stock shot from the first film, the voice of Cameron Mitchell as Jesus Christ is heard as Demetrius kneels at the foot of the Cross during the Crucifixion.

MARCELINO PAN Y VINO (Marcelino, Bread and Wine)
1954
Spain
Chamartin
90 minutes B/W
Director: Ladislas Vajda
Screenplay: Ladislas Vajda & Jose Maria Sanchez-Silva,
          from the novel by Jose Maria Sanchez-Silva
Photography: Enrique Guerner
Editor: Julio Pena
Music: Pablo Sorozabal
      CAST: Pablito Calvo (Marcelino), Rafael Rivelles (Father Superior), Antonio Vico (Brother "Door"), Juan Calvo (Brother "Cooky"), Jose Marco Davo (Blacksmith), Adriano Dominguez (Brother "Baptism"), Juan Jose Menendez (Brother Giler), Mariano Azana (Brother "Bad"), Joaquin Roa (Brother "Ding Dong"), Isabel De Pomes (The Mother), Rafael Calvo (Don Emilio), Jose Prada (Uncle Roque), Fernando Rey (Brother Moderno), Jose Nieto (Civil Guard Commander), Carmen Carbonell (Alfonsa).
      Set in the Middle Ages, this Spanish production tells the story of Saint Marcelino. It is the tale of a young boy (Pablito Calvo) who offers a life-sized crucifix bread and wine, and of how Jesus Christ comes to life from the cross in the monastery and talks to the small boy.
      The film was issued in the United States as MARCELINO by the United Motion Picture Organization in 1956. It was also called THE MIRACLE OF MARCELINO.

THE PRODIGAL
1955
Metro-Goldwyn-Mayer
114 minutes   Color
Producer: Charles Schnee
Director: Richard Thorpe
Screenplay: Maurice Zimm

Adaptation: Joe Breen Jr. & Samuel James Larsen
Photography: Joseph Ruttenberg
Editor: Harold F. Kress
Music: Bronislau Caper
Art Directors: Cedric Gibbons & Randall Duell
        CAST: Lana Turner (Samarra), Edmund Purdom
(Micah), Louis Calhern (Nahreeb), Audrey Dalton (Ruth),
James Mitchell (Asham), Neville Brand (Rhakim), Walter
Hampden (Eli), Taina Elg (Elissa), Francis L. Sullivan
(Bosra), Joseph Wiseman (Carmish), Sandra Descher (Yas-
min), John Dehner (Joram), Cecil Kellaway (Governor),
Philip Tonge (Barber/Surgeon), David Leonard (Blind Man),
Henry Daniell (Ramadi), Paul Cavanagh (Tobiah), Dayton
Lummis (Caleb), Tracey Roberts (Tahra), Jarma Lewis
(Uba), Jay Novello (Merchant), Phyllis Graffeo (Miriam);
Dorothy Adams, Pete De Bear, Patricia Iannone, Eugene
Mazzola, George Sawaya, Richard Devon, Ann Cameron,
Gloria Dea, John Rosser, Charles Wagenheim.
        The New Testament parable of the Prodigal Son,
from the Book of Luke, first came to the screen in 1911*
in France, in Eclair's THE PRODIGAL SON. Director
Raoul Walsh made a more definitive version in 1925's THE
WANDERER (q.v.). This 1955 outing was made in Eastmancolor and CinemaScope. Despite all its spectacular trappings, however, this third version may well be the least
satisfying of the lot.
        Made basically as a vehicle for Lana Turner, the
film retold the Biblical story of Micah (Edmund Purdom),
the favorite son of a Jewish family, who takes his inheri-
tance to Damascus where he wastes it on a prostitute,
Samarra (Lana Turner), the high priestess of the goddess
Astarte. Despite the attempts of Samarra and her pagan
friends, Micah refuses to denounce his God, and eventually
sees the error of his ways.
        The New York Times commented on the film: "This
big, expensive, gaudily-arrayed and absolutely atrocious
whangdang of a movie represents Hollywood at its costly
worst--not a cheap film, just a big, vulgar, blinding eye-
sore."
        Although miscast Lana Turner was the main box of-
fice attraction in the film, the role of Micah was the central

---

*Eclair also made another early silent film based on the
New Testament, HERODIAS (1911). Also from the French
studio Urban-Eclipse came the 1911 film ST. PAUL AND
THE CENTURION.

figure, but was blandly played by Edmund Purdom, who had
appeared in such ancient world features as JULIUS CAESAR
(Metro-Goldwyn-Mayer, 1953) and THE EGYPTIAN (20th
Century-Fox, 1954) and who would later star in ERODE IL
GRANDE (Herod the Great) (q. v.) in 1958.

THE SILVER CHALICE
1955
Warner Brothers
144 minutes   Color
Producer-Director: Victor Saville
Associate Producer-Screenplay: Lesser Samuels
Story: Thomas B. Costain
Photography: William V. Skall
Editor: George White
Music: Franz Waxman
  CAST: Virginia Mayo (Helena), Pier Angeli (Debor-
ra), Jack Palance (Simon), Paul Newman (Basil), Walter
Hampden (Joseph), Joseph Wiseman (Mijamin), Alexander
Scourby (Luke), Lorne Greene (Peter), David J. Stewart
(Adam), Herbert Rudley (Linus), Jacques Aubuchon (Nero),
E. G. Marshall (Ignatius), Michael Pate (Aaron), Natalie
Wood (Helena as a Girl), Peter Reynolds (Basil as a Boy),
Mort Marshall (Benjie), Booth Colman (Hiram), Terence de
Marney (Sosthene), Robert Middleton (Idbash), Ian Wolfe
(Theron), Lawrence Dobkin (Ephraim), Philip Tonge (Ohad),
Albert Dekker (Kester), Beryl Machin (Eulalia).
  THE SILVER CHALICE was a CinemaScope produc-
tion interpolating Biblical characters in a fictional story
about the Greek sculptor (Paul Newman) who designed the
framework for the cup used at the Last Supper by Jesus.
The melodramatic plot further showed the sculptor's involve-
ment with the revolution to overthrow Roman rule in the
Holy Land.
  A big, glossy, empty and terribly dull film, THE
SILVER CHALICE is best remembered today as actor Paul
Newman's screen debut.   The New York Times said the
film "is perfectly awful, with all the appeal, credibility and
pacing of a sleepwalking elephant. "

CELUI QUI DOIT MOURIR (He Who Must Die)
1956
France-Italy

Indusfilms/Prima-Films/Cinetel/Filmsonor/Da. Ma. Cine-
    matografica
124 minutes   B/W
Director: Jules Dassin
Screenplay: Ben Barzman & Jules Dassin, from the novel
            O Christos Xanastauronetai (Christ Recrucified)
            by Nikos Kazantzakis
Dialogue: Andre Obey
Photography: Jacques Natteau
Editors: Pieree Gillette & Roger Dwyre
Art Director: Max Douy
Music: Georges Auric
        CAST: Carl Mohner (Lukas), Roger Hanin (Pannayo-
taros), Melina Mercouri (Katernina), Jean Servais (Fotis),
Pierre Vaneck (Manolios), Gregoire Aslan (Agha), Gert
Froebe (Patriarcheas), Teddy Bilis (Hadji Nikolis), Rene
Lefevre (Yannakos), Lucien Raimbourg (Kostandis), Dimos
Starenios (Ladas), Fernand Ledoux (Pope Grigoris), Maurice
Ronet (Michelis), Nicole Berger (Mariori).
        Set in a Greek village in Asia Minor in 1921, this
feature told of a village under truce with its Turkish mili-
tary occupants and how the citizens are set to perform their
annual Easter Passion Play when a horde of starving, dis-
placed people wander into the streets.   The film showed
how the performers in the Passion Play began to associate
the roles they played with their activities in real life.   The
local shepherd boy, Manolios (Pierre Vaneck), is chosen to
play Jesus, and eventually he is one of the leaders who stand
up to the village government and offer to help the strangers,
which will inevitably incur the wrath of the Turks.
        The film was released in the United States in 1958
as HE WHO MUST DIE.

THE STAR OF BETHLEHEM
1956
Great Britain
90 minutes   Color
Director: Lotte Reiniger
        Lotte Reiniger, a German director who is credited
with being one of the inventors of the silhouette film, made
this color film in Great Britain, although she had directed
the original, DER STERN VON BETHLEHEM (q. v.), in her
homeland in 1921.   Like the original silent feature, this
film was made in the animated silhouette format.

ERODE IL GRANDE (Herod the Great)
1958
Italy-France
93 minutes   Color
Executive Producer: Gian Paolo Gigazzi
Director: Arnoldo Genoino
Screenplay: Damiano Cerchio & W. Tourjansky
Photography: Massimo Dallamano
Editor: Antoinetta Zitta
       CAST: Edmund Purdom (King Herod), Sylvia Lopez
(Miriam), Sandra Milo (Sarah), Alberto Lupo (Aaron), Massimo Girotti (Octavius), Elena Zareschi (Elena); Renato
Baldini, Corrado Pani.
       ERODE IL GRANDE, also called LE ROI CRUEL
(The Cruel King), takes place as the power of the Roman
Empire is beginning to crumble in the Middle East.   Herod
(Edmund Purdom), the King of Judea, feels his position is
endangered, especially with the defeat of his ally, Roman
general Octavius (Massimo Girotti).   Herod is torn between
saving his kingdom and the fear that his queen has been unfaithful, and the two problems drive him to insanity.
       By the time this dubbed spectacle made it to the
United States in 1960, issued as HEROD THE GREAT by
Allied Artists, the film had little appeal.   It had been several years since British actor Edmund Purdom had starred
in spectacles like JULIUS CAESAR (M-G-M, 1953) and THE
EGYPTIAN (20th Century-Fox, 1954) and his box office draw
was minimal by the time this film was released.

IL MAESTRO (The Teacher)
1958
Italian
Gladiator-Union
88 minutes   B/W
Producer-Director: Aldo Fabrizi
English Version Directors: Carol & Peter Riethof
Screenplay: Aldo Fabrizi, L. Lucas, J. Gallardo & Mario
                 Amendlola
Photography: Antonio Masasoli & Manuel Merino
Music: Carlo Innocenzi
       CAST: Aldo Fabrizi (Giovanni Merino), Eduardo
Nevola (Antonio), Marco Paoletti (Gabriel), Alfredo Mayo
(Principal), Mary Lamar (Teacher), Felix Fernandez (Porter), Julio San Juan (Doctor), Jose Calvo (Chauffeur), Julia

Caba Alba (Portress).

A teacher (Aldo Fabrizi) loses his faith and will to live after his beloved son (Eduardo Nevola) is killed by an auto. A new pupil (Marco Paoletti), however, arrives and restores the man's faith and lust for life, then vanishes. The teacher searches for the boy and traces him to a church, where he finds the lad is identical to the figure of Jesus in a statue of the Madonna and Child.

Released in the United States in 1961 by President Films as THE TEACHER AND THE MIRACLE, this charming little film was mainly aimed at juvenile audiences. Sadly, it was cut by some 12 minutes from its original 100-minute running time.

POWER OF THE RESURRECTION
1958
Family Films
60 minutes   Color & B/W versions
Director: Harold Schuster
Screenplay: Henry Denker
Assistant Directors: Lou Perlof & Clancy Herne
CAST: Richard Kiley (Peter), Jon Shepodd (Jesus Christ), Jan Arvan (Judas), Carl B. Reid (Annas), Robert Cornthwaite (Caiaphas), Charles Maxwell (Investigator), Stephen Joyce (John), Booth Colman (James), Joseph Sonessa (Young Man), Dorothy Morris (Mary, Sister of Lazarus), Dan Riss (Thomas), John Zaremba (Samuel), John Close (Sentry), Charles Wagenheim, Marc Krah, Ralph Neff (Merchants), William Hughes, Christopher Alcaide (Officers), William Pullen (Guard), Gil Rankin (Joseph of Arimathea), Lisa Pons (Mary Magdalene), James Bronte, Jim Oberlin (Roman Officers), Judd Holdren (Temple Officer), Norman Alden (Gate Guard), Belle Mitchell (Woman), Ralph Smiley (Servant), Mary Patton (Mother Mary), Walter Maslow, Troy Patterson (Roman Soldiers), Warren Parker (Andrew), Richard O'Shea (Thaddeus), Milt Hamerman (Matthew Levi), George Khoury (Phillip), Mark Mitchell (Bartholomew), Harry Jackson (James Lesser), Vic Tayback (Simon Canaanite), Kenneth Drake (Marcus).

Toward the end of his life in a Roman prison, Peter (Richard Kiley) tells the drama of Christ's (Jon Shepodd) last days to a young Christian (Joseph Sonessa), who is imprisoned with him. Peter relives Jesus' final visit to Jerusalem, His growing conflict with the priesthood establishment, the Last Supper with His arrest, trial, Crucifixion

Joseph Sonessa and Richard Kiley in THE POWER OF THE RESURRECTION (Family Films, 1958).

and the Resurrection. The power of Peter's story gives the young man courage as he awaits unknown tortures and possible death, and it cements his faith.

POWER OF THE RESURRECTION was made at Hollywood's Keywest Studio and was intended for church and television distribution. A well done feature, with a fine Hollywood cast, the film was especially intended for Easter and Watch Night (New Year's Eve) showings. The film was designed to be effective for teenage audiences; hence the plotline framework of having Peter tell his story to a teenage Christian being persecuted for his faith.

BEN-HUR
1959
Metro-Goldwyn-Mayer
217 minutes   Color
Producer: Sam Zimbalist

Charlton Heston in BEN-HUR (MGM, 1959).

Director: William Wyler
Associate Directors: Andrew Marton, Yakima Canutt &
          Mario Soldati
Screenplay: Karl Tunberg, from the novel by Lew Wallace
Photography: Robert L. Surtees, with Harold E. Wellman &
          Pietro Portalupi
Editors: Ralph E. Winters & John D. Dunning
Music: Miklos Rozsa
Art Directors: William A. Horning & Edward Carfagno
Costumes: Elizabeth Haffenlen
Assistant Directors: Gus Agosti & Alberto Cardone
          CAST: Charlton Heston (Ben-Hur), Jack Hawkins
(Quintus Arrius), Stephen Boyd (Messala), Haya Harareet
(Esther), Hugh Griffith (Sheik Ilderim), Martha Scott (Miri-
am), Sam Jaffe (Simonides), Cathy O'Donnell (Tizah), Finlay
Currie (Balthasar), Frank Thring (Pontius Pilate), Terence
Longden (Drusus), Andre Morrell (Sextus), Marina Berti
(Flavia), George Ralph (Tiberius), Adi Berber (Malluch),
Stella Vitelleschi (Amrah), Jose Greci (May), Lawrence
Payne (Joseph), John Horsley (Spintho), Richard Coleman
(Metellus), Duncan Lamont (Marius), Ralph Truman (Tiberi-
us' Aid), Richard Hale (Caspar), Reginald Lal Singh (Mel-
chior), David Davies (Quaestor), Dervis Ward (Jailer),
Claude Heater (Jesus Christ), Mino Doro (Gratus), Robert
Brown (Chief Rower), Tuttle Lemkow (Leper), Howard Lang
(Hortator), Ferdy Mayne (Rescue Ship Captain), John Le
Mesurier (Doctor), Stevenson Lang (Blind Man), Aldo Mozele
(Barca), Dino Fazio (Marcello), Michael Cosmo (Raimondo),
Remington Olmstead (Decurian), Hugh Billingsley (Mario),
Aldo Silvani (Man in Nazareth), Cliff Lyons (The Nubian),
Joe Yrigoyan (The Egyptian), Joe Canutt (Sportsman);
Thomas O'Leary, John Glenn, Maxwell Shaw, Emile Carrer,
Noel Sheldon, Hector Rose, Bill Kuehl, Diego Pozzetto, A.
Pini, Victor De La Fosse, Enzo Fiermonte, Tiberio Mitri,
Pietro Tordi, Jerry Brown, Otello Capanna, Luigi Marra,
Edward J. Auregui, Alfredo Danesi, Raimondo Van Riel,
Mike Dugan.
          Movie spectacles have always appealed to movie-going
audiences and this is probably the best explanation for the
success of both versions of BEN-HUR, both poor melodramas
in their own right. This 1959 version is a remake of the
1925 feature (q. v.) and, like its predecessor, the film was
hugely successful financially and also with some critics. It
won nine Academy Awards, including best picture of the year.
Outside of Yakima Canutt's wonderfully excitingly staged
chariot race sequence, the film tends to move at a crawl
for its incredibly long 217 minutes.

This remake followed the original pretty closely, both being based on Lew Wallace's popular novel, and told how Ben-Hur (Charlton Heston) and his family were affected by brief encounters with Jesus Christ (Claude Heater). Christ is seen in the film only as a passing figure; His face is not shown and the character has no dialogue. One very disappointing sequence has a long buildup to the Sermon on the Mount, which is never heard.

THE BIG FISHERMAN
1959
Buena Vista/Centurion Films
180 minutes   Color
Producer: Rowland V. Lee
Director: Frank Borzage
Screenplay: Howard Estabrook & Rowland V. Lee, from the novel by Lloyd C. Douglas
Photography: Lee Carmes
Editor: Paul Weatherwax
Music: Albert Ray Malotte
Musical Director: Joseph Gershenson
Art Director: Julia Heron
Production Design: John DeCuir
Makeup: Bud Westmore & Frank Westmore
    CAST: Howard Keel (Simon Peter), Susan Kohner (Fara), John Saxon (Voldi), Martha Hyer (Herodias), Herbert Lom (Herod Antipas), Ray Stricklyn (Deran), Marian Seldes (Arnon), Alexander Scourby (David Ben-Zadok), Beulah Bondi (Hannah), Jay Barney (John the Baptist), Charlotte Fletcher (Rennah), Mark Dana (Zendi), Rhodes Reason (Andrew), Henry Brandon (Menicus), Brian Hutton (John), Thomas Troupe (James), Marianne Stewart (Ione), Jonathan Harris (Lysias), Philip Pine (Lucius); Leonard Mudie, James Griffith, Peter Adams, Joe Di Reda, Stuart Randall, Herbert Rudley, Francis McDonald, Perry Ivins, Ralph Moody, Tony Jochim, Don Turner, Joe Gilbert, Michael Mark.
    Rev. James K. Friedrich's Centurion Films produced this lavish spectacular about the life of Simon Peter (Howard Keel), set against the love story of a prince and princess. The film also showed Christ's miracles and God killing an evil man. Christ was not shown in the film. His presence was indicated by His hand or the bottom of His robe. His voice (by an unbilled actor) was dubbed onto the soundtrack.
    The film, released by Walt Disney's distribution company, Buena Vista, got only lukewarm reviews. A rather

bland outing, the film showed Christ to have no enemies, thus negating any reason for the Crucifixion, which was not shown in the feature.

LOS MISTERIOS DEL ROSARIO (The Mysteries of the Rosary)
1959
Spain
Cruzade del Rosario en Familia
93 minutes   Color
Producer: Rev. Patrick Payton
Associate Producer: Father Jerome Lawyer
Director: Joseph I. Breen Jr.
Screenplay: Tom Blackburn, Robert Hugh O'Sullivan, John
        T. Kelley & James O'Hanlon
Photography: Edwin Du Par
Art Director: Enrique Alacron
Music: David Raskin (English Soundtrack); Jose Munoz-
        Molleda (Spanish Soundtrack)
        CAST: Luis Alvarez (Jesus Christ), Macdonald Carey
(Voice of Jesus Christ), Sebastian Cabot (Prologue/Epilogue
Narrator), Maruchi Fresno (Virgin Mary), Antonio Vilar
(Pontius Pilate), Felix Acaso (Caiaphas), Manuel Monvay
(Judas), Carlos Casaravilla (Herod); Virgilio Texeira, Jose
Marco Davo, Hebe Donay, Jacinto San Emeteria, Felix De
Pomas, Antonio Casas, Carlota Bilboa, Francisco Avenzana.
        The last three days of Jesus Christ, from Judas' be-
trayal through the horrors of the Cross to the Resurrection,
are told in this Spanish-made feature.   Produced by Rev.
Patrick Payton, head of the Family Rosary Crusade, mostly
from small donations collected worldwide, the film did not
get United States distribution until several years after its
original production.   Filmed at Sevilla Studios outside Ma-
drid, Spain, in 1957, the feature was finally shown in the
United States late in 1965.
        Although a faithful adaptation of Christ's final three
days, the film was not widely shown and it often irritated
viewers by never showing the face of the Saviour.   Further-
more, the use of the voice of Macdonald Carey, a popular
movie and television actor, dubbed on the soundtrack only
served to distract viewers from the feature itself.
        The film was released in the United States as THE
REDEEMER by Empire Films.

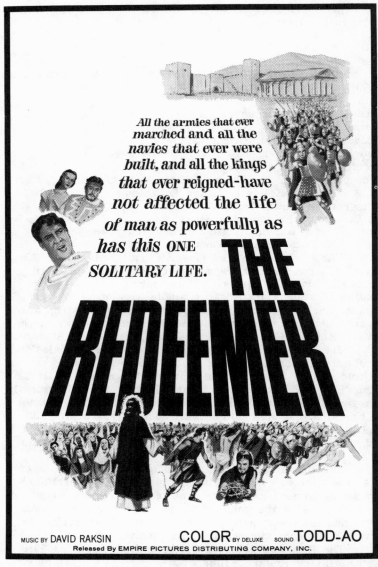

Advertisement for THE REDEEMER (Empire, 1965), American release title of the Spanish film LOS MISTERIOS DEL ROSARIO (1959).

Yvonne De Carlo and Jorge Mistral in LA SPADE E LA
CROCE (Liber Film, 1959).

LA SPADE E LA CROCE (The Sword and the Cross)
1959
Italy
Liber Film
105 minutes   Color
Producer: Ottavio Poggi
Director: Carlo Ludovico Bragaglia
Screenplay: Alessandro Continenza
Photography: Raffaele Masciocchi
Music: Roberto Nicolosi
    CAST: Yvonne De Carlo (Maria Maddalena), Jorge
Mistral (Caio Marcello), Rossana Podesta (Marta), Massimo
Serato (Anan); Mario Girotti, Andrea Aureli, Rossano Rory,
Philippe Hersent.
    Released in the United States as MARY MAGDALENE
(Amex, 1960).
    During a revolt in Judea, Roman centurion Caio Mar-
cello (Jorge Mistral) rescues Maria Maddalena (Yvonne De
Carlo), a beautiful courtesan, from the hands of her captor,
Barabbas.   The two fall in love but the girl flees to Jeru-
salem before the Roman can find out about her past.   There

she meets an old lover (Massimo Serato) and soon she begins to hear strange tales about a man named Jesus and finally she has a vision. Deeply troubled and disgusted by her shameful past, Maria becomes a Christian after the death of her brother, Lazarus. She leaves the Roman after realizing she has been called upon for a greater mission.

Filmed in Ferraniacolor and Supercinescope, this lavish spectacle was nothing more than fiction using Biblical names. The film was basically a vehicle for beautiful Yvonne De Carlo (who later said she detested the film), who had scored so well as the wife of Moses in Cecil B. DeMille's THE TEN COMMANDMENTS (q. v.) in 1956. Although popular in Italy, the film got little release outside that country. In 1960 it showed up on French television and a dubbed version was issued in the United States with no fanfare. One French critic, Jean d'Yvoire in Telerama, scored the production for its bad taste, melodramatic flavor and the use of pseudo-significant dialogue. To date the film has yet to be issued for U. S. television.

ULTIMI GIORNI DI POMPEII (The Last Days of Pompeii)
1959
Italy-Spain
Cineproduzioni/Procusa
103 minutes   Color
Director: Mario Bonnard
Screenplay: Ennio De Concini, Sergio Leone, Duccio Tessari & Sergio Corbucci
Photography: Antonio Ballesteron
Editor: Eraldo Da Roma
Music: Angelo Francisco Lavagnino
        CAST: Steve Reeves (Glaucus), Christine Kauffman (Ione), Barbara Carroll (Nydia), Anne Marie Baumann (Julia), Mimmo Palmara (Gallinus), Fernando Rey (High Priest), Carlo Tamberlini (Christians' Leader), Angel Aranda (Antonius), Mino Doro (Second Consul), Guillermo Marin (Askinius), Mario Berroatua, Angel Ortiz (Guards).

Edward Bulwer-Lytton's 1843 novel The Last Days of Pompeii has been adapted to the screen at least a half-dozen times, mostly in Italy where versions were produced in 1908, 1913 and 1925 prior to this 1959 outing. There was also an American version in 1935 and one in France in 1950. Only the 1935 version (q. v.) and this one attempted to include the story of Jesus Christ and the Crucifixion with the later eruption of Vesuvius. The 1935 film, however, was far more religious than this standard spectacle, which opted to accentuate its arena and orgy sequences.

For this version Steve Reeves, who had already scored with HERCULES (Warner Brothers, 1957) and HER-CULES UNCHAINED (Warner Brothers, 1959), starred as gladiator Glaucus, who returns home to Pompeii in 79 A. D. after fighting on the frontier to find his family killed and the city being sacked, supposedly by Christians. Later he learns that an evil woman (Anne Marie Baumann) is responsible for the terror. When he spurns her affections he and the daughter (Christine Kaufmann) of a high official are thrown into the arena with the Christians, with whom they have become sympathetic, but they are saved from harm by the arrival of Glaucus' friends. At that moment Vesuvius erupts and Glaucus and the girl are led to safety before the city is buried in lava ash.

Only a brief retelling of the story of Christ qualifies this sand and sandal epic as even a marginal religious film. A colorful but empty outing, the feature was issued in a dubbed version in the United States by United Artists as THE LAST DAYS OF POMPEII.

KING OF KINGS
1961
Metro-Goldwyn-Mayer
168 minutes   Color
Producer: Samuel Bronston
Associate Producers: Alan Brown & Jaime Prades
Director: Nicholas Ray
Screenplay: Philip Yordan
Narration Writer: Ray Bradbury
Photography: Franz F. Planer, Milton Krasner & Manuel
            Berenguer
Editors: Harold Kress & Renee Lichtig
Music: Miklos Rozsa
Sets & Costumes: Georges Wakhevitch
Set Decorator: Enrique Alacron
Makeup: Maria Van Riel & Charles Parker
Cinematograph Special Effects: Lee LeBlanc
Special Effects: Alex C. Weldon
        CAST: Jeffrey Hunter (Jesus Christ), Robert Ryan (John the Baptist), Siobhan McKenna (Mary), Hurd Hatfield (Pontius Pilate), Ron Randell (Lucius), Viveca Lindfors (Claudia), Rita Gam (Herodias), Carmen Sevilla (Mary Magdalene), Brigid Bazlen (Salome), Harry Guardino (Barabbas),

Jeffrey Hunter in KING OF KINGS (20th Century-Fox, 1961).

Rip Torn (Judas), Frank Thring (Herod Antipas), Guy Rolfe
(Caiaphas), Maurice Marsac (Nicodemus), Gregoire Aslan
(Herod), Royal Dano (Peter), Eric Connor (Balthazar),
George Coulouris (Camel Driver), Conrado San Martin (Gen-
eral Pompey), Gerard Tichy (Joseph), Jose Antonio (Young
John), Luis Prendes (Good Thief), David Savies (Burly Man),
Jose Nieto (Caspar), Ruben Rujo (Matthew), Fernando Sancho
(Madman), Michael Wager (Thomas), Felix de Pomes (Joseph
of Arimathea), Adriano Rimoldi (Melchior), Barry Keegan
(Bad Thief), Rafael Luis Calvo (Simon of Cyrese), Tino Bar-
rero (Andrew), Francisco Moran (Blind Man), Orson Welles
(Narrator).

Producer Samuel Bronston filmed this remake of the
1927 Cecil B. DeMille classic, KING OF KINGS (q. v.), in
Spain, but any similarity between the two films ends with
their titles and the fact they dealt with the life of Christ.
Where the DeMille film is considered one of the finest of
its genre, the remake was basically reviled by critics and
the movie-going public was apathetic toward it. Time magazine called it, "Incontestably the corniest, phoniest, ickiest,
and most monstrously vulgar of all the big Bible stories
Hollywood has told in its last decade." The New York
Times was a bit less harsh; it said, "there are too many
conventional trappings of melodramatic costume movies and
too much random action to allow a living personality for
Him."

For a time the blame was placed squarely on Jeffrey
Hunter's passive performance as Christ in the movie, but in
retrospect he was judged to have given the portrayal "taste-
ful simplicity" (New York Times). Hunter was approximate-
ly the same age as Christ (early 30s) and he brought a quiet
dignity and self-control to the part. Unfortunately the film's
failure hurt his career. The fact he was a teenage idol did
not endear him to the critics when they reviewed the film.
The supporting performances are basically good, especially
Robert Ryan's brief role as John the Baptist.

The true blame for the failure of KING OF KINGS
must rest with director Nicholas Ray and screenwriter Philip
Yordan. Ray seemed out of his element with a big-budget
spectacle, while Yordan turned out a terribly hokey script
which was frequently at odds with the Scriptures. Yordan
basically followed the pattern set by DAY OF TRIUMPH
(q. v.): he had Judas (Rip Torn) and Barabbas (Harry Guar-
dino) as members of a Jewish revolutionary group out to
overthrow the Romans, with Christ becoming a pawn in the
proceedings. Among other script weaknesses were the dele-
tion of important Biblical events, including all the major

miracles, while fictional events (like Christ visiting John the Baptist in jail) took their place. The film showed Christ without enemies and the events leading up to and including the Crucifixion as basically a series of accidents and mis-understandings. Spectacle events, such as two large battles between the Romans and Jews, were overplayed while Biblical events were downplayed. For example, the violent events at the Crucifixion were practically overlooked--the earthquake that rent the temple in the Scriptures became just a storm in the movie. Finally, no mention of Jesus Christ's divinity was made in the film.

In contrast to the vapid screenplay, Ray Bradbury's narrative was exceedingly well done and, at times, is all that saves the film.

This version of KING OF KINGS is a classic example of a film that had all the ingredients needed for a superb movie, but through lack of understanding of its subject, turned out to be a disappointing and lackluster production. Some critics even dubbed it "I Was a Teenage Jesus."

SIN OF JESUS
1961
Film-maker's Coop
40 minutes   B/W
Director: Robert Frank
Story: Isaac Babel
Photography: Gert Berliner
Music: Morton Feldman
        CAST: Julie Bovasso, Roberts Blossom, George Brian.

SIN OF JESUS is a silly amateur production about Jesus Christ refusing mercy to a woman and thus forcing her into a life of sin. When He asks her for forgiveness, she refuses. A sub-plot had Jesus giving the woman a guardian angel whom she seduces. When he refuses to take off his wings before getting into bed, she smothers him.

BARABBAS
1962
Italian
Columbia
144 minutes   Color
Producer: Dino de Laurentiis

Associate Producer: Luigi Luraschi
Director: Richard Fleischer
Screenplay: Christopher Fry, Ivo Perilli, Diego Fabbri &
         Nigel Balchin, from the novel by Pär Lagerkvist
Photography: Aldo Tonti
Editors: Raymond Poulton & Alberto Gallitti
Music: Mario Nascimbene
Art Director: Mario Chiari
Costumes: Maria De Matteis
Sets: Maurizio Chiari
      CAST: Anthony Quinn (Barabbas), Silvana Mangano
(Rachel), Arthur Kennedy (Pontius Pilate), Katy Jurado
(Sara), Harry Andrews (Peter), Vittorio Gassman (Sahak),
Jack Palance (Torwald), Ernest Borgnine (Lucius), Norman
Wooland (Rufio), Valentina Cortesa (Julia), Michael Gwynne
(Lazarus), Douglas Fowley (Vasario), Robert Hall (Gladiator
Captain), Lawrence Payne (Disciple), Arnold Foa (Joseph of
Arimathea), Roy Mangano (Jesus Christ), Ivan Triesault
(Emperor), Enrico Glori (Important Man), Carlo Giustini
(Officer), Rino Braido (Tavern Reveller), Gustavo De Nardo
(Man in Potter's Store), Tullio Tomadoni (Blind Man),
Mario Zanubi (Beggar), Friedrich Ledebur (Second Officer),
Guido Calano (Scorpio), Spartaco Nale (Overseer), Gianni
De Benedetto (Third Officer), Vladimiro Picciafuochi (Farm
Superintendent), Joe Robinson (Gladiator); Nando Angelini,
Marcello Di Martire.
      This is a fictional film about a real person--
Barabbas, the war chief who was saved when Christ went
to the cross in his place. A hazy character at best in the
Bible, Barabbas' life is shown here as one that is eventual-
ly touched and saved by his fleeting association with The
Saviour. Unfortunately the film is overlong, and despite
its expensive spectacle trimmings, quickly loses interest
after the opening scenes.
      Jesus Christ (Roy Mangano) is seen mainly in the
film's opening sequences, which include His trial before
Pilate (Arthur Kennedy), the crowning with thorns, the walk
to Calvary with Jesus pausing to stare at the spared Barabbas, and the Crucifixion, where only His feet are seen
dangling from the cross.
      Parents' Magazine said of this feature, "an excel-
lently made Biblical spectacle that is genuinely religious.
For those of faith it will be a profoundly moving experience. For the skeptical it will be an intellectual stimulus....
For history lovers the most rewarding element will be the
recreation of Pagan Rome at its must cruel." Many film
critics and organizations listed BARABBAS as one of the
top ten feature films of 1962.

PRO MUNDI VITA
1962
West Germany
Filmkommission des Eucharistischen Weltkongressen
137 minutes   Color
Director: Rudolf Reiber
Photography: Georg Thurmair
Music: Heinz Terworth
 A documentary issued by a Munich company, PRO MUNDI VITA showed the events of the 37th Eucharistic World Congress in Munich.   The film also showed such historical spots as the Colosseum in Rome and the Via Appia, along with a recreation of one of the earliest reappearances of Jesus Christ from the Domitilla catacombs in Rome.   This documentary was little seen outside its native land.

VASEN (Passion)
1962
Czechoslovakia
Color
Producer-Director-Screenplay-Art Director: Jiri Trnka
 VASEN was a color Czech production of the venerable "Passion Play" with a twist--animated puppets tell the story instead of live actors.

ROGOPAG
1962
Italy
Arco Film-Cineriz-Lyre Film
125 minutes   B/W
Producer: Alfred Bini
Music: Carlo Rustichelli

"Illibatezza" (Virginity):
Director-Screenplay: Roberto Rossellini
Photography: Luciano Trasatti
 CAST: Rosanna Schiaffino, Bruce Balaban, Maria Pia Schiaffino, Carol Zappavigna.

"Il Pollo Ruspante" (The Range-Grown Chicken):
Director-Screenplay: Ugo Gregoretti
Photography: Mario Bernardo

CAST: Ugo Tognazzi, Lisa Gastoni, Riky Tognazzi, Antonellia Taito.

"Il Nuovo Mondo" (The New World):
Director-Screenplay: Jean-Luc Godard
Photography: Jean Robier
CAST: Jean Marc Bory, Alexandra Stewart.

"La Ricotta" (Cream Cheese):
Director-Screenplay: Pier Paolo Pasolini
Photography: Tonino Delli Colli
CAST: Orson Welles, Mario Cipriani, Laura Betti, Edmonda Aldini, Ettore Garofolo.

An episodic film from Italy, ROGOPAG (the title is said to be made up of letters from its individual segments) contains a 40-minute portion called "La Ricotta" ("Cream Cheese") in which director-writer Pier Paolo Pasolini anticipates his THE GOSPEL ACCORDING TO ST. MATTHEW (q. v.) by telling a story about the filming of The Passion Play. This segment was somewhat censored in Italy and in some circles it was called sacrilegious.

"La Ricotta" attempted to show the contrast between the solemn filming of The Passion Play and the obnoxious behavior of the actors between takes. Looking at the events, with detached cynicism, was the director, played by Orson Welles. One scene that drew critical ire shows an underpaid player, who portrays one of the two thieves crucified with Jesus Christ, actually dying on the cross during the filming due to overeating the free food from the production company's commissary.

PONZIO PILATO (Pontius Pilate)
1964
Italy-France
Glomer Film/Lux C. C. F.
100 minutes   Color
Executive Producer: Enzo Merolla
Director: Irving Rapper
Screenplay: Gino De Sanctis
Photography: Massimo Dallamano
Music: A. F. Lavagnino
CAST: Jean Marais (Pontius Pilate), Jeanne Crain (Claudia Procula), Basil Rathbone (Caiaphas), Leticia Roman (Sarah), Massimo Serato (Nicodemus), Gianni Garko (Jonathan), John Drew Barrymore (Jesus Christ/Judas), Riccardo

Garrone (Calba), Livio Lorenzon (Barabbas); Roger Treville, Carlo Giustini, Dante Di Paolo, Paul Muller, Alfredo Varelli, Manoela Ballard, Emma Baron, Raffaella Carra.

This little seen Italian-French co-production told the story of Pontius Pilate (Jean Marais), focussing on his political troubles from the time he took office as the Roman ruler in Palestine until his recall to Rome after the Crucifixion of Jesus Christ (John Drew Barrymore). Unfortunately Jean Marais played the part of Pilate very passively, and without a strong central figure the film proved uninteresting, especially in its dubbed version which got little release in America by U. S. Films.

Jesus Christ is presented in the film mostly in His confrontation with Caiaphas (Basil Rathbone), chief rabbi of the Temple in Caesarda, who tries to turn His words into heresy because Caiaphas fears Christ is a threat to his position of power. Christ is also shown at the trial, with Pilate finally ordering that a plaque be nailed to the Cross, reading "Jesus of Nazareth, King of the Jews." In one of his few forceful moments in the feature, Pilate overrules Caiaphas' objections to this decision. Perhaps the most ironic thing about PONZIO PILATO is that John Drew Barrymore played the roles of both Jesus and Judas. Of the performances, Basil Rathbone's cold, calculating Caiaphas is easily the best. Rathbone, years before, had enacted the role of Pilate in THE LAST DAYS OF POMPEII (q. v.).

IL VANGELO SECONDO MATTEO (The Gospel According to
        St. Matthew)
1964
Italy-France
Continental
142 minutes   Color
Producer: Alfredo Bini
Director-Screenplay: Pier Paolo Pasolini
Photography: Tonino Delli Colli
Editor: Andrea Fantucci
Music: Luis E. Bacalor
Art Directors: Nino Baragli & Luigi Scaccianoce
Special Effects: E. Catalucci
        CAST: Enrique Irazonqui (Jesus Christ), Marherita Caruso (Young Mary), Susanna Pasolini (Older Mary), Marcello Morante (Joseph), Mario Socrate (John the Baptist), Settimo Di Porto (Peter), Otello Sestili (Judas), Ferruccio Nuzzo (Matthew), Gracomo Morante (John), Alfonso Gatto

(Andrew); Enzo Siciliano, Giorgio Agamben, Guido Cerretani, Luigi Barfini, Marcello Galdini, Elio Spaziani, Rosario Nigale, Rodolfo Wilcock, Alessandro Tasca, Amerigo Bevilacqua, Francesco Leonetti, Franca Cupane, Paolo Tedesio, Rosana Di Rocco, Elseo Boschi, Natalia Ginsburg, Renato Terra.

Pier Paolo Pasolini, a Communist, wrote and directed this version of the life of Jesus Christ (Enrique Irazonqui), based on the writings of St. Matthew. Many critics took this feature, co-produced by Italy and France, to be "a Communistic view of the story of Christ." Instead, the film turned out to be a very reverent version of the life of The Saviour and, unlike some films made in Christian countries (e.g., the remake of KING OF KINGS) showed Christ performing many of the miracles related in The Bible.

Although some critics and viewers considered this film, released in the United States in 1966 as THE GOSPEL ACCORDING TO ST. MATTHEW, to be the best film version of the life of Christ in the 1960s, it was basically a low-budget effort and was over-long and draggy, not very well produced and poorly dubbed for U.S. release. Still, the film does have its moments and Enrique Irazonqui gives a good performance as Christ and several scenes are well staged, especially the Crucifixion. The musical score for the film is also interesting; it interpolates the works of Bach, Mozart, Prokofiev and Webern with a new background composed by Luis E. Bacalor.

Despite the fact that THE GOSPEL ACCORDING TO ST. MATTHEW was a widely discussed film when it played in the United States, it was not widely distributed and probably got most of its showings on college campuses after its initial theatrical release.

THE GREATEST STORY EVER TOLD
1965
United Artists
260 minutes   Color
Producer-Director: George Stevens
Executive Producer: Frank I. Davis
Associate Producers: George Stevens, Jr. & Antonio Vellani
Screenplay: George Stevens & James Lee Barrett, from the book by Fulton Oursler, the writings of Henry Denker and The Bible.
Photography: William C. Mellor & Loyal Griggs

Max von Sydow in THE GREATEST STORY EVER TOLD
(United Artists, 1965).

Editors: Harold F. Kress, Argyle Nelson & Frank O'Neill
Music: Alfred Newman
Choral Supervisor: Ken Darby
Art Directors: Richard Day, William Creber & David Hall
Costumes: Vittorio Nino & Novarese
Second Unit Directors: Richard Talmadge & William Hale
Creative Associate: Carl Sandburg
        CAST: Max von Sydow (Jesus Christ), Charlton Heston (John the Baptist), Dorothy McGuire (Virgin Mary), Michael Anderson, Jr. (James the Younger), Pat Boone (Angel at the Tomb), Jose Ferrer (Herod Antipas), Richard Conte (Barabbas), Victor Buono (Sorak), David Hedison (Phillip), Martin Landau (Caiaphas), Angela Lansbury (Claudia), Robert Loggia (Joseph), Van Heflin (Bar Amand), Janet Margolin (Mary of Bethany), David McCallum (Judas Iscariot), Roddy McDowall (Matthew), Sal Mineo (Uriah), Claude Rains (Herod), Ed Wynn (Old Aram), Shelley Winters (Woman of No Name), Telly Savalas (Pontius Pilate), Sidney Poitier (Simon of Cyrene), Nehemiah Persoff (Shemiah), Donald Pleasence (The Dark Hermit/Satan), John Wayne (Roman Centurion), Carroll Baker (Veronica), Robert Blake (Simon the Zealot), Burt Brinckerhoff (Andrew), John Considine (John), Jamie Farr (Thaddeus), Peter Mann (Nathanael), Gary Raymond (Peter), Tom Reese (Thomas), David Sheiner (James the Elder), Ina Balin (Martha of Bethany), Michael Tolan (Lazarus), Joanna Dunham (Mary Magdalene), Joseph Schildkraut (Nicodemus), Paul Stewart (Questor), Johnny Seven (Pilate's Aide), Harold J. Stone (General Varus), Robert Busch (Emissary), John Crawford (Alexander), Russell Johnson (Scribe), John Lupton (Speaker of Capernaum), Abraham Sofaer (Joseph of Arimathea), Chet Stratton (Theophilus), Ron Whelan (Annas), John Abbott (Aben), Rodolfo Acosta (Lancer Captain), Michael Ansara (Herod's Commander), Philip Coolidge (Chuza), Dal Jenkins (Philip), Joe Perry (Archelaus), Marian Seldes (Herodias), Frank De Kova (Tormentor), Joseph Sirola (Dumah), Cyril Delvanti (Melchior), Frank Silvera (Caspar), John Pickard (Peter's Second Accuser), Celia Lovksy (Woman Behind Railings), Mickey Simpson (Rabble Rouser), Richard Bakalyan (Good Thief), Marc Cavell (Bad Thief), Renata Vanni (Weeping Woman); Frank Richards, Harry Wilson, Dorothy Neumann, Inbal Dance Theatre of Israel.
        Presented in Ultra Panavision 70, and originally in Cinerama, THE GREATEST STORY EVER TOLD hardly lived up to its title. The film opened to critical drubbings and audience apathy. With each of its releases, the film's running time got less and less. Originally it ran 260 minutes,

then it was cut to 238 minutes; it ran at 197 minutes when issued in Great Britain, and it finally ended up at 190 minutes in the U. S.   When it runs on television these days it is usually in two parts.   The film was made between October, 1962 and July, 1963.

Perhaps the greatest fault of this feature was that it tried too hard to be the ultimate in religious films and in doing so, failed miserably.   It was too long, there was stilted and some unintentionally amusing dialogue, and the film was overly dominanted by cameo appearances by name stars, to the distraction of the viewing audience.   The result was an opulent, empty film which lacked the thing it needed most to succeed--inspiration.   As a result, the feature did not do well at the box office.

There were, however, some good points to THE GREATEST STORY EVER TOLD.   Max von Sydow gave a good performance as Jesus Christ and many of the supporting players were excellent, especially Claude Rains as the aging King Herod and Dorothy McGuire as the Virgin Mary. Several sequences in the film were well staged and quite well done, in particular the raising of Lazarus, the walk to Calvary and the Crucifixion.   Also the film contained a fine film score by Alfred Newman.

Donald Pleasence also deserves praise for his unique portrayal of Satan.   He used no makeup (no horns on his head or a sharp-pointed tail as in the films of old) but his sly voice and darkened presence personified the essence of evil.   After trying to tempt Christ, and failing, the Devil reappears throughout the film, always working against the Saviour.   Charlton Heston also deserves praise for his role as John the Baptist.   His angry dialogue with Herod is among the best in Biblical films.

The ending of the film is quite good, with Caiaphas (Martin Landau) finding Christ's tomb empty and pondering, "No matter, the whole thing will have been forgotten by tomorrow," while Nicodemus (Joseph Schildkraut) replies, "I wonder?"   The film's final scene, with Christ appearing from the clouds and giving His final message of love, is most touching, especially as handled by Max von Sydow.

THE GREATEST STORY EVER TOLD is not the best film interpretation of the life of Jesus Christ by any means, but it succeeds more often than it fails.

HVEZDA BETLEMSKA (The Star of Bethlehem)
1969

Czechoslovakia
10 minutes
Producer-Director: Hermina Tyrlova
This Czech color short was an animated telling of the birth of Christ. In the United States it was shown as THE STAR OF BETHLEHEM.

GAS-S-S-S! (Gas or It Became Necessary to Destroy the
        World in Order to Save It)
1970
American-International
79 minutes   Color
Producer-Director: Roger Corman
Screenplay: George Armitage
Photography: Ron Dexter
Editor: George Van Noy
Music: Country Joe and the Fish & Barry Melton
Art Director: David Nichols
Sets: Stephen Graham
Makeup: Dean Cundy
Sound: James Tannenbaum
        CAST: Robert Corff (Coel), Elaine Giftos (Cilla), Bud Cort (Hooper), Talia [Shire] Coppola (Coralie), Ben Vereen (Carlos), Cindy Williams (Marissa), Alex Wilson (Jason), Lou Procopio (Marshall McLuhan), Phil Borneo (Quant), Jackie Farley (Ginny), George Armitage (Billy the Kid), Pat Patterson (Demeter), Alan Braunstein (Dr. Drake), Country Joe and the Fish (Themselves).
        A mysterious gas is released from an Alaskan defense plant and it kills everyone on Earth over 25 years of age, thus throwing the world's power into the hands of youths. At the finale, the ground opens up and world leaders like the Kennedys, Che Guevara and Martin Luther King return to life while God is heard talking to Jesus Christ about the "new world."
        Originally made in 1968 in New Mexico, the plotline of GAS-S-S-S! was intended to have God as a major character but after the film was finished, American-International re-edited the work and excised this portion. The film received some minor playdates in the early 1970s and has since joined a multitude of films in the limbo of television syndication, where it gets no more exposure than it did in theatres. Perhaps the only thing the film has going for it is that it features a number of future stars, including Talia Shire, then billed under her real name of Talia Coppola; Cindy Williams, Ben Vereen, Elaine Giftos and Bud Cort.

MULTIPLE MANIACS
1970
Dreamland Productions
90 minutes B/W
Producer-Director-Screenplay-Photography-Editor: John
Waters
CAST: Divine (Lady Divine), David Lockary (Mr.
David), Mary Vivian Pearce (Bonnie), Mink Stole (Herself),
Cookie Mueller (Cookie), Paul Swift (Steve), Rick Morrow
(Ricky), Edith Massey (Barmaid), George Figgi (Jesus
Christ), Michael Renner, Jr. (The Infant of Prague), Susan
Lowe, Howard Gruber, Vince Peranio, Jim Thompson, Dee
Vitolo, Ed Peranio, Tom Wells, Gilbert McGill (The
Freaks), Bob Skidmore, Margie Skidmore, Jack Walsh,
Susan Walsh, Pat Moran, Harvey Freed, Mark Lazarus
(The Straight People).
Filmed in Baltimore, Maryland, this violent and
grotesque low-grade feature told of an obese woman (Divine)
who runs a traveling freak show, which deals in blackmail
and murder, with her boyfriend (David Lockary). When she
finds out that he is cheating on her she plans to kill him and
his lover (Mary Vivian Pearce), but she is seduced in a
church by a religious fanatic and, as a result, has hallucin-
atory visions of a blasphemous crucifixion and of Christ
(George Figgi) performing the miracle of the loaves and
fishes--only this time the result is tons of packaged bread
and cans of tuna.
Fortunately this film got little exposure. Its poking
fun at religion, in the context of such an awful and disgusting plotline, hardly can be termed humorous.

LA VOIE LACTEE (The Milky Way)
1970
France-Italy
U-M Productions/Greenwhich/Medusa
102 minutes Color
Producer: Serge Silberman
Director-Music: Luis Buñuel
Screenplay: Luis Buñuel & Jean-Claude Carrière
Photography: Christian Matias
Editor: Liusette Mautecoeur
Art Director: Pierre Guffroy
CAST: Paul Frankeur (Pierre), Laurenz Terzieff
(Jean), Alain Cuny (Cape), Edith Scob (Virgin Mary), Fran-
çoise Maistre (French Clergyman), Claude Cerval (Brigadier),

Muni (Mother Superior), Julien Bertheau (Maitre d'), Ellen Bahl (Mrs. Carnier), Michel Piccoli (Marquis), Agnes Capri (Teacher), Michel Etcheverry (Inquisitor), Pierre Clementi (Devil), Georges Marchal (Jesuit), Bernard Verley (Jesus Christ), Jean Piat (Jansenite), Denis Manuel (Rodolph), Daniel Pilon (François), Claudio Brook (L'Eveque), Julien Gruomier (Spanish Clergyman), Marcel Peres (Innkeeper), Delphine Seyrig (Prostitute).

An episodic fantasy film on the theme of heresy, LA VOIE LACTEE told of a pair of modern-day pilgrims who journey to a shrine. On their trek they have visions and religious experiences. They then go back in time, where they meet the Virgin Mary, witness the teachings of Jesus Christ, see His Crucifixion, and later meet the Marquis De Sade.

EL CRISTO DEL OCEANA (The Christ of the Ocean)
1971
Spain-Italy
100 minutes   Color
Director: Nino Del Arco
Screenplay: Manuel Oliveras Tovar, Frederico De Urrutia,
             Alfred Manas & Luciano Martino
Story: Anatole France
Photography: Julio Sanchez Caballero
      CAST: Nino Del Arco, Paolo Gozlino, Pilar Velaz-ques, Leonard Mann, Jose Suarez.

Aimed at children, this very charming Spanish-Italian co-production centers on a small boy, an orphan, who makes a living by fishing, although he is alway sad. One day he meets Jesus Christ in a sea cavern and the Saviour cheers the lad by performing miracles for him and telling him great stories. When Christ vanishes, the boy is content with his life, one he had once thought was dreary.

THE DEVILS
1971
Great Britain
109 minutes   Color
Producers: Robert H. Solo & Ken Russell
Director: Ken Russell
Screenplay: Ken Russell, from the novel The Devils of
             Loudun by Aldous Huxley

Photography: David Watkin
Editor: Michael Bradsell
Music: Peter Maxwell Davies
Art Director: Robert Cartwright
Makeup: Charles Parker
Set Design: Derek Jarman
   CAST: Vanessa Redgrave (Sister Jeanne), Oliver
Reed (Father Urbain Grandier), Dudley Sutton (Baron de
Laubardemont), Max Adrian (Ibert), Gemma Jones (Made-
leine), Murray Melvin (Mignon), Michael Gothard (Father
Barre), Georgina Hale (Philippe), Brian Murphy (Adam),
Christopher Logue (Cardinal Richelieu), Graham Armitage
(Louis XIII), John Woodvine (Trincant), Andrew Faulds
(Rangier), Kenneth Colley (Legrand), Judith Paris (Sister
Judith), Catherine Willmer (Sister Catherine), Iza Teller
(Sister Iza).

   If a few other Biblical films smack of blasphemy,
THE DEVILS tops them all in sheer grossness.   Set in the
17th century, the film deals with power-mad Cardinal Richelieu (Christopher Logue) trying to bring down the self-
governing city of Loudun by accusing the powerful local
priest (Oliver Reed) of causing the possession of a number
of nuns by the Devil.   Totally anti-religious, the film was
best described by Baxter Phillips in Cut: The Unseen
Cinema (1975):   "No medieval painting of Hell exceeded
[Ken] Russell's images of sexual degradation--and the crucifixion of the suffering Oliver Reed, playing Urbain Grandier, both in the fantasies of his mistress and the realities
of the stake.   But it was the antics of the naked nuns, pos-
sessed with devils of obscenity and blasphemy, which brought
out the censors all over the world in an orgy of hacking the
sequences of the madness. ...   If there was ever a case for
the total ban of a film for religious and social reasons,
THE DEVILS was that film---and it passed even the censors
at Venice, despite the Vatican. "
   In one sequence in THE DEVILS Oliver Reed appears
as the figure of Jesus Christ, complete with a crown of
thorns.   The rape, torture, burning and final crucifixion of
Christ in the film are among its most disgusting aspects.

JOHNNY GOT HIS GUN
1971
Cinemation
100 minutes   Color & B/W
Producer: Bruce Campbell

Director-Screenplay: Dalton Trumbo, from his novel
Photography: Jules Brenner
Editor: William P. Dornich
Music: Jerry Fielding
        CAST: Timothy Bottoms (Joe Bonham), Kathy Fields
(Kareen), Marsha Hunt (Joe's Mother), Jason Robards (Joe's
Father), Diana Varsi (Fourth Nurse), Donald [Don "Red"]
Barry (Jody), Donald Sutherland (Jesus Christ), Sandy Brown
Wyeth (Lucky), Charles McGraw, Eduard Franz, Bruce Morrow.
        Based on screenwriter Dalton Trumbo's little known
pacifistic novel of the same title, JOHNNY GOT HIS GUN
was released at the height of the anti-Vietnam War feeling.
Although aimed at the "youth cult" of the period, the picture
got little exposure and today it remains about as obscure as
its source.
        Taking place after World War I, the film tells about
a young soldier (Timothy Bottoms) who has been left but one
thing after a battle--his mind.   The young man has no arms,
legs, or face and is kept alive by machines.   His brain,
however, is normal and active and most of the picture con-
sists of flashbacks as he recalls portions of his life, such
as making love to his girlfriend (Kathy Fields) just before
going off to war.   The soldier also creates his own fantasies, including one where he has a conversation with Jesus
Christ (Donald Sutherland).   Christ talks to him for a while,
and even plays a game of cards with him, but comes to the
conclusion that the soldier is a "real downer," so he "splits."
        Unlike the harrowing book, the film makes little
sense and Donald Sutherland's self-indulgent performance as
Christ does not help matters.

GREASER'S PALACE
1972
Cinema 5
91 minutes   Color
Producer: Cyma Rubin
Director-Screenplay: Robert Downey
Photography: Peter Powell
Editor: Bud Smith
Music: Jack Nitszche
Set Design: David Foreman
        CAST: Allan Arbus (Jesus Christ/Zoot Suit/Jessy),
Albert Henderson (Seaweedhead Greaser), Elsie Downey (The
Woman), Luana Anders (Cholera Greaser), Woodrow Cham-

bliss (Father), Michael Sullivan (Lamly Greaser), James Antonio (Vanon), George Morgan (Coo Coo), Ron Nealy (Card Man/Ghost), Larry Moyer (Captain Good), John Paul Hudson (Smiley), Jackson Haynes (Rope Man), Lawrence Wolf (French Padre), Alex Hitchcock (Nun), Pablo Ferro, Toni Basil (Indians), Stan Gottlieb (Spitunia), Herve Vellechaize (Mr. Spitunia), Rex King (Turquoise Skies), Don Smolen (Gip), Joe Madden (Man With Painting), Donald Calfe (Morris).

GREASER'S PALACE is one of those films that is so full of "inside" jokes that no one but its producers could understand its "humor" or "meaning." As a result, the film could not find a distributor and the producers released it themselves. It was greeted with a critical shellacking and audience apathy.

The so-called "humorous" plot had Jesus Christ (Allan Arbus), dressed in a zoot suit, parachuting into a small Western town to recreate His final three years. The Holy Ghost arrives in a bed sheet and Christ walks on water and performs many other miracles, including His resurrection of a gunfighter.

SALOME
1972
Italy
Italnoleggio Films
77 minutes   Color
Producer-Director-Screenplay-Art Director: Carmelo Bene
Photography: Mario Masini
Editor: Mauro Contini
        CAST: Veruschka (Salome); Lydia Mancinelli, Donyale Luna, Piero Vida, Alfiero Vincenti, Giovanni Davali.

This version of SALOME from Italy is a brutal, ugly little film. It begins with Jesus Christ being tortured and mocked, and eventually crucifying Himself on the Cross. The story then switches to John the Baptist and Salome (Veruschka), the latter obtaining the former's death because he rejects her.

Full of violence and nudity, this version of SALOME was the most explicit of all the films made on the seductress who danced the dance of the seven veils. The early scenes with Christ are overly violent and filled with blood, while the seduction sequences between Salome and John the Baptist are extremely explicit. This outing may well be the worst version of SALOME ever to reach the screen.

GODSPELL
1973
Columbia
103 minutes   Color
Producer: Edgar Lansbury
Associate Producer: Kenneth Utt
Director: David Greene
Screenplay: David Greene and John-Michael Tebelak, from
     the Broadway play by John-Michael Tebelak and
     Stephen Schwartz & The Book of Matthew
Editor: Alan Helm
Music: Stephen Schwartz
Choreographer: Sammy Bayes
   CAST: Victor Garber (Jesus Christ), David Haskell
(John the Baptist/Judas Iscariot), Merrell Jackson, Jerry
Stroka, Jeffrey Mylatt, Katie Hanley, Joanne Jonas, Robin
Lamont, Lynne Thigpen, Gilmer McCormick (The Disciples).

   The musical GODSPELL was derived from the Broadway play of the same title, which, in turn, was based on the
writings of St. Matthew.   Appearing after JESUS CHRIST
SUPERSTAR (q. v.), it scored big at the box office but it
was an obvious copy and, like most copies, it was not as
good as the original.   Although it has some very fine moments, GODSPELL has some very poor scenes as well.
The film was obviously aimed at the youth market and tries
to combine the Gospels with the "in-youth" feelings of the
early 1970s--only half succeeding.
   Opening in New York City, the film tells of eight
young people who are caught in the hassles of modern-day
living.   Appearing before one of these youths is a man
dressed in colorful hobo rags who says he is the "new"
John the Baptist (David Haskell).   He blows his horn and
summons the other distraught youths together.   They as-
semble in a park and frolic at a fountain, which is the
symbol of John baptizing them.   Suddenly John sees a
strange figure at the end of the park, a man who is dressed
only in blue shorts.   There is make-up on His face to sym-
bolize that He is different.   As the stranger moves closer,
John yells, "I baptize you with water, but He who comes
after me is mightier than I.   I'm not worthy to take off His
shoes.   And He will baptize you with the Holy Spirit, and
with fire!"   The mysterious stranger waves his arms and
demands to be "washed up" or baptized.   The figure turns
out to be Jesus Christ (Victor Garber), and He tells John,
"We do well now to do all that God has commanded. "
   John baptizes Jesus and as He arises from the water

Victor Garber and David Haskell in GODSPELL (Columbia, 1973).

He is dressed in a blue shirt with an "S"--the Superman emblem on it--and red and white pants and clown shoes. As Christ comes out of the water He sings "Save the People." Christ and John then skip along through the countryside and the eight youths join them; they are now His disciples. The group then rests in an old deserted junk yard, sings songs and retells the parables from Matthew, only this time in a "hip" vogue.

Up to this point the film has been very light but it changes as John, now possibly Judas (David Haskell played both parts in the film) points to Christ and says, "Blessed are Ye, when men shall persecute You and defile You and say all manner of evil against You--falsely." The group then runs into an ugly black machine that shoots out dark smog, the machine-creature representing the "authority or government" that will crucify Jesus. He becomes angry at the machine and destroys it in a violent rage; this is supposed to represent the destruction of the sin-city of Jerusalem by Jesus, in the Gospel according to St. Matthew.

Christ realizes what He has been forced to do, and in a very moving scene He says, "How often I have longed to gather your children as a hen gathers her brood under her wings, but you would not let me." He goes to pray in solitude. The disciples come to Him and the girls sing a touching song, "By My Side." During this number, Judas is seen betraying Jesus. The group then skips through some beautiful New York City scenery to the tune of "Beautiful City," a song written especially for the film. A backdrop of the statues of angels highlights this scene.

The final stop is within a deserted area at night; there Christ sits with His disciples and sings another touching song, "On the Willows." He then tells them that "one of you among us will betray me." Christ then has His final meal and bids farewell to His disciples.

The disciples fall asleep and Judas brings the police. They string Jesus up to a wire fence and He is crucified. The disciples, Judas among them, mourn His death and carry His body out of the yard to the melody of "Long Live God." When morning comes the group vanishes and is replaced by the modern-day city. A reprise of the song "Day By Day" ends the film.

Many conclusions can be drawn from GODSPELL, but most likely the film is telling people to rejoice in what they have and to slow down their pace of living. Whatever the conclusions, the film begins slowly, becomes very dull, picks up toward the last half-hour and has a beautiful finish. Although Victor Garber is good as a "hip" Jesus, it is David

Haskell in the roles of John the Baptist and Judas who dominates the film. He dominates every scene in which he appears, has the best singing voice and is the most talented actor in the film. Perhaps one reason Haskell dominates over the lead Garber is that it is very difficult to accept the role of Christ as a clown, and that is just how He is dressed in this feature.

Like all musicals, GODSPELL must also be judged on its score. The one saving grace of the scene where the parables are retold is the song "Day By Day," sung by Robin Lamont, which turned out to be the movie's biggest musical success. Some of the other numbers are not so fortunate: "Turn Back, O' Man" is a terrible song done in a Mae West imitation and "Bless the Lord" is a complete failure. "All Good Gifts" has a few good moments (especially when Christ interrupts it to tell about the "lilies of the field") but it too is generally a failure. "Light of the World" is another dull tune in the score. "All for the Best" is a fine production number by Haskell and Garber, who sing it on top of a tall building with the logo "Accutron by Bulova" flashing below them.

The film was the subject of a television special on PBS called "Godspell Goes to Plimoth Plantation for Thanksgiving with Henry Steele Commager," which was aired in a 60-minute time period on November 18, 1973, just a few months after the film's theatrical release. The program featured the Boston cast of the play "Godspell" at Plimoth Plantation, with Henry Steele Commager hosting the event.

GOSPEL ROAD
1973
20th Century-Fox
93 minutes   Color
Producers: June Carter Cash & Johnny Cash
Director: Robert Elfstrom
Screenplay: Johnny Cash & Larry Murray
Photography: Robert Elfstrom & Tom McDonough
Editor: John Craddock
Music: Larry Butler & Johnny Cash
CAST: Robert Elfstrom (Jesus Christ), June Carter Cash (Mary Magdalene), Larry Lee (John the Baptist), Paul Smith (Peter), Alan Bates (Nicodemus), Robert Elfstrom, Jr. (Child Jesus), Gelles La Blanc (John), Terrance Winston (Matthew), Thomas Leventhal (Judas), John Paul Kay (James), Sean Armstrong (Thomas), Lyle Nicholson (Andrew), Steven

Chernoff (Phillip), Stuart Clark (Nathaniel), Ulf Pollack (Thaddeus), Jonathan Sanders (Simon), Johnny Cash (Narrator).

Country music performer Johnny Cash masterminded this production, which is a mixture of different formats: a tour of the Holy Land, songs about Christ, and actors acting out scenes from the life of Christ. Some found this odd conglomeration interesting; others did not. Many viewers complained that the film presented Christ and his apostles as a bunch of hippies and appealed mainly to the "Country Jesus" crowd. Ironically, the film did not fare particulary well in theatres and eventually ended up being shown in churches, the direct opposite of DAY OF TRIUMPH (q. v.), which was made for churches but was so good that it did quite well in theatrical release.

Director and co-photographer Robert Elfstrom appears on screen briefly as Jesus Christ and his performance is mediocre, even though he has no lines. Johnny Cash is the on-screen narrator, and also appears in several tiny parts in the film; he performs the eight songs he wrote for the production. Perhaps the most laughable casting was that of Cash's country comedienne wife, June Carter Cash, in the role of Mary Magdalene.

JESUS CHRIST SUPERSTAR
1973
Universal
103 minutes   Color
Producers: Norman Jewison & Robert Stigwood
Associate Producer: Patrick Palmer
Directors: Norman Jewison & Robert Stigwood
Screenplay: Merlyn Bragg, Norman Jewison & Robert Stigwood, from the Rock Opera and Record by Tim Rice
Music: Andrew Lloyd Webber & Tim Rice
Music Conductor: Andre Previn
Orchestrations: Andrew Lloyd Webber
CAST: Ted Neeley (Jesus Christ), Carl Anderson (Judas Iscariot), Yvonne Elliman (Mary Magdalene), Joshua Mostel (Herod), Barry Dennen (Pontius Pilate), Larry T. Marshall (Simon Zealotes), Kurt Yaghjian (Annas), Bob Bingham (Caiaphas), Philip Toubus (Peter), Pi Douglass, Jonathan Wynne, Richard Molinare, Jeffrey Hyslop, Robert Lupone, Thommie Walsh, David Devir, Richard Orbach, Shooki Wagner (Apostles), Darcel Wynne, Sally Neal, Vera Biloshisky,

Ted Neeley in JESUS CHRIST SUPERSTAR (Universal, 1973).

Wendy Maltby, Baayork Lee, Susan Allison, Ellen Hoffman, Judith Daby, Adaya Pilo, Marcia McBroom, Leeyan Granger, Kathryn Wright, Denise Pence, Wyetta Turner, Tamar Zafria, Riki Oren, Lea Kestin (Women), Zvulun Cohen, Meir Israel, Itzhak Sidranski, David Rfyivon, Amitz Razi, Avi Ben-Haim, Haim Bashi, David Barkan (Priests), Steve Boockvor, Peter Luria, David Barkan, Danny Basevitch, Cliff Michaelevski, Tom Guest, Stephen Denenberg, Didi Liekov (Roman Soldiers), Doron Gaash, Noam Cohen, Zvi Lehat, Moshe Uziel (Temple Guards).

JESUS CHRIST SUPERSTAR was a powerful media-event that swept the youth of America in the mid-1970s. The project began in 1968 when it was created as a double record album by composer Andrew Lloyd Webber and lyricist Tim Rice. The album became a record classic, selling millions of copies. Concerts were created around the record by Robert Stigwood and David Land and by 1970 these were attracting capacity crowds across the country. Next the project was fashioned into a stage show and it played around the world to international recognition. The most important element, however, was the music and it was used as a powerful weapon to spread the spirit of Jesus Christ to the youth of America and the world.

By 1971, Universal announced that JESUS CHRIST SUPERSTAR would be produced as a motion picture, to be directed by Norman Jewison, who had already scored with FIDDLER ON THE ROOF (United Artists, 1971). Both David Cassidy, of television's "The Partridge Family," and Micky Dolenz, a former child star and drummer for the rock group "The Monkees" in the 1960s, were mentioned for the lead role of Jesus Christ, but the part went to newcomer Ted Neeley. Neeley turned out to be an excellent choice for the role and played Christ with power, sympathy and feeling.

The film JESUS CHRIST SUPERSTAR transcended the boundaries of both set and stage to become what is now considered a statement of historical and contemporary significance. The film "turned on" a whole generation of lost youth to Jesus Christ and this alone makes the entire project more than worthwhile.

Director Norman Jewison filmed the project in Israel, entirely on location, in Technicolor and Todd-AO 35. The natural settings made the music seem even more inspirational. Andre Previn, brought in to conduct the musical score, turned in a masterful performance. Jewison's direction blended the traditional and modern--besides the ancient weapons, one also sees modern ones, such as tanks and guns.   There is much of this mixing throughout the movie.

To play Judas Iscariot, a black actor, Carl Anderson, was selected.   This caused a bit of controversy in the black community but Anderson gives a powerful performance as Judas.   He portrays Judas not as an entirely evil person but almost a sympathetic one; certainly, his performance is not that of the traditional "bad guy in black."   The rest of the cast is also fine, especially Yvonne Elliman as Mary Magdalene.   Though not an experienced actress, Elliman makes up for it with her excellent vocals.   Indeed, her song from the film, "I Don't Know How to Love Him," became a best-selling pop single for her.

To this writer (Richard H. Campbell), JESUS CHRIST SUPERSTAR is the best of all Biblical films, although it is more inspirational than historically accurate.   But inspiration, after all, is what religious movies are supposed to be all about.

The film begins with a busload of teenagers arriving in Israel.   They unload and proceed to erect sets and to dress and act out the story of Jesus Christ as a musical. The teenagers dress one of their own in a white robe, as he is to play Jesus Christ (Ted Neeley).   Meanwhile, a lone wolf, an intense-looking black actor (Carl Anderson), as Judas Iscariot, walks away from the group and climbs into the mountains, where he vows to betray Jesus.

Next the scene moves to Bethany, on a Friday night, as Roman guards patrol the area dressed in hard hats, sweatshirts and armbands and carrying spears.   Christ and His disciples are located in a cavern beneath the earth. The cave is full of Apostles who are of all nationalities and colors, all dancing together.   Mary Magdalene (Yvonne Elliman) enters to "cool down" Christ's* face.   Judas appears, mystified that "a man like (Jesus) can waste His time on a woman of her kind."   Jesus blasts Judas, "Who are you to criticize her?"   The scene ends with an enraged Jesus shouting that no one cares if He comes or goes.

Meanwhile Caiaphas (Bob Bingham) is in his court, which is shown as nothing more than old, broken battlements. He is upset over the teachings of Christ and Annas (Kurt Yaghijian) arrives to comfort him, assuring Caiaphas that Jesus is "just another scripture-thumping hack from Galilee."

---

*Christ is portrayed as a virile young man in this film and He responds to the affections of Mary Magdalene.   Fundamentalists in various cities picketed this rock opera on grounds of blasphemy.

Caiaphas, however, feels that "Jesus is important" and he is determined to see Christ killed before he is forced out of political power.

Back in the cave, Judas argues with Jesus, but He tells Judas to "look at the good things you've got! Think, while you still have me. Move, while you still see me. You'll be lost and you'll be sorry when I'm gone." With this, Jesus and Judas clutch hands in a very powerful and emotional sequence.

Next it is Jerusalem on Sunday. Caiaphas and Annas have called together their council, who appear on the broken battlements like birds on a fence, waiting to devour their prey. Jesus and His followers calmly walk past the castle. "No riots, no army, no fighting, no slogans--one thing I'll say for Him, Jesus is cool," says Caiaphas, who continues to say that he must crush "this Jesusmania" at any cost. Saying, "So like John before Him, this Jesus must die," Caiaphas convinces the council that Christ must be killed.

To the beat of "Hosanna," a very beautiful number, Christ teaches His people. But the crowd asks Jesus if He "will die for me," and Jesus' worried face is freeze-framed, providing a very powerful scene. During the next number, Simon (Larry T. Marshall) devotes himself to Christ, with young girls dancing in and out of thin air.

By Monday Jesus arrives in Jerusalem, which is a city of sin. Seedy-looking characters sell everything from picture post cards to United States currency and machine guns. Sex is pushed by the prostitutes and dope by the junkies. Jesus charges into the scene, destroying every-thing in sight with a club. "My temple should be a house of prayer, but you have made it a den of thieves. Get out," He shouts. Judas and the other Apostles look on, shocked by His display of violence.

Jesus then goes to the mountains to meditate and lepers appear, as if they have come to life from the moun-tainsides. They are bundled in black and there are hundreds of them, all wanting Jesus to heal them. "There's too many of you," He screams, "Leave me alone!" There are, in-deed, too many and His pleas are to no avail as the lepers surround and smother Him. It is an ugly, terrifying scene, yet very effective and necessary. Next Mary Magdalene sings "I Don't Know How to Love Him," wondering why she is so attracted to Christ and why He is so different.

Judas, meanwhile, has decided to betray Jesus. He is confused, as if he is doing something he cannot help. Caiaphas offers Judas thirty pieces of silver to betray Jesus. "I don't want your blood money," Judas screams,

but Caiaphas convinces him to take it. After Judas tells
Caiaphas that he can locate Jesus in the Garden of Gethsemane, tanks appear over a hill to pursue Judas, a wry
reference to the Vietnam war.

The next day the Last Supper takes place. The
Apostles sing a very beautiful song, "Trials and Tribulations." Jesus becomes angry, saying that He will not be
remembered and that one of the Disciples will deny Him.
Judas calls Jesus a "sad pathetic man" and leaves to betray Him. On Friday, in the Garden of Gethsemane, Judas
betrays Jesus with a kiss and the guards escort Jesus to
Caiaphas, who, in turn, sends Him to Pilate (Barry Dennen) for trial. Meanwhile, Peter denies Jesus.

Pilate questions Christ: "This broken man cluttering
up my hallway ... are you king of the Jews?" Pilate sends
Him to Herod, who is portrayed as an ugly, fat slob of a
man. He sits in front of a sea of beautiful water, with
Christ humbly standing on the opposite side. Herod (Joshua
Mostel) is surrounded by an odd-looking group of youths,
teenagers with painted faces and purple hair. The king
sings a song mocking Jesus and ends by saying He is nothing but a fraud. He sends Jesus back to Pilate for trial.

Next comes a beautiful scene with Peter and Mary
Magdalene singing "Could We Start Again Please?" Christ
sadly turns His head and walks away, turns to stretch out
His arms, then turns away again. Distraught, Judas won-
ders why he has been chosen to be "saddled" with the murder of Christ. Finally, unable to cope with his guilt, he
hangs himself.

Meanwhile, Pilate does not want to execute Jesus;
instead, he sentences Him to thirty-nine lashes. This is
not enough for the crowd, however, and the people demand
that Christ be crucified. Pilate tries to help Christ but
fails and washes his hands of the affair; the water in which
he washes turns red.

Jesus, broken, beaten and in tattered rags, turns
and His white robe, no longer torn, now glows. The backdrop turns black and He is now in Heaven. Judas swings
down on a star, accompanied by a band of beautiful angels,
all dancing to rock music. Here the song "Superstar"
comes into play.

Then comes the Crucifixion, with guards nailing
Jesus to the Cross. Jesus prays to God and demands to
be shown that He "would not die in vain." He is answered
by some of the world's best paintings of Him as they are
flashed across the screen, all showing Him on the cross.
The scene is very beautiful and intense.

The crew then packs up and gets on board the bus--but the youth who "played" Christ is not among them. The actor who was Judas takes a long look at the three crosses and faintly sees a figure of a crucified man. Then the bus drives away.

HIM
1974
Hand in Hand Films
Color
Producer: Edward D. Louie

When pornographic feature films surfaced in the late 1960s and early 1970s, nothing remained sacred.* SURE-LICK HOLMES mocked Sherlock Holmes, SOUPERMAN parodied "The Man of Steel," and there was even a pornographic Frankenstein film, HOLLOW MY WEENIE, DR. FRANKEN-STEIN. Sadly, it was not long before the skin-flicks took aim at the image of Jesus Christ.

HIM is an X-rated film that declares Christ was a homosexual. The plot had a young man, who is a homosexual, becoming obsessed with the sex life of Jesus and declaring that Christ and His Apostles were all lovers, thus finding "startling" new insights into the hidden meanings of the New Testament.

The advertisements for this film asked, "Are You Curious About HIS Sex Life?" The answer was an overwhelming "NO," both to the question and to this garbage film.

PROCESCO A JESUS (Trial of Jesus)
1974
Spain
Aldebaran Films, S.A.
109 minutes   Color
Producer: Diego Fabbri
Director: Jose Luis Saenz de Heredia
Screenplay: Jose Luis Sanchez Silva & Jose Luis Saenz de

---

*Variety (April 17, 1974) reported that plans to film the love life of Christ in Copenhagen, Denmark caused such an outrage in 1973 that the production was "scuttled for lack of cooperation and location privileges."

Heredia
Photography: Luis Cuadrado
Music: Ruiz de Luna
        CAST: Jose Maria Rodero, Monica Randall, Julia
Gutierrez Caba, Andres Mejuto, Armando Calvo, Maria
Cuadra, Lili Muratti, Alfredo Mayo, Diana Lorys, Tomas
Blanco, Carlos Lemos, Agustin Gonzalez, Miguel Angel.
        A group of Sephardic Jews write a play called
"Trial of Jesus" so that Christian audiences may judge
whether or not there was justification to condemn Him in
accordance with the laws of that age. In an ancient synagogue in Toledo, Spain, the public becomes involved in the
realism of the debate, causing the play to remain without a
verdict, although it is clear that His death was that of an
innocent person and one that 2000 years later still weighs
heavily on humanity.
        While a modern-day film, this Spanish production
did include a recreation of the trial of Jesus in an ancient
synagogue, in the dress of the period.

THE TRIAL OF BILLY JACK
1974
Warner Brothers
170 minutes   Color
Producer: Joe Cramer
Director: Frank Laughlin
Screenplay: Frank & Teresa Christian
Photography: Jack A. Maria
Music: Elmer Bernstein
Production Manager: William Beaudine, Jr.
        CAST: Delores Taylor (Jean Roberts), Tom Laugh-
lin (Billy Jack), Victor Izay (Doc), Teresa Laughlin (Carol),
Riley Hill (Posner), Sparky Watt (Sheriff Cole), Russell
Lane (Russell), William Wellman, Jr. (National Guardsman),
Michelle Wilson (Michelle), Geo Anna Sosa (Joanna), Lynn
Baker (Lynn), Gus Greymountain (Blue Elk), Sacheen Little-
feather (Patsy Littlejohn), Michael Bolland (Danny), Jack
Stanley (Grandfather), Sandra Ego (Rolling Thunder); Trini-
dad Hopkins, Marianne Hall, Jason Clark, Johnny West,
Buffalo Horse, Dennis O'Flaherty, Bong Soo Han, Michael
J. Singezone, Kathy Cronkite, Alexandra Nicholson.
        Tom Laughlin created the character of "Billy Jack,"
the half-Indian martial-arts master, in BORN LOSERS
(American-International, 1968). This was followed by the
hugely successful BILLY JACK (Warner Brothers, 1971),

with THE TRIAL OF BILLY JACK coming as the third in
the series.   Made at a cost of $7.8 million, THE TRIAL
OF BILLY JACK grossed over $35 million in the United
States alone, although it reportedly did not do well in for-
eign markets.   Portions of the motion picture were shot in
Monument Valley and the Grand Canyon.

THE TRIAL OF BILLY JACK begins where BILLY
JACK ended, with the shoot-out at the Reservation School.
The teacher (Delores Taylor) relates the story from her
hospital bed.   Billy Jack is released from prison, where
he has been detained for a murder he committed in the
second film, and returns to the mountains where he was
raised.   There he meets an old Indian sage who helps him
find "the inner peace of the third level."   Billy then begins
a mystical trek which transcends time and space.   He
learns that the "first level" is to return violence with violence, while the "second level" is to use a verbal defense
against physical actions.   He discovers that the "third
level" is one of total non-resistance, of pure love and total
peace.   It is on this level that Billy Jack encounters Jesus
Christ, who briefly teaches him the "third level" lesson.
As Billy Jack returns to reality he is told there is a "fourth
level," which no person has yet been able to reach.   Inter-
mixed with this philosophy were Billy Jack's continuing battles with bigots, politicians and the National Guard.

Some people consider the "Billy Jack" films to be
among the best series ever produced.   On the other hand,
many, including most critics, greatly dislike the series.
Regarding THE TRIAL OF BILLY JACK, Charles Champlin
wrote in the Los Angeles Times, "It is one of the longest,
slowest, most pretentious and self-congratulatory ego trips
ever put on film."   The Wall Street Journal said it was
"unintentionally funny" and Judith Crist wrote in TV Guide,
"[It is] an incoherent muddle of racial-fascist jargon...."
When the film was aired on television it was cut from 170
to 144 minutes.

The financial success of THE TRIAL OF BILLY
JACK resulted in a fourth film, BILLY JACK GOES TO
WASHINGTON (Taylor-Laughlin, 1977), a loose remake of
MR. SMITH GOES TO WASHINGTON (Columbia, 1939), but
it was a financial bust.   It should be noted that Tom Laugh-
lin and Delores Taylor, the stars of the series, are mar-
ried, and that Frank Laughlin, the director of THE TRIAL
OF BILLY JACK, is their son, while daughter, Teresa
Laughlin, played Carol in that film.

THE PASSOVER PLOT
1976
United States-Israel
Atlas Films
128 minutes   Color
Producer: Wolf Schmidt
Executive Producer: Menahem Golan
Associate Producer: Yoram Globus
Director: Michael Campus
Screenplay: Millard Cohan & Patricia Knop, from the book
          by Dr. Hugh J. Schonfield
Photography: Adam Greenbert
Editor: Dov Hoenig
Music: Alex North
Art Director: Kuli Sander
Costume Designer: Mary Wills
Special Effects: Jack Rabin
        CAST: Zalman King (Yeshua [Jesus] of Nazareth),
Harry Andrews (Yohanan [John] the Baptist), Hugh Griffith
(Caiaphas), Donald Pleasence (Pontius Pilate), Scott Wilson
(Judah), Dan Ades (Andros), Michael Baseleon (Mattai),
Lewis van Bergen (Yoram), William Burns (Shimon), Daniel
Hedaya (Yaacov), Helena Kallianiotes (Visionary Woman),
Kevin O'Connor (Irijah), Robert Walker (Bar Talmi), William Watson (Roman Captain).
        Advertisements for this Israeli-filmed production
called THE PASSOVER PLOT "the first major motion picture to challenge two thousand years of history!" and asked
the question, "Did Jesus really die on the Cross?"   Based
on the best-selling novel by Dr. Hugh J. Schonfield, the
film attempted to show that Christ (Zalman King) was an
opportunist who set out to capitalize on the social unrest of
the time, thus to overthrow Roman rule and fulfill the Jewish prophecy of the promised Messiah by making Himself
king of Israel.
        Although expensively mounted, well acted and photo-
graphed, the film was at its weakest when trying to prove
its point.   Nearly all of the supposed frauds surrounding
Christ were shown off-camera and only discussed in the
film.   The finale has Christ drugged on the Cross so that
He appears to be dead, but the "Passover Plot" is foiled
when one of the Roman guards stabs Him in the side before
the body is claimed.   The next day, before He dies, Christ
is seen, and word spreads that the prophecies have been
fulfilled and the Messiah has risen.
        THE PASSOVER PLOT is really a little known feature
film because it failed to get wide distribution.   As a direct

confrontation with Christian thinking, the film was basically
ignored and it has been given the obscurity it rightly deserves.

JESUS OF NAZARETH
1977
NBC-TV
390 minutes   Color
Producer: Vincenzo Labella
Executive Producer: Bernard J. Kingham
Associate Producer: Dyson Lovell
Director: Franco Zeffirelli
Script: Anthony Burgess, Suso Cecchi d'Amico & Franco
          Zeffirelli
Additional Dialogue: David Butler
Photography: Armando Nennuzzi & David Watkins
Editor: Reginald Mills
Art Director: Gianni Quaranta
Music: Maurice Jarre
Costume Design: Marcel Escoffier & Enrico Sabbatini
Scenic Design: Francesco Fedeli
Choreography: Alberto Testa
          CAST: Robert Powell (Jesus Christ), Anne Bancroft
(Mary Magdalene), Ernest Borgnine (The Centurion), Claudia
Cardinale (The Adulteress), Valentina Cortese (Herodias),
James Farentino (Simon Peter), James Earl Jones (Baltha-
sar), Stacy Keach (Barabbas), Tony Lo Bianco (Quintilius),
James Mason (Joseph of Arimethea), Ian McShane (Judas
Iscariot), Laurence Olivier (Nicodemus), Donald Pleasence
(Melchior), Christopher Plummer (Herod Antipas), Anthony
Quinn (Caiaphas), Fernando Rey (Caspar), Ralph Richardson
(Simeon), Rod Steiger (Pontius Pilate), Peter Ustinov (Herod
the Great), Michael York (John the Baptist), Olivia Hussey
(Virgin Mary), Cryil Cusack (Rabbi Yehuda), Ian Holm
(Zerah), Yorgo Voyagis (Joseph), Ian Bannen (Amos), Re-
gina Bianchi (Anna), Marina Berti (Elizabeth), Oliver Tobias
(Joel), Maria Carta (Martha), Lee Montague (Habbukuk),
Renato Rascel (Blind Man), Norman Bowler (Saturninus),
John Phillips (Proculus), Robert Beatty (Naso), Ken Jones
(Jotham), Nancy Nevinson (Abigail), Renato Terra (Abel),
Roy Holder (Enoch), Jonathan Adams (Adam), Christopher
Reich (Circumsicion Priest), Lorenzo Monet (Jesus at Age
12), Robert Davey (Daniel), Oliver Smith (Saul), George
Camillier (Hosias), Murray Salem (Simon the Zealot), Tony
Vogal (Andrew), Isabel Mestres (Salome), Michael Cronin

Frank De Wolfe, Anne Bancroft, James Mason and Robert Powell in JESUS OF NAZARETH (NBC-TV, 1977).

(Eliphaz), Forbes Collins (Jonas), Steve Gardner (Phillip), John Duttine (John the Evangelist), Michael Haughey (Nahum), Keith Skinner (Obsessed Boy), Cyril Shaps (Obsessed Boy's Father), Jonathan Muller (James), John Tordoff (Malachi), Keith Washington (Matthew), Sergio Nicolai (James II), Antonello Campodifiori (Ircanus), Renato Montalbano (Jairus), Bruce Liddington (Thomas), Mimmo Crao (Thaddeus), Derek Godfrey (Elihu).

Originally telecast on NBC-TV's "The Big Event" program in two parts on April 3 and April 10, 1977, JESUS OF NAZARETH ran six and one-half hours. When it was retelecast April 1, 2, 3 and 8, 1979, it was expanded to a total of eight hours. As indicated by its expansive running times, the feature told the life of Christ in great detail, resulting in "the best film of its kind" (Judith Crist in TV Guide).

Filmed primarily in Morocco and Tunisia between September, 1975 and May, 1976, this project was originally called THE LIFE OF JESUS, and even before it was telecast it ran into a great deal of controversy. Because the film questioned several major accepted "facts" about the life of Christ, it came under fire from fundamentalist groups. After the telecast, however, it was generally agreed that the film was a reverent and inspirational retelling of the life of The Saviour. The main area of disagreement with accepted texts was that the film contended that Zerah (Ian Holm), a Temple priest, was the betrayer of a well-intended Judas (Ian McShane) and that he also manipulated the Pilate's (Rod Steiger) lack of interest in bringing about the Crucifixion.

As a total unit, JESUS OF NAZARETH is a beautiful film and it has become a yearly tradition on network television, usually re-broadcast at either Thanksgiving or Christmas in a mini-series format. The film details every aspect of Christ's life, from His birth to His death and Resurrection, and it does so brilliantly. The acting and production values are top-notch and Robert Powell gives both a powerful and sympathetic portrayal of Jesus Christ.

A good example of the beauty of the film is seen in its finale, with Christ rising from the tomb three days after the Crucifixion. As Mary Magdalene (Anne Bancroft) rushes away from the empty tomb she sees a blur of a man who tells her not to worry and asks, "Why do you seek the living with the dead?" As Jesus is reunited with His Disciples (appearing shadow-like at the doorway), He tells them to go and spread His word. Simon Peter (James Farentino) begs Him, "Master, do not go for the day is short and the night is almost upon us." Christ comforts him by saying, "Do not worry, for I am with you always, every day, in every way, now until the end of time ... and beyond."

Judith Crist wrote in TV Guide that it was "a truly epic six-hour film of the life of Christ, confirming its status as one of the fine religious films of our time. Taste, subtlety and scholarship are its base; impeccable performances and a vivid recreation of time and place are its strengths, with its spiritual values left to the heart of the beholder."

The script for JESUS OF NAZARETH was novelized by William Barclay.

THE LOST YEARS
1977
Aura Productions
90 minutes   Color
Producer-Photography: Richard Bock
Screenplay: Richard Bock, Janet Bock & Gilda Franklin
Narrators: Rod Colbin & William Marshall

THE LOST YEARS is a choppily-made documentary that claims to fill in the "lost years" in the life of Jesus Christ, from the ages of 13 to 29, which are not mentioned in the Scriptures.

According to this outing, which is as much a colorful travelogue as a religious drama, Jesus traveled in those years from Palestine to Asia Minor, India, Rome, and Egypt before returning to Palestine to fulfill His destiny. The bulk of the documentary, which was filmed in India, Italy, and Germany, takes place in India where Jesus supposedly studied with that country's great masters. Also the film contends that Jesus and one St. Esa, who dwelled in India and Tibet, were the same person.

Other portions of THE LOST YEARS cover St. Thomas' coming to India in 52 A.D. and establishing a church; the prophecies of Edgar Cayce regarding Christ; the history and authenticity of the Shroud of Turin, which is thought to be the burial cloth of Christ; and the Spear of Longinus, which is said to have pierced Jesus while He was on the Cross and has since given powers to its owners.

In telling its story, this documentary interpolates the opinions of Biblical scholars like Rev. John C. Trevor, various Indian holy men and nuclear scientist Ralph Graeber, who believes in the authenticity of the Shroud of Turin. The film also uses many religious paintings to present its point of view.

Although THE LOST YEARS is in some ways an interesting film, its poverty row origins take away from what might have been a most convincing argument as to the whereabouts of Christ during his "lost years."

The film has been issued to television by Gold Key Entertainment.

BEYOND AND BACK
1978
Sunn Classics Pictures
93 minutes   Color
Producer: Charles E. Sellier Jr.
Director: James L. Conway
Screenplay: Stephen Lord, from the book by Ralph Wilkerson
Photography: Henning Schellerup
Editor: James D. Wells
        CAST: Brad Crandall (Narrator), Vern Adix (Plato), Shelley Osterloh (Louisa May Alcott), Beverly Rowland (Mrs. Harry Houdini).

Another in the series of Sunn Classic Pictures' media-blitz exploitation pictures, BEYOND AND BACK concerned itself with "the death experience" and claimed it would tell its audience what happens to the soul after death.   The film, however, does not answer any questions and leaves the viewer knowing little more about the inevitable than before seeing it.

The film recounts supposed true events in the lives of persons who died and then returned to life.   Many such incidents involve the victims seeing Jesus Christ as they die. Historical figures such as Louisa May Alcott and Harry Houdini and their experiences with death are also covered, as is the theory of Dr. Duncan MacDougal, who claims that the soul of a person leaves the body at death and that it weighs three-fourths of an ounce.

Of all the so-called documentary films from Sunn Classics Pictures, this one is the least satisfactory.   Interestingly, when the film debuted on network television after its theatrical run, it was cut by more than one-third and fitted into a one-hour time period.

THE NATIVITY
1978
ABC-TV/20th Century-Fox

Madeline Stone and John Shea in THE NATIVITY (ABC-TV, 1978).

100 minutes   Color
Producer: William P. D'Angelo
Executive Producers: Ray Allen & Harvey Bullock
Director: Bernard L. Kowalski
Script: Millard Kaufman & Mort Fine
Photography: Gabor Pogany
Editors: Robert Phillips & Jerry Dronsky
Music: Lalo Schifrin
Art Director: Luciano Spadoni
   CAST: Madeline Stone (Mary), John Shea (Joseph),
Jane Wyatt (Anna), Paul Stewart (Zacharias), Leo McKern
(Herod), Audrey Totter (Elizabeth), George Voskovec
(Joachim), Julie Garfield (Zipporah), Kate O'Mara (Salome),
Barrie Houghton (Preacher), Jamil Zakkai (Menachem),
Freddie Jones (Diomedes), John Rhys-Davies (Nestor), Mor-
gan Shephard (Flavius), Geoffrey Beevers (Eleazar), Jacob
Witkin (Census Taker), Jack Lynn (Innkeeper).
   When THE NATIVITY, a feature made for television,
was telecast on ABC-TV on December 17, 1978, it was ad-
vertised as "the greatest family story of all time" about "a
man, a woman, and the Child who changed the world." To
its credit, the telefeature is a reverent retelling of the
events that led up to the birth of Jesus Christ. However,
TV Movies rightly reported that it is "hampered by pedestrian performances by the two leads and so-so direction."
The main highlights of the film are the performance of film
veterans Jane Wyatt, as Anna, and Leo McKern's portrayal
of King Herod.
   With all its shortcomings, however, THE NATIVITY
is far better than another telefilm dealing with the same
subject, MARY AND JOSEPH: A STORY OF FAITH (q. v.),
which NBC-TV telecast the next year.

JESUS (The Public Life of Jesus)
1979
Warner Brothers-Genesis Project
117 minutes   Color
Producer: John Heyman
Associate Producer: Richard Dalton
Directors: Peter Sykes & John Kirsh
Screenplay: Barnet Fishbein
Costumes: Rochelle Zaltzman
   CAST: Brian Deacon (Jesus Christ), Rivka Noiman
(Mary), Yossef Shiloah (Joseph), Niko Nitai (Simon Peter),
Gadi Rol (Andrew), Itzhak Ne'eman (James), Shmuel Tal

(John), Kobi Assaf (Phillip), Michael Varshaviak (Bartholo-mew), Mosko Alkalai (Matthew), Nisim Gerama (Thomas), Leonid Weinstein (James), Rafi Milo (Simon Zelotes), Eli Danker (Judas Iscariot), Eli Cohen (John the Baptist), Talia Shapira (Mary Magdalene), David Goldberg (Judas, Son of James), Richard Peterson (King Herod), Miki Mfir (Simon the Pharisee), Peter Frye (Pontius Pilate), Alexander Scour-by (Narrator).

JESUS, which was also issued as THE PUBLIC LIFE OF JESUS, is an adaptation of the Book of Luke, but unlike most Biblical films it is a faithful version of its source. Filmed in Israel on a $6 million budget, Variety said the film is "a Classics Comics version ... [that] skims through the Saviour's life quickly ... hitting all the high spots, but leaving little time for contemplation or depth of character."

Although the incidents in JESUS have been filmed many times before, this production, over all, is a good one and Brian Deacon is very good in the title role, using his soft English accent to present the Luke Gospel word for word. The film is, however, graphically violent in show-ing the tortures inflicted on Christ before the Crucifixion, but these are done in a realistic manner. The film con-cludes with Christ returning from the grave three days af-ter His death.

The Genesis Project, the production company for the film, has announced plans for a series of motion pictures about Jesus Christ, all based exactly on each of the Gospels in the New Testament. With JESUS as a good start, the company could very well produce a group of high-quality religious films.

MARY AND JOSEPH: A STORY OF FAITH
December 9, 1979
NBC-TV
180 minutes   Color
Producer: Gene Corman
Executive Producers: Lee Rich & Harold Greenberg
Director: Eric Till
Script: Carmen Culver
Photography: Adam Greenberg
Editor: J. Howard Terrill
Music: Robert Farnon
Art Director: John Blezard
Sound: Cyril Collick
      CAST: Blanche Baker (Mary), Jeff East (Joseph),

Colleen Dewhurst (Elizabeth), Murray Matheson (Zacharias);
Lloyd Bochner, Shay Duffin, Paul Hecht, Marilyn Lightstone,
Stephen McHattie, Tuvia Tavi, Yossi Yadin, Liron Nirgod,
Joseph Bee, Yehudh Ephroni, Dino Doran, Yakar Semach,
Gabi Amroni, Israel Biderman, Amos Makadi, Noam Kedem,
Jacob Ben Sira.

In an attempt to duplicate the success of its JESUS
OF NAZARETH (q. v.), NBC-TV filmed the story surrounding the birth of Jesus and called it MARY AND JOSEPH: A
STORY OF FAITH. Unlike the former film, this outing
limped along for three long hours, and the New York Times
commented, "The art of meaninglessness has rarely been so
well served. "

The film relates how Joseph (Jeff East) and Mary
(Blanche Baker) meet, with Joseph getting involved with the
Zealots, a Jewish group seeking to overthrow the yoke of
Roman rule in Palestine. Unfortunately the film portrayed
both Mary and Joseph as early-day hippies and it is void of
miracles and good taste, and distorts all known Biblical
facts surrounding the pre-Nativity.

Filmed on location in Israel by Lorimar Productions,
in association with CIP-Europaische Treuhand A. G. of West
Germany, the film was a dud from start to finish. Variety
noted that the film "veers from contemporary viewpoints to
historical posing, from pop to pap, with no sense of vivacity."

Originally called MARY AND JOSEPH, the film was
shot in the summer of 1979 at a cost of $4 million and was
issued theatrically outside North America by a Canadian
company, Astral Bellevue-Pathé.

THE DAY CHRIST DIED
1980
CBS-TV/20th Century-Fox
180 minutes   Color
Producer: Martin Manulis
Associate Producer: Ted Butcher
Director: James Cellan Jones
Script: James Lee Barrett & Edward Anhalt, from the book
        by Jim Bishop
Photography: Franco Di Giacamo
Editor: Barry Peters
Music: Lawrence Rosenthal
Art Director: Gianni Quaranta
Costumes: Dada Scaligeri
First Assistant Director: Carlo Cotti

Religious Advisor: Rev. Terrance A. Sweeney
Consultants: Dr. Eugene J. Fisher & Rev. Patrick J.
      Sullivan
      CAST: Chris Sarandon (Jesus Christ), Colin Blakely
(Caiaphas), Keith Michell (Pontius Pilate), Jonathan Pryce
(King Herod), Barrie Houghton (Judas), Jay O. Sanders
(Peter), Eleanor Bron (Mary), Tim Pigott-Smith (Tullius),
Delia Boccardo (Mary Magdalene), Hope Lange (Claudia),
Oliver Cotton (John), Gordon Gostelow (Nicodemus), Harold
Goldblatt (Annas), Gary Brown (Aaron), Leonard Maguire
(The Demoniac), Marne Maitland (Jacob), Tony Vogel (First
Temple Guard), Brian Coburn (James), Emma Jacobs (Le-
liah), Ralph Arliss (Matthew), Anna Nogara (Ruth), Dov Got-
tesfeld (Andrew), Anthony Langdon, Donal O'Brien (Roman
Soldiers), Rodd Dana (Abenadar), John Savident (Aide to
Herod), Thomas Milian Jr. (Mark), Joseph Murphy, Ted
Rusoff (Temple Guards), Charles Boromel (Second Witness),
Donal Hodson (Joseph of Arimethea), Veronica Welles (Sara),
Leonardo Treviglio (Thomas), Cyrus Elisa (Herod's Messen-
ger), Fabrizio Jovine (Phillip), Nando Paone (Thaddeus),
Samuele Cerri (Nathaniel), Marie-Cristine Dunham (Deborah),
Jean-Paul Boucher (James the Younger), Mattia Machiavelli
(Simon).
      Loosely based on the book by Jim Bishop, this tele-
feature dramatized the arrest, trial and Crucifixion of Jesus
Christ (Chris Sarandon) in the politically troubled Roman-
occupied city of Jerusalem. The film reconstructed the
world of ancient Jerusalem at the fateful time when Jesus
of Nazareth entered the city to face the events which changed
the course of the world.
      The film begins as Jesus and His disciples prepare
to return to Jerusalem to celebrate the Passover, which is
to be the Last Supper. There is secrecy about the return
because of the commotion created by Jesus' arrival into the
city the preceding Palm Sunday and his confrontation with the
money changers at the Temple. Among those closely viewing the events are Pontius Pilate (Keith Michell), the Procurator of Judea under the Romans, who fears political unrest; and Caiaphas (Colin Blakely), who believes Jesus'
teachings offend Hebrew teachings and that His activities
might cost Caiaphas his powerful position within the church.
Under the urging of his advisors, Pilate is persuaded to offer the life of Jesus in return for that of the convicted thief
Barabbas, a dissident whose death could provoke an uprising.
Pilate then contrives to draw Caiaphas into his plans and
Christ's own disciple, Judas (Barrie Houghton), confused and
torn over his teacher's words and the belief that Jesus may

be courting martyrdom, is coaxed into betraying Christ. Jesus, aware of the actions of His enemies, then sets out to prepare His followers for His Crucifixion.

Filmed in Tunisia, THE DAY CHRIST DIED was billed as "the greatest story as it's never been told before." Unfortunately, the story of Christ's last days were never told more vapidly, as the film downplayed the religious aspects of the story to speculate on the political intrigues that led to the Crucifixion. CBS-TV, which telecast the film on March 26, 1980, feared it might be controversial, but found that their expensive product was merely dull. Jim Bishop was so dissatisfied with it that he took his name off the final product.

THE DAY CHRIST DIED, although well acted, had no miracles, no teachings, no power and no meaning, and telling Christ's story without these elements led only to boredom. In a three-hour time slot the film was much too long; it is sad to see such a potentially fine premise end up so poorly conceived and executed.

FOR THIS CAUSE
1980
60 minutes   Color
FOR THIS CAUSE was billed as a "feature-length audio-visual production of the life of Jesus Christ with scenes photographed in Israel. Three screens, six projectors, audio-visual programmer, stereo music and vivid color. See the birth, life and death of Christ. Relive His miracles and teachings. Thrill to His grand prophecies."

Not much else is known about this production, except that it got some release, at least in the Pittsburgh, Pennsylvania area in 1980.

IN SEARCH OF HISTORIC JESUS
1980
Schick Sunn Classics
91 minutes   Color
Producers: Charles E. Sellier, Jr. & James L. Conway
Associate Producer: Bill Conford
Director: Henning Schellerup
Screenplay: Marvin Wald & Jack Jacobs, based on the book
              by Lee Roddy & Charles E. Sellier, Jr.
Photography: Paul Hipp

Editor: Kendall S. Rase
Music: Bob Summers
Production Design: Paul Staheli
Special Effects: John Carter
Set Decorator: Randy Staheli
Art: Doug Vanderfrif

CAST: John Rubenstein (Jesus Christ), John Anderson (Caiaphas), Nehemiah Persoff (Herod Antipas), Brad Crandell (Narrator), Andrew Bloch (Apostle John), Morgan Brittany (Mary), Walter Brooke (Joseph), Annette Charles (Mary Magdalene), Royal Dano (Prophet), Anthony De Longis (Peter), Lawrence Dobkin (Pontius Pilate), Jeffrey Druce (Thomas).

While Variety called IN SEARCH OF HISTORIC JESUS "exploitation ... it mocks the art of film," the movie actually followed in the footsteps of other Schick Sunn Classics' productions (i. e., THE LINCOLN CONSPIRACY, IN SEARCH OF NOAH'S ARK [q. v.], BEYOND AND BACK [q. v.]) in attempting to solve a historical mystery in an entertaining manner and at the same time provide a vehicle for the vastly neglected audience for G-rated movies. Despite the critical drubbing it received, the film accomplished what its producers intended.

The film, which was finely acted, examines some of the "missing years" in the life of Jesus Christ (John Rubenstein) and offers some explanations, including that He may have spent a few years with an Indian tribe in the Americas--thus answering the riddle of why American Indians often worshipped a white deity. Also explored is the Shroud of Turin, which many believe is the actual burial cloth of Christ.

Like all Schick Sunn Classics, the film was advertised in a media-blitz with blurbs on radio and television advertising the film in certain locales. Like previous Sunn productions, the film was very profitable as a result of this method. Many people saw this harmless feature which offers no actual answers to the questions it raises.

PART III

SELECTED TELEVISION PROGRAMS

ACTOR'S STUDIO
1949
CBS-TV
30 minutes

"A Child is Born" December 20, 1949
        CAST: Jean Muir; Marc Connelly (Host).
        The early days of television were not chronicled with
much accuracy, but as far as can be determined this was
perhaps the first religious/seasonal TV production. This
adaptation of the story by Stephen Vincent Benèt told about
the birth of Jesus Christ.

THE LUX VIDEO THEATRE
1951-55
NBC-TV
30 minutes B/W

"A Child is Born" December 25, 1950
        CAST: Gene Lockhart (Innkeeper), Fay Bainter (Inn-
keeper's Wife).
        Another early television adaptation of the Stephen
Vincent Benèt story of the birth of the baby Jesus.

STUDIO ONE
1948-57
CBS-TV
30 minutes B/W

"Pontius Pilate" April 7, 1952
        CAST: Geraldine Fitzgerald, Cyril Ritchard, Francis
L. Sullivan.
        This was number 147 of the series and it was an ad-
aptation of the Broadway play, The Most Honourable Gentle-
man by Michael Dyne. Telling the story of Pontius Pilate,
this high-quality production (a fine example of the golden
age of television) was sponsored by Westinghouse and produced by Worthington Miner.

"The Nativity" December 22, 1952
        CAST: Miriam Wolfe, Hurd Hatfield, Paul Tripp,
Tom Chalmers.
        Another television adaptation of the events leading up
to the birth of Jesus Christ. The same plot and title were
used for a 1979 (q. v.) television movie.

YOU ARE THERE
1953-57
CBS-TV
30 minutes   B/W
Host: Walter Cronkite

"The Plot Against King Solomon" November 28, 1954
        "Everything is happening exactly as it happened then,
except ... " is how each episode of YOU ARE THERE
started. Host Walter Cronkite would take a TV crew back
in time to recreate history. This episode dealt with court
intrigue surrounding King Solomon of The Old Testament.

THE KRAFT TELEVISION THEATRE
1947-58
NBC-TV
30 minutes   B/W

"A Child is Born" December 23, 1954
        Still another television adaptation of the Stephen Vin-
cent Benet story of the birth of Christ.

"The Other Wise Man" December 25, 1957
        CAST: Richard Kiley, Dolores Vitina.
        Robert J. Crean adapted the story by Henry Van Dyke
about the fictional fourth Wise Man, who traveled across the

world to see the baby Jesus. Along the way events kept
happening to delay his trip and at the finale he must choose
between seeing Jesus and saving the life of a village girl.
He saves the girl, and in doing so, is killed.   Although he
never saw Christ in this world, his good deeds guaranteed
that he would walk with Him in the world beyond.

"The Other Wise Man" was adapted for television
many times, including GENERAL ELECTRIC THEATRE
(q. v.) and on several Sunday morning religious anthology
programs, including THIS IS THE LIFE in 1979.

OMNIBUS
CBS-TV
1952-59
60 minutes   B/W

"Salome" December 18, 1955
        CAST: Eartha Kitt (Salome), Leo Genn (Herod),
Patricia Neal (Herodias), Elsa Lanchester.
        William Spier produced and Alistair Cooke hosted
this prestigious series, which was education-oriented and
often presented adaptations of famous plays.   Here Oscar
Wilde's drama about the temptress Salome and her dance
of the seven veils was shown.   The dramatization marked
the television debut of Eartha Kitt in the title role.   It
was something of a media first, with the part played by a
black actress.

MATINEE THEATRE
NBC-TV
1955-58
60 minutes   B/W
Host: John Conte

"The Book of Ruth" March 30, 1956
Director: Lamont Johnson
Script: Howard Rodman
        CAST: Sarah Churchill (Ruth), Katharine Warren
(Naomi), Fay Bainter, Lamont Johnson (Narrator).

"The Story of Joseph" April 19, 1957
Script: Howard Rodman
        CAST: Brett Halsey (Joseph), Forrest Taylor (Jacob).

"The Story of Sarah" September 22, 1957
Script: Marjorie Duhan Adler
   CAST: Tom Tryon (Abraham), Marian Seldes (Sarah).

"The Prophet Hosea" March 5, 1958
Script: Marjorie Duhan Adler
   CAST: Joseph Wiseman (Hosea).
   This fine dramatic series was one of the few staples
of television that presented Biblical adaptations, outside the
realm of the weekly religious network and syndicated series.
The four dramas listed above were adaptations from the Old
Testament and all four were good quality dramas presented
in this weekday afternoon time-slot series.

THE HALLMARK HALL OF FAME
NBC-TV
1951-
90 minutes B/W

"The Green Pastures" October 17, 1957
Script: Marc Connelly, from his play
   CAST: William Warfield (De Lawd); Eddie "Roches-
ter" Anderson, Frederick O'Neal, Earle Hyman, Terry
Carter.

"The Green Pastures" March 27, 1959
Script: Marc Connelly, from his play
   CAST: William Warfield (De Lawd); Eddie "Roches-
ter" Anderson, Frederick O'Neal, Earle Hyman, Terry
Carter, Butterfly McQueen, Estelle Hemsley, Avon Long,
Mantan Moreland.
   Marc Connelly adapted his famous play, which had
already been filmed by Warner Brothers in 1941 (q. v.), to
television. After its initial showing, the drama was re-
staged the next season with much the same cast.

"Give Us Barabbas!" March 24, 1961
Producer-Director: George Schaefer
Script: Henry Denker
   CAST: James Daly (Barabbas), Kim Hunter (Mara),
Dennis King (Pontius Pilate), Robinson Stone (Phineas),
Leonardo Cimino (Caleb), Ludwig Donath (Joseph), Keir
Dullea (Elisha), Muni Seroff (Samuel), John Gerstad (Le-
muel), Kermit Murdock (Peter), Allen Nourse (Centurion),
Eric Sinclair (Officer), John Straub (John), Richard Thomas

(David), Theodore Tenley (Zachary), Toni Darnay (Mary).

This acclaimed drama presented the circumstances surrounding the choice between the thief Barabbas and Jesus Christ for execution. The story shows how Pilate washed his hands of the choice, giving the decision to the mob, and it also looked into the evolution of Barabbas from a vicious criminal to a man of awakening conscience. This drama was telecast four times, the last being on March 28, 1969.

Ironically, the very first telecast of THE HALLMARK HALL OF FAME, on December 24, 1951, was the religious opera, "Amahl and the Night Visitors." This story, about a young boy who meets and follows The Magi to the birthplace of Christ in Bethlehem, was restaged each year for many seasons, but it was either done live or on tape, and not filmed.

GENERAL ELECTRIC THEATRE
1953-61
CBS-TV
30 minutes   B/W
Host: Ronald Reagan

"The Other Wise Man"   December 25, 1960
CAST: Harry Townes (Artaban), Francis X. Bushman (Abgarus), Abraham Sofaer (Rabbi).

Adapted from Henry Van Dyke's Christmas classic story, this program told of a wealthy Persian nobleman (Harry Townes), who sells all his possessions to buy three gems: a ruby, a sapphire and a pearl. He plans to give these as gifts to the Christ Child, who, it has been prophesied, will be born in Bethlehem.

A well staged and finely acted drama, "The Other Wise Man" was hosted by Ronald Reagan and his wife, Nancy Davis, and their children Patricia Ann and Ronald, from their California home. Two decades later, Ronald Reagan would be celebrating the holidays as the president-elect of the United States.

THE TIME TUNNEL
1966-67
ABC-TV
20th Century-Fox/Irwin Allen Productions
60 minutes   Color

Robert Colbert and James Darren in THE TIME TUNNEL (ABC-TV, 1966-67)

"The Walls of Jericho" January 27, 1967
Producer: Irwin Allen
Director: J. Juran
Script: Ellis St. Joseph
      CAST: James Darren (Tony Newman), Robert Colbert (Douglas Philips), Lee Meriwether (Ann), Whit Bissell (Kirk), John Zaremba (Swain), Rhodes Reason (Joshua), Myrna Fahey (Rahab), Arnold Moss (Malek), Lise Gaye (Ahza), Abraham Sofaer (Father), Michael Pate (Captain), Cynthia Lane (Shala), Tiger Joe Marsh (Torturer).
      Producer Irwin Allen, who did THE STORY OF MANKIND (q. v.) in 1957, created this science-fiction program which had scientists Tony Newman and Douglas Philips lost in their own creation, a "time tunnel," and each week the duo drifted helplessly through the void of time, arriving on board the Titanic one week or at the Alamo the next. Occasionally they would encounter aliens from the future, or team-up with mythical heroes such as Robin Hood or Merlin the Magician.
      In this episode the duo is in Biblical times and they act as two "strangers" (as The Bible terms it) who act as

spies, helping Joshua and his troops to topple the walls of Jericho. Both an earthquake and a miracle are presented as ideas for bringing down the walls, but unbelieving scientist Ann, who views the events from her laboratory set in 1968, is sure the walls fell from natural causes. As the battle ends, Tony and Doug again find themselves lost in time and space.

THE TIME TUNNEL was an excellent television program, running for one season of thirty episodes. The stories were fascinating and intelligent but the show was cheaply produced, and "The Walls of Jericho" segment, for example, relied greatly on stock footage. The series, however, was redeemed by good actors, intelligent writers and good special effects. "The Walls of Jericho" was one of the program's better episodes.

THE LITTLE DRUMMER BOY (Books I and II)
December 12, 1968 & December 14, 1975
NBC-TV
30 minutes each episode   Color
Producers-Directors: Arthur Rankin & Jules Bass
Narrator: Greer Garson
          CAST: Jose Ferrer, Paul Frees (Voices for Book I); Zero Mostel, David Jay (Voices for Book II).
          This fable, based on the song by Katherine Davis, Henry Onorati and Harry Simeone, tells of the poor little drummer boy who has no gift to give to the Baby Jesus.
          In 1968 the story was produced for television using puppets, and seven years later the sequel was telecast. Both are fair for children, although Book II has nothing to do with Christ.

CHRISTMAS IS
1970
Lutheran Television
Syndicated
30 minutes   Color
Producers: Rev. Ardon D. Albrecht & Dr. Martin J. Neeb
             Jr.
Director: Leonard Gray
Script: Don Hall
          CAST: Hans Conried (Voice).

CHRISTMAS IS, an animated cartoon first syndicated in 1970, still appears each year at Christmas time. It tells of a little boy named Benjy and his pet dog, Waldo, who travel back in time to witness the birth of Jesus Christ.

This tale was made for children, but it has enough charm to captivate adult audiences. A sequel, EASTER IS (q. v.), appeared five years later.

EASTER IS
1975
Lutheran Television
Syndicated
30 minutes   Color
Producers: Rev. Ardon D. Albrecht & Dr. Martin J. Neeb Jr.
Director: Leonard Gray
Script: Don Hall
CAST: Hans Conried, Leslie Uggams (Voices).

EASTER IS was produced as a follow-up to CHRISTMAS IS (q. v.) and it has the main characters from the original, the small boy Benjy and his dog Waldo, going back in time to witness the Crucifixion of Jesus Christ, in order to learn the true meaning of Easter.

This syndicated program is not nearly as good as its predecessor, but children will enjoy a few minutes of it.

THE NIGHT THE ANIMALS TALKED
1975
ABC-TV
30 minutes   Color

This cartoon, which aired in prime time on ABC-TV, centers on the animals in the manger where Christ was born. The film showed that these animals gained the ability to "talk" on the night Jesus was born.

Juvenile, even for children, this cartoon was poorly produced, with mediocre animation.

IN SEARCH OF ...
1975-
Syndicated
30 minutes   Color

Producer: Alan Landsburg
Host-Narrator: Leonard Nimoy

IN SEARCH OF ... is a popular syndicated series which explores unsolved mysteries, such as missing persons, UFO's, myths and monsters. The series presents well-produced programs of speculation, which give no answers and do not claim to, but always manage to inform and entertain. Among the program's top-quality episodes have been those dealing with The Bible.

The episodes are:

1) "The Dead Sea Scrolls." In 1945 a Bedouin shepherd boy discovered writings which are over 2,000 years old, and the program looks at these scrolls and the effect they have had on organized religion.

2) "The Garden of Eden." It has been claimed that the Garden of Eden was located near the coast of Saudi Arabia, in what is now Iran. The program looks at efforts to locate the Garden of Eden.

3) "Noah's Flood." This episode looks into the scientific methods used to prove the Flood as described in The Bible.

4) "Sodom and Gomorrah." Scientists look into the theory that the remains of these wicked cities are on the very site of a crater now filled by the Dead Sea.

5) "The Ten Commandments." A look at Mt. Sinai, where Moses was supposed to have received the Ten Commandments from God.

During the program's fourth season, 1979-80, two of its episodes dealt with the New Testament:

6) "The Shroud of Turin" (Episode 74). This segment began the series' fourth season and it examines the authenticity of the Shroud of Turin, which many believe is the actual burial cloth of Christ and that it bears His image.

7) "John the Baptist" (Episode 88). Here an examination is made of bones found in a North African monastery, which are said to be those of John the Baptist. The program features a sequence which recreates John baptizing Jesus; it is excellently done, if not a little too flashy.

The program's 1980-81 season had the following episode from The New Testament:

"The Holy Grail." A brilliant documentary on the fascinating legend of the Holy Grail, the silver chalice which Christ used at the Last Supper. The cup was preserved by Joseph of Arimathea, who took some of Christ's blood in it at the Crucifixion, making it "holy" and "sangreal." Eventually Joseph fled to Britain, taking the grail with him. It was left to be guarded by holy men there but it vanished because of the impurity of its guardians. Although the Biblical legend ends at this point, the Holy Grail is also a part of the King Arthur legend, in which Sir Galahad is sent on a quest for it. In this century a golden cup was discovered, with a silver cup inside, and it was believed to be the Holy Grail. Since then, however, many historians have felt it was not the grail because it came from a later age.

THE SILVER CHALICE (q. v.) also deals with this legend but the 1974 comedy film, MONTY PYTHON AND THE HOLY GRAIL, was nothing less than an insult to the legend.

MARY'S INCREDIBLE DREAM
January 22, 1976
CBS-TV
60 minutes   Color
Producer: Jack Good
Directors: Gene McAvoy & Jaime Rogers
Script: Jack Good & Mary Tyler Moore
Music: Ray Pohlman

CAST: Mary Tyler Moore (Woman/Angel/Devil/Eve), Ben Vereen (Noah/Man/Satan), Doug Kershaw (Adam/War/Devil).

In 1976 Mary Tyler Moore, who was appearing on her own "Mary Tyler Moore Show" on CBS-TV, starred in this television special, best described as a musical fantasy. There is no storyline, at least none that makes any sense, but such Biblical characters as Noah, Adam, Eve and Satan do appear. In all, it was a very entertaining special and the songs, costumes and production values were top-notch. However, the special came under heavy critical attack and has not been re-telecast.

NOAH'S ANIMALS
April 5, 1976

ABC-TV
30 minutes   Color
Producer: Charles G. Mortimer
Director: Shamus Culhane
        CAST: Paul Soles, Judy Sinclair (Voices).
        A Westfall Production, this cartoon aired on ABC-TV
and was aimed at children.   The film tells of the events that
lead up to Noah preparing the ark for the Great Flood.

GARDEN OF EDEN
1977
Lutheran Church Television
30 minutes   Color
        CAST: Walter Matthau (Adam), Edward Asner (God).
        A serio-comedy, GARDEN OF EDEN centers on Adam
(Walter Matthau) being visited by God (Edward Asner).   Adam
is dressed in overalls and God wears a business suit.   They
have a lengthy discussion about the world in general.   The
film was a very fine combination of humor and warmth.

NESTOR, THE LONG EARED CHRISTMAS DONKEY
December 3, 1978
ABC-TV
30 minutes   Color
Producers-Directors: Arthur Rankin & Jules Bass
        CAST: Don Messick, Brenda Vaccaro, Roger Miller
(Voices).
        Another Rankin-Bass puppet-cartoon, this one is about
the weary klutz of a donkey, Nestor, who is chosen to carry
Mary to Bethlehem, where she will give birth to Jesus Christ.
Country music singer-songwriter Roger Miller sang the songs
in this outing.

THE THIRTEENTH DAY: THE STORY OF ESTHER
November 18, 1979
ABC-TV/Universal
60 minutes   Color
Producer: Stefanie Kowal
Executive Producer: David Victor
Supervising Producer: Robert F. O'Neill
Director: Leo Penn
Script: Norman Hudis

Olivia Hussey and Tony Musante in THE THIRTEENTH DAY: THE STORY OF ESTHER (ABC-TV, 1979)

Story: Norman Hudis & Robert Bruce
Photography: Enzo A. Martinelli
Editor: Edwin F. England
Music: Morton Stevens
 CAST: Olivia Hussey (Esther), Tony Musante (King Ahasuerus), Harris Yulin (Haman), Nehemiah Persoff (Mordecai), Elizabeth Shepherd (Hegai), Erica Yohn (Sura), Kario Salem (Dalphon), Tom Troupe (Teresh), Ted Wass (Simon).
 Aired as a one-hour special on ABC-TV, this drama told the Old Testament story of a young queen who had to defend both herself and her people after a power-mad advisor convinces her husband that she must die. The story had Jewish girl Esther (Olivia Hussey) marrying King Ahasuerus (Tony Musante), whose minister Haman (Harris Yulin) tried to kill him. The plot was thwarted by a Jew. To get revenge, Haman convinces the king that the Jews are a threat to his throne, although neither man knows that beautiful young Esther is also Jewish. Since the king's order to kill her people cannot be reversed, the queen has to find a way to save her people and at the same time reveal to the king the true nature of the treacherous Haman.
 A well-done television drama, the program's familiar

plotline had been used before for the features QUEEN
ESTHER and ESTHER AND THE KING (qq. v.).

AND DAVID WEPT
1980
Syndicated
60 minutes   Color
Music: Ezra Laderman & Joe Darion
    The story of David and Bathsheba, told in cantata
form, is the basis for this television film syndicated in
1980.

CLOSING REMARKS

Although the framework of this volume closes with 1980, feature films and television programs based on The Bible continue to be announced and produced.

As its presentation for the 1981 Easter season, CBS-TV telecast PETER AND PAUL, a five-hour, two-part telefeature chronicling the foundation of the Christian church. Produced in Greece late in 1980 under the working title THE ACTS, the film was written by Christopher Knopf and directed by Robert Day. Anthony Hopkins starred as Saul of Tarsus, who later became Paul, the apostle of the gentiles, while Robert Foxworth was Peter, the rock of the Christian church. The supporting cast included Raymond Burr as Agrippa, Herbert Lom as Barnabas, Eddie Albert as Festus, Jean Peters as Priscilla, Jon Finch as Luke and Jose Ferrer as Gamaliel. The film was telecast April 12 and 14, 1981.

Another 1981 television program based on the New Testament was the syndicated INSIGHT: RESURRECTION, a 30 minute color production of Paulist Television. A surreal teleplay, it told of Christ (Richard Beymer) awakening in a modern-day hospital after the Crucifixion and being tempted by sex and fame before overcoming these temptations and returning for His resurrection on Easter Sunday.

A duo of early 1981 theatrical films have also dealt with Jesus Christ. THE FINAL CONFLICT, 20th Century-Fox's last film in its trilogy about the Anti-Christ (who had appeared earlier in THE OMEN in 1976 and DAMIEN: OMEN II two years later), presented the Second Coming of Christ and His final confrontation with the Anti-Christ. FEAR NO EVIL, issued by Avco-Embassy, was a low-budget effort concerning a high school student (Stefan Arngrim) who discovers he is the Anti-Christ. The film contained the re-creation of the death of Jesus Christ as the high school students enact "The Passion Play."

Several theatrical films have been announced for production that deal with aspects of the Bible. WHITE POP
JESUS is a Spanish musical about the life of Christ. From
France comes another version of THE QUEEN OF SHEBA
and several biblical characters are in Mel Brooks' THE
HISTORY OF THE WORLD PART I. An untitled all-black
version of the life of Jesus has been announced by an inde-
pendent film company while THE RAIDERS OF THE LOST
ARK features the holy ark of Moses.

Finally, in a book of this type and scope there are
bound to be last minute film additions or titles that deserve
further research. Among these are GIACOBBE ED ESAU
(Jacob and Esau), a 1964 Italian production based on the Old
Testament, and BART LA RUE'S THE ARK OF NOAH, a
1976 documentary about Noah's Ark. This 95 minute feature
is available to television from Gold Key Entertainment. Apparently released theatrically were SODOM AND GOMORRAH:
THE LAST SEVEN DAYS and THE MYSTERY OF THE SA-
CRED SHROUD. The former title is an XXX-rated feature
produced by Jim and Artie Mitchell on a $600,000 budget.
A porno hardcore version of the events surrounding the
destruction of the twin cities of sin, the film was premiered
in 1976 in San Francisco. THE MYSTERY OF THE SACRED
SHROUD is a 1979 documentary narrated by Richard Burton
and as its title implies it deals with the Shroud of Turin.

TITLE INDEX

(Titles in quotation marks are television programs.)

THE AUTHORS

RICHARD H. CAMPBELL, a free-lance writer whose interests include religion, music, television and films, was born in Latrobe, Pennsylvania on February 7, 1959. He has contributed to such cinema journals as Japanese Giants, Inertia, and Fanta Zine, as well as having published his own periodical, Godzillamania, a fan letter dealing with the Japanese horror cinema. For several years he co-produced, with Wayne R. Smith, the underground comic book cult classic The Gang, which ended in 1977 but is still highly praised today. He is a member of the James Bond 007 Fan Club, the Japanese Fantasy Film Society, the Cartoon/Fantasy Organization, and the Irving Forbush Appreciation Society. He is preparing another book, Super Heroes on Screen, which will deal with super-powered heroes on film and television.

MICHAEL R. PITTS has written nine other books for Scarecrow Press, including Famous Movie Detectives, Hollywood on Record, Radio Soundtracks, and The Great ... Pictures series. He is also the author of Horror Film Stars (McFarland & Co., 1981) and has contributed to eight other books. His magazine articles have been published both in the United States and abroad and Mr. Pitts writes a monthly column on record collecting for The Big Reel magazine. A member of the Madison County (Ind.) Historical Society, the Hank Snow Fan Club, the Frankie Laine Society of America, and the Slim Whitman Appreciation Society, Mr. Pitts resides in Chesterfield, Indiana, with his wife, Carolyn, and his daughter, Angela.